LIFE IN BRAMPTON
WITH 63 PUBLIC HOUSES

David Moore

February 2007.

LIFE IN BRAMPTON
WITH 63 PUBLIC HOUSES

DAVID MOORAT

HiP
HISTORY INTO PRINT

First published by
History into Print, 56 Alcester Road,
Studley, Warwickshire B80 7LG in 2006
www.history-into-print.com

© David Moorat 2006

All rights reserved

ISBN 1 85858 313 6

The moral right of the author has been asserted

A Cataloguing in Publication Record
for this title is available from the British Library

Typeset in Bembo
Printed in Great Britain by
Cromwell Press Ltd.

CONTENTS

Acknowledgements	vii
Introduction	viii
Under Starter's Orders	ix
The Nag's Head	1
The Nag's Tail	6
The George and Dragon Inn	8
The Sportsman Inn	12
The Jolly Butcher	15
The Half Moon Inn	18
The Black Bull	21
Brampton Public Houses and Politics	25
The Samson Inn	28
But, why are there so many Public Houses around?	31
The Shoulder of Mutton	37
Modlen's Spirit Vaults	41
The Shepherd and The Lion and the Lamb	44
The Blue Bell	48
The Nursery Arms	51
The Barley Stack or The Barley Mow	53
The Greyhound and The Hare and Hounds	56
The Horse and Farrier and The Crown	58
The Alma	63
The Red Lion	64
The Lord Nelson	67
The Crown and Cushion/The Crown and Thistle	70
The Howard Arms	71
The Pack Horse Inn	77
The Fat Ox Tavern	81
The Broom	84
The Board	85
Crime and Punishment in Brampton 1800–1900	86
The Grapes	93

The Joiner's Arms	95
The Salutation Inn	98
The Globe Inn	99
The Board and Goodburn's Spirit Vaults	102
The White Lion	104
The Plough	107
The Graham Arms	109
The White Hart	112
Elliot's Spirit Vaults	115
The Highland Laddie	117
The Kings Arms	119
The Wheatsheaf	123
The Scotch Arms	127
Poverty, unemployment, drunkenness – Poor relief and friendly societies	133
The Tom and Jerry	144
The Ship, The Punchbowl, The Coach and Horses	147
The Tom and Jerry – Ewarts Buildings	151
The General Wolfe	153
The Klondyke Bar	154
The Anchor Inn	156
The Tom and Jerry, or is it The Star?	159
The Freemasons Arms	162
The String of Horses and The Board	166
The Bush	169
The Commercial Inn	173
The Three Crowns	176
The Willie Brewed	178
The Tom and Jerry – Moatside	179
The Wellington and The Earl Grey	181
The Sand House Inn and The Three Lions	184
The Coal Waggon	188
The Bay Horse, The Horse and Groom and The Ridge House	190
The Black Bull Inn, Lanercost	194
The Johnson Arms	197
The Hare and Hounds	200
The Graham Arms	203
The Oddfellows and The Pavier	206
Last Orders Please! – The Temperance Movement is coming	213
Bibliography and Primary Sources	222
Index	224

ACKNOWLEDGEMENTS

I am greatly indebted to many people who have been so helpful during the course of research for this publication: Staff at Carlisle Record Office for their cheerfulness, forbearance and professionalism; Stephen White of The Lanes Library Carlisle for access to The Jackson Collection, and Dennis Perriam Carlisle Historian for much guidance.

Most of the old photographs are reproduced with kind permission of Iain Parsons. I am grateful to Hon Philip Howard and to Mr John Lee for permission to use the illustration of "The Blue Lady", and for their help with proof reading.

The cover illustration is reproduced from a print by Brampton artist Stephen Warnes BA. RGA.

Last but by no means least I am very grateful to my personal friends who have urged me on and given much support when my spirits were low.

INTRODUCTION

In 1790, there were ten public houses in Brampton, but by 1845 this number had grown to well over fifty, and later, to 63. However, following the end of the 19th Century, the number of public houses in Brampton had fallen back to that which had existed 100 years previously.

What were the reasons for this sudden mushrooming of new public houses, and why, some fifty years later did their number decline, almost as rapidly as they had grown?

This paper sets out to identify where each of these public houses was and to identify the building, if any, that currently occupies its place. The study also traces events, retells incidents which took place, and discusses the social and political circumstances which brought about their rapid increase and what contributed to their sudden demise.

Those who trace the whereabouts and stories of the public houses of Brampton, very quickly come upon several contradictions and uncertainties:

Public Houses often changed their names.
Some changed their location – taking their old name with them.
Several changed their names 3 or 4 times.
Often, there were two or more public houses with the same name.
On very many occasions, licensees changed houses.
Several proprietors are recorded as having other trades or professions
at the same time as being a public house keeper.

Details have been collated from Directories, Magistrate Court Records, Carlisle Journal 1790–1900, Carlisle Patriot 1790–1900, The North Cumberland Reformer, Magistrates Public House Licensing Records, Census of 1851, First Edition Ordnance Survey maps, Brampton Tithe Map, Peter Burn's "Memoirs of When I was young in Brampton", Rev. Arthur Penn's lesson notes "Public houses in Brampton"; a study of records of property sales, archives, merchants ledger records and discussions with several of today's property owners in Brampton.

UNDER STARTER'S ORDERS

Come with me now on a "pub crawl" of a life-time! I use these words respectfully. Our objective is not to consume large quantities of drink in the shortest possible time, but to visit each public house in the Brampton of 1800–1900, at a very slow pace.

We will stop at each one to hear about its history, the people who owned or ran the house, the events which took place there, and to see for ourselves what life was like at that time for the common man.

I use the term pub-crawl of a "life-time," as we will visit all of the 63 public houses that existed. But, they did not all exist at the same time. In 1800 there were only ten; and a hundred years later again there were only ten, however over the hundred years between, a further 53 came into and went out of existence. We will on the way, find out why there was such an increase in the number during the first 30 years of the century and why there was such a dramatic reduction in the last 30 years of the century.

A word of caution before we start, about our behaviour.

It is now the year 1800. We will be served with "small beer" which will cost us only half a penny a pint, but it will be fairly weak so we must not indulge ourselves by taking too much of this "foolish beverage." We must avoid drunkenness at all costs, because the 19th Century has some surprises for us:

Drunkenness
The terms used in Brampton and Carlisle to describe someone who was drunk were:

"He hath whipped the cat"
"He has been bit by the barn weasel"
"He hath seen the French King"

For those who were bit by the barn weasel, or who had seen the French King too often, and who became a public nuisance, there were ways in Brampton for dealing with such people:

Brampton Magistrates

"Drunkenness excuses no crime – he who is guilty of any crime whatsoever through his voluntary drunkenness shall forfeit five shillings or be confined to the stocks for 6 hours in the Market Place."

Carlisle Patriot, 1815

So, if you are found guilty of being drunk, which would you choose? To forfeit five shillings (about £15 in today's money), or to be confined to the stocks in the Market Place on full public display for six hours?

Jwohnnie Steenson

The last person to be punished in the stocks at Brampton was Jwohnnie Steenson, a well known local character who was regularly to be found in the Nag's Head, usually in a drunken state, often falling over things – and people, and using the foulest of language in the process.

Peter Burn, Brampton's poet and historian of the 19th Century records the event in his lecture notes "A fireside Crack":

On one occasion, Jwohnnie, having trawled the depths of his vocabulary of swear words and profanities to such an extent that irritated the locals, the constable was sent for, and Jwohnnie was marched off by the collar and the seat of his breeches to be locked into the stocks to teach him a lesson. The Brampton Magistrate's record later describes;

"He had been sentenced by the constable to expiate his crime for being drunk and disorderly to spend 24 hours in the stocks."

Jwohnnie had to sit in the stocks with his legs manacled, in full display of everyone in humiliation. It was raining and Jwohnnie's discomfort was further accentuated by water dripping off the Moot Hall roof above, on to his shoulders. However, Jwohnnie had many friends. He was a popular fellow despite his regular drunkenness and very soon, an umbrella was provided and a relay of his mates from The Nags Head was organised around the clock to keep him company. Other local sympathisers came up to Jwohnnie and *"alleviated his sufferings by a plentiful supply of liquor."* Whilst in the stocks a good number of people came up to him and placed a copper or two in his pocket out of sympathy.

After several hours, Jwohnnie was *"wet without and wet within."* The Brampton doctor Dr. Armstrong took pity of Jwohnnie in such a wet and cold state, that he requested the constable to release him.

Upon release, what did Jwohnnie do? Did he go home to get changed into some dry clothes and get his supper? No. Did he go home to sleep it off? No such thing!

Armed with his pockets rattling with coppers from his sympathisers and a body well lubricated with liquor to keep out the cold, he returned triumphantly with his mates to The Nag's Head to spend his hard earned takings. No record has been seen as to whether he changed his behaviour as a result of his being locked in the stocks.

It seems appropriate therefore to begin our journey to the public houses of Brampton at The Nag's Head – in the Market Place.

Iron Stocks

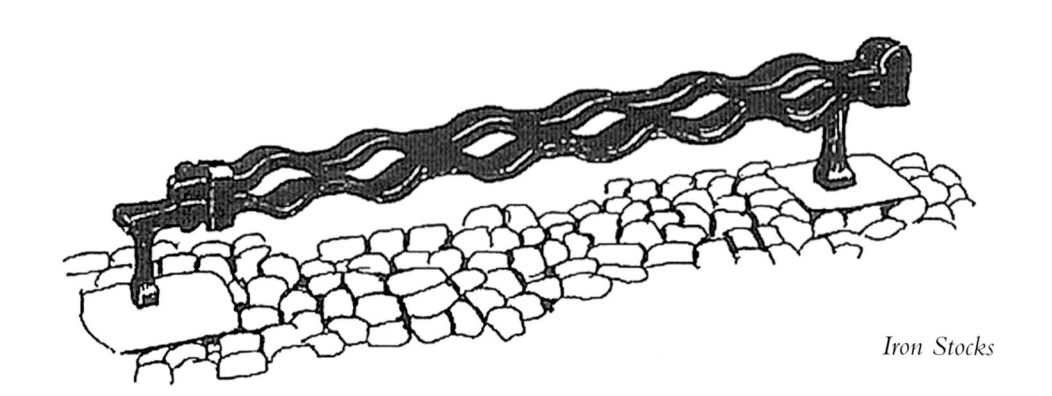

1
THE NAG'S HEAD

The Nag's Head was already a well established coaching inn by 1800, providing rooms upstairs for travellers to stay overnight, stables for horses, and yards for coaches and carts to be parked safely. There were store houses for fodder and accommodation for coachmen and staff. Of the staff who worked here were Elisabeth Farish and Margaret Thomson, both maidservants 24 years of age and an ostler age 27 by the name of Thomas Parker. All were under the management of the innkeeper, Francis Atkinson.

The Nag's Head of today occupies the same site as in 1800 but the stables, yards and outhouses have been converted to bars, kitchens, and dining areas.

Life in Brampton with 63 Public Houses

Nag's Head or Horse's Head?
The Nag's Head has also been known as The Horse's Head. In 1815 John Brown is mentioned as innkeeper of The Horse's Head in the Carlisle Patriot when recording a murder, whilst for the same year Bulmer's Directory records "John Brown Innkeeper Nag's Head." The 1851 Census records James Armstrong innkeeper of The Horse's Head whilst the directories of that same year show him as innkeeper of the Nag's Head. Further, in 1880 John Nixon according to Slater's Directory is recorded as innkeeper at both The Nag's Head and The Horse's Head. It can be safely concluded therefore that The Nag's Head and The Horse's Head have been one and the same place.

Brampton's balloted Militia man absconds
Brampton was in Eskdale Ward of Cumberland and, like all parishes, had to draw up a list of men between the ages of 18 and 45 years of age. The list was called The Militia List and was drawn up by the constable by visiting each house in the parish. According to the total number of eligible men in each ward, the County of Cumberland

> ABSCONDED.
> WHEREAS, EDWARD ATKINSON, Junior, by trade a Nailor, of Brampton, about 5 feet 8 inches high, of fair complexion, being balloted to serve in the CUMBERLAND MILITIA, for BRAMPTON-QUARTER, in Eskdale Ward, and having since absconded,
> Notice is hereby given,
> that a reward of FIVE GUINEAS will be paid by the Members of the NAG'S HEAD CLUB, in Brampton, to any Person or Persons who shall apprehend the said Edward Atkinson.

Carlisle Journal, 1808.

allocated a quota to each parish, to provide sufficient men to be sent off for military training with The Cumberland Militia, which amounted to four weeks each year, rather like today's Territorial Army.

Having prepared the list, the constable was then responsible for arranging a ballot which would take place at a public meeting when all of the names would be put in a hat and the appropriate number of names representing the Parish' quota drawn out. Men with two or more children were excluded from the ballot. Those whose names were drawn were obliged by law to leave their job, their family, their home and present themselves for military training.

Clearly Edward Atkinson did not fancy the life of a soldier, and after finding out that it was his name that had been pulled out of the hat, he decided to make himself scarce! The result of this action was that the Brampton Parish would be made to hold another ballot to draw a replacement for Edward Atkinson. So, it is understandable that the Nag's Head Club would be keen to find the absconder rather than having to send someone else in his place.

Here is the Militia List that was used for the above ballot, and Edward Atkinson's name is shown below that of his brother Thomas, both of whom we shall meet later.

1. The Nag's Head

Being a twenty year old nailor it would be unlikely that he would be able to afford to escape and live independently elsewhere without soon being discovered by the local constable. By absconding, Edward Atkinson put himself at great risk of being arrested and made to serve in the militia for even longer service as punishment; he also clearly risked alienating himself from the people of Brampton.

The Nag's Head Club which had placed the advertisement in the newspaper was formed by all the men of the parish aged between 18 and 45, each person paying a fee of 1 Guinea. Any one whose name had been drawn in the ballot, and did not wish to serve in the Militia, could, on the payment of a further 4 Guineas, ask for financial help from the club to find a substitute willing to serve in his place.

A new Coach Service for Brampton – 1837

During the late 1830s plans were well advanced for the building of a railway line from Newcastle to Carlisle and many business people saw this as a threat as well as an opportunity. Several horse drawn coach companies were pleased to find that the new railway line was not to come into the town of Brampton:

> "On June 3rd 1837, a light 2 horse post Coach to carry 4 people inside and 9 outside passengers will commence running everyday in the week except Sundays as follows: From the HORSE HEAD INN Market Place Brampton at 8 o'clock in the morning and at 4 o'clock in the afternoon every day except Wednesdays when it will leave Brampton at 7 o'clock in the morning.
>
> Fares: 1s. 6d inside and 1s. 0d outside to, or from Brampton or Carlisle. No gratuities to coachman. Parcels under 14lbs–4d. each."
>
> Carlisle Patriot, 3rd June 1837

Life in Brampton with 63 Public Houses

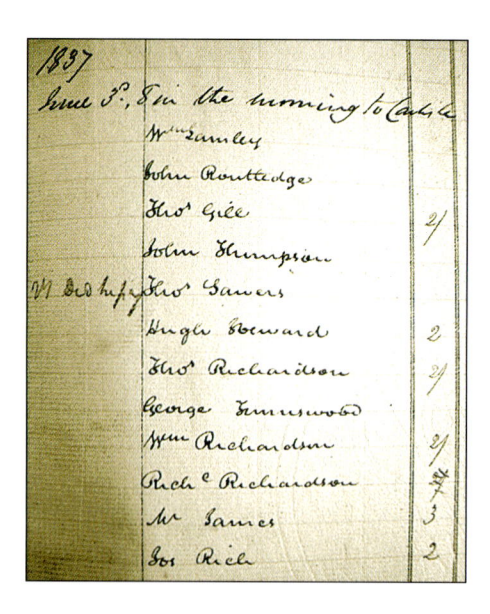

The Coach was called "THE INDEPENDENT" and on the inaugural journey of the 3rd June 1837, there was only one empty place, as shown by the list. The passengers and parcels for the return Journey were: William Elliot, A gentleman, John Ewart, John Halliburton, Thomas Routledge and One Basket of Fish.

The Carlisle Patriot was hopeful for the success of this venture and commented:

"A new coach service has commenced running between Brampton and Carlisle by way of Crosby on Eden. The proprietors who are said to be numerous – the landlord of the Horse Head is included – assign the origin of their opposition to the railroad carriages to be chiefly the charge of the conveyances required in travelling that route, and the distance each person has to walk in order to reach the centre of the town. The proprietors of this newspaper are very sanguine of the success of this new undertaking."

Murder at The Nag's Head

"On Monday last, a Coroners inquest was taken at Brampton, on the body of Hector Goodfellow, who died in consequence of violent kicks and blows he had received on the preceding Wednesday night at the Horse Head public house, from a William Richardson of the town – a clockmaker. It appeared from the evidence from Mr Joseph Brown innkeeper, that Goodfellow went into the kitchen of The Horse's Head and called for a pint of ale. Soon after, William Richardson pitched on the table with William Bell for a gill of Rum, which was won by the former. They played two more games which Richardson won also. The deceased proposed that Bell should play with Richardson for a note – a quarrel ensued,

1. The Nag's Head

Richardson struck and kicked the deceased in the lower part of the belly who fell and lay inanimate and in this state was trailed out of the house into the passage. The deceased was described as a quiet man not given to quarrelling. A surgeon declared that his death was the consequence of a kick to the belly. The Coroner concluded that Hector Goodfellow came by his death as a result of blows given to him by Richardson. A warrant has been issued for his arrest but he has absconded."

Carlisle Patriot, December 1815

The Nag's Head survived the century well. The days of being a successful coaching and posting inn provided sufficient experience and income to withstand the challenges from The Temperance Movement which put intense pressure on magistrates to close many of the public houses, not only in Brampton, but also nationally. The 1892 Return of Public Houses and Beer houses describes this public house as:

"8 Sleep; 12 Dine; 12 Horses; Next nearest public house – 100 yards. Owner Mrs Ann Latimer."

The following innkeepers are recorded at The Nag's Head/The Horse's Head:

1790 Francis Atkinson
1815 John Brown
1829–1835 Joseph Lee – he was also a wheelwright
1847–1851 James Armstrong
1855–1858 John Smith
1861–1873 James Reay
1879–1884 John Nixon – he was also a potato dealer
1884–1894 Samuel Shipley

Before we leave the Nag's Head, there is a "tale" to tell.

The number of public houses on our list to visit in Brampton is not diminished by one because we have discovered that the Horse's Head and the Nag's Head are one and the same place. So, why does the number stay at 63? Well, because at the same time as the Nag's Head was busy with coaches, overnight guests, hiring carts, gigs and post horses, a small cottage at the rear of the Nag's Head set itself up and called itself – very appropriately, as "The Nag's Tail."

2
THE NAG'S TAIL

This public house was owned by Mrs Anne Dodd from the early 1800s. The census and the Tithe map show that she was still innkeeper in 1841 and owned three cottages at the rear of the Nag's Head close to the entrance of the Bowling Green.

Mrs Anne Dodd is recorded in the directories as innkeeper at "The Board" in the Market Place, but in the same year she is reported in the newspapers as being innkeeper at The Nag's Tail. Later, this is confirmed in Mr Modlen's (spirit merchant) account book which records the order for a gallon of brandy to "Mrs A. Dodd of the Nag's Tail."

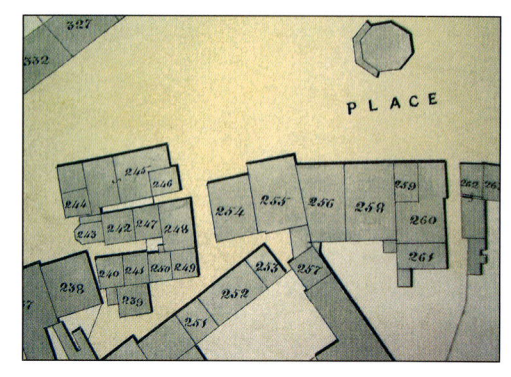

Money goes missing at the Nag's Tail

"Thomas Allen age 30 years was charged with feloniously stealing from the breeches pocket of James Jardine at Brampton, a gold ring valued at £1 and a quantity of silver. James Jardine had attended Brampton Market on the Wednesday and was quartered with Mrs Dodd. I saw Thomas Allen in the room where I slept. I had occasion to get a £5 note changed – I got 2 sovereigns and the rest silver. I had a gold ring in my breeches pocket but the silver and sovereigns were in my waistcoat. I placed the breeches on the window during the night – the money went missing later. Mrs Dodd the innkeeper of The Nag's Tail searched Allen and found some silver and a gold ring. Thomas Allen said that someone else must have put the ring there but the silver was his own. The Magistrate found Thomas Allen not guilty."

Carlisle Patriot, 1832

2. The Nag's Tail

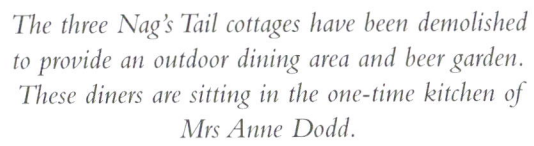

The three Nag's Tail cottages have been demolished to provide an outdoor dining area and beer garden. These diners are sitting in the one-time kitchen of Mrs Anne Dodd.

The 1851 census shows Anne Dodd as a 75 year old widow and innkeeper still here at The Nag's Tail living with her 48 year old son Joseph, a master tailor. Following Anne's death in 1860 the public house ceased trading and in 1868, Joseph Dodd advertised the premises as three dwelling houses for sale:

Dwelling Houses for Sale

> *"To be sold by private treaty, three dwelling houses situate behind the Horse Head Inn Brampton. Apply to Joseph Dodd the owner, behind the Horse Head, Brampton."*
>
> Carlisle Journal, 14th February 1868

Walking down the cobbled Horse Head Lane our route takes us across the Market Place to our next public house, The George and Dragon Inn.

Horse Head Lane has been named after the public house, as prior to 1895 this lane was called New Bank Street.

7

3
THE GEORGE AND DRAGON INN

At no 3 Market Place today stands a white three storey building where for more than 150 years, The George and Dragon traded as one of the busiest coaching inns of Brampton.

Like the Nag's Head, The George and Dragon was already a well established coaching inn at the beginning of the 19th century, and because of its success, continued to prosper well into the 20th century despite great efforts by the Temperance Movement to close it down. The property of John Gill, an influential business man of Brampton in 1800, this was a very popular venue for social occasions and official functions. Public auctions of property were regularly held here, as were inquests by the County Coroner. Farmers hired labourers and met merchants here, and sealed deals over a pint of ale. Fights, wrestling competitions and other pass-times were regular entertainment at The George and Dragon, so as we enter, what do we find?

Gormandising

"On Saturday last, a young man undertook for a trifling wager, to hop on one leg while he ate twelve penny pies. He commenced his operation in a manner which left little room to doubt his success; after devouring the 7th pie, he confessed reluctantly that although not tired of hopping, he was of eating!"

Carlisle Patriot, 1810

Again:

"The Assembly held at The George and Dragon Inn at Brampton on the 30th was well attended. Great credit is due to Mr and Mrs Graham for their polite attention to the ladies and gentlemen. After supper a certain gentleman – who may be very properly denominated "A Knight of the Trencher" undertook for a trifling wager of 2s 6d – to eat a chicken of no ordinary size and drink 2 quarts of ale in the space of 5 minutes – which treat he accomplished considerably within the limited time to the no small admiration of the beholders."

Carlisle Journal, 1809

3. The George and Dragon Inn

And again!

"Brampton – Yesterday week at a public house, for a wager of 1 gallon of ale, a bi-ped of the name of Robert Hope – a joiner of Brampton whose capaciousness of stomach appears to be his chief qualification, devoured 33 hard boiled eggs – the greater part of a six penny loaf, a half pound of butter in 33 minutes – after having just eaten half a pound of dried beef and drunk the greater part of two pints of beer."

Carlisle Journal, 1810

The George and Dragon had a reputation for being the "IN" place in Brampton for entertainment – it is where people often went to enjoy themselves, to be entertained and to be "seen":

Concert at Brampton

"The inhabitants of Brampton and its vicinity were highly gratified by a musical treat of a very superior description held at The George Inn on Friday 26th June 1821. numerously and responsibly attended. The overtures, glees, and tunes. Miss Shipley sang "Rest warrior rest" and a Scotch air in a pleasing manner was rapturously applauded. The deep rich bass voice of Mr Turpin was heard to advantage in "The Death of Nelson" and "The Wolf." Miss Gibson – an interesting little girl – sang "The sisters" with great sweetness and Mr Foster sang "Farewell Farewell Farewell" with great taste."

Carlisle Patriot, 31st January 1829

Ball at Brampton

"A Ball under the auspices of the Tradesman of Brampton will take place at The George Inn 10th April 1851. Tickets: Gentlemen 3s 6d: Ladies 2s 6d. An excellent Quadrille Band has been engaged."

Carlisle Journal, 28th March 1851

Life at The George and Dragon however was not always sweetness and light: There were events which illustrated more serious aspects of the times:

A Robbery at Brampton

"A robbery was committed at Brampton on Thursday night. A person named Proud – a cheese merchant from Carlisle, who attends Brampton Market each Wednesday, put his cart with the cheeses he had left into the barn belonging to Mr Joseph Graham of the George and Dragon inn. In the course of the night, the barn was broken open and three of the heaviest cheeses were taken away."

Carlisle Patriot, 17th August 1816

Inquest into the death of a baby at Brampton

"An inquest was held at The George and Dragon Inn, on the body of a new born baby – a male – found by John Dryden a farmer whilst attending to hedges in the Meeting House field near Brampton. The child was dead when found, was newly born and wrapped in a white cloth. Verdict found dead."

Carlisle Journal, 25th February 1826

Drunken driving

Drunken driving is not a 21st century phenomenon as the following report shows:

Just imagine the ignominy of losing your hat and whip and a mere guard taking over your job as driver – and being fined £5! The Carlisle Journal of March 1808 records another embarrassing episode here – to the landlord this time:

> On Wednesday last, the 14th inst., Thomas Stubbs, Driver of the Newcastle Mail-coach, between Brampton and Carlisle, was convicted in the penalty of £5, for being drunk when on duty. The coach left Brampton at the usual hour, about 9 o'clock at night, and had not proceeded far before Stubbs fell from his box into the road; the Guard immediately quitted his seat and was fortunate enough to stop the horses. Stubbs was taken up and placed on the top of the coach, and brought to Carlisle with the loss of his hat and whip; the Guard performing the duty of driver.

Carlisle Patriot, 1815.

3. The George and Dragon Inn

Landlord loses his clothes

> On the 25th ult. a person on horseback, of respectable appearance, stopped at the George and Dragon Inn, Brampton, where he resided that night. On the morning, the stranger early arose, and having hired a horse from a neighbour, decamped with a suit of clothes belonging to his landlord, leaving his own behind. The host's servant, getting information of the circumstance, instantly pursued, and nearly succeeded in apprehending the villain. The latter, however, was too alert: he left his horse, and taking refuge in a wood near Naworth Castle, eluded the vigilance of his pursuers.

We would hope that the hapless landlord Joseph Graham had an alternative set of clothes to wear whilst dealing with his customers that day. A recently discovered accounts ledger belonging to Isaac Bird grocer and wholesale spirit merchant of High Cross Street, records the supply of 20 gallons of Rum over the year of 1818 to Mr Joseph Graham innkeeper of The George Inn for the price of £15. A gallon of wine for the same year cost 17 shillings which would be very expensive by comparison.

From the Directories, Magistrates records, advertisements, and the Licensing Registers, the following were innkeepers at The George and Dragon:

1790 John Gill	1871–1880 Hannah Graham
1790–1861 Joseph and Mrs Graham	1892–1897 Martha Edgar
1861 George Graham	1900 William Lightfoot
1869 Thomas Graham	

The 1892 Return of Public Houses and Beer houses describes the George and Dragon as:

"8 Sleep, 40 Dine, 6 Horses. Next nearest public house – 20 yards."

So, now a stroll of just 20 yards around the corner will take us to number 4 Main Street our next public house – The Sportsman.

4
THE SPORTSMAN INN

At Number 4 Front Street today there is a tanning studio which is through the arch in the corner of Front Street, and along a passage way. This passage was once a lane which led to the back yards of The George and Dragon Inn and where there was previously a butchers shop.

The stone archway of the 1800s gives this corner much greater appeal than today's iron mesh door. The Sportsman is first recorded in 1811 with a Mr William Edmondson as owner, and Mr James Haston as landlord.

Because of restricted access and limited accommodation, this public house was never a coaching inn; there were neither stables nor yard for horses, coaches or carts, but it did have accommodation for 6 overnight guests. The Sportsman was essentially a drinking den, and this was reflected in the many unsavoury incidents which took place here; cheating at cards, thieving and fights many involving the landlord often being reported in the newspaper and in Magistrates Court appearances.

Cheating at Cards at The Sportsman

"A Brampton man with a rueful luck complained that he had been trepanned into playing a game of cards at The Sportsman Inn and was cheated of a considerable sum of money. On the evening of Wednesday last John Hetherington met James Haston landlord of the Sportsman Inn and two packmen – brothers called Miller and agreed to a card game of Loo. Hetherington, on entering the public house, had £12.10s. – a sum which he lost in a short time. Then one of the company bought his watch for £2.18s. Having been stripped of a further £2.16s. and 6d, Hetherington declared "You two are cheating" Hetherington then noticed a card sticking out of the breeches of one of the Millers, and a card at the sleeve of the other – one of them an ace and the other trumps. The Magistrates verdict: "It was beyond the jurisdiction of the Police."
Carlisle Patriot, 1821

Imagine the impact of losing £14.16s. and 6d. – more than three month's wages!

In 1829 Mr Edmondson died leaving The Sportsman in his will to his family of five children. The next report is of a Magistrates Court Case, and helps to give some idea of the layout of the lanes and streets of Brampton in 1844.

4. The Sportsman Inn

Police Superintendent attacked in Brampton

"Richard Pearce – "I am a police Superintendent at Brampton. I was on duty at Routledge's corner archway in Brampton (Routledge's corner was here at the archway close to The Sportsman where Joseph Routledge was innkeeper.) John Mark and Isaac Dawson came from under the arch having been drinking at The Sportsman. I proceeded in the direction of Souter How, I met two others – Armstrong and Dixon and passed them opposite The George and Dragon Inn on my way. I went to Forsters shop and stood there. Mark struck me and I hit him with my stick and a fight ensued." Isaac Dawson said "We came in front of The George where Mr Pearce was. We were past Forster's corner when Pearce came up to us and pushed us on the shoulder. We stopped at Swallow's corner (George Swallow was innkeeper of The Freemasons Arms – now Hamilton's shoe shop) Pearce came up again and struck Mark with his stick and beat him – this was close to Swallow's back door near one end of the Beck. We found Mark and Pearce lying on the ground at the corner of Swallow's house." Mark was found guilty by the Magistrate of common assault upon a Police Officer and sent to gaol with hard labour."

Carlisle Journal, January 1844

It seems that the life of a policeman in Brampton at this time was not a happy one! Superintendent Pearce features in another fight the following year as we shall see when we visit the Jolly Butcher shortly. The Sportsman attracted police attention in other ways:

Brampton landlord waters down the whisky

"George Blaylock, landlord at The Sportsman Inn Brampton was charged with selling whisky under the legal standard. Superintendent Parks said that he had purchased half a

pint of whisky and had sent one third of it to the County Analyst who certified that the whisky was 28.8 degrees below the required proof. He was fined 10 shillings with costs."
Carlisle Journal, 21st December, 1881

The Licensing magistrates appear to have been quite lenient in giving George Blaylock only a ten shilling fine, without issuing a warning, or endorsement of the public house licence. In 1894, The Sportsman Inn kept up its record of attracting trouble when the landlord George Nixon appeared before the Brampton Magistrates to answer a charge of assault upon William Wilkinson, labourer of Brampton, both of whom were also charged with being drunk at the same time. In the same year, William Graham of Longtown was found guilty of being drunk and disorderly and causing affray. Sergeant Brown witnessed landlord George Nixon throwing Wilkinson out of The Sportsman inn:

"Both wanting a fight, becoming noisy, swearing loudly and becoming a public menace."
North Cumberland Reformer, May 1894

At the end of the 19th century, the magistrates called for a six month assessment to be made of the condition and reputation of all public houses of Brampton, and of The Sportsman, the Superintendent of Police reported the following:

"The Sportsman Inn is occupied by Mr G. Nixon. This bar by Brampton Beck is low, dark and difficult to supervise. The front door opens into a passage way then an arch into Front Street. There is no urinal and people come out and commit a nuisance."
North Cumberland Reformer, September 1892

Accommodation at The Sportsman was cramped in the two downstairs drinking rooms, and it was difficult to avoid becoming involved in the conversations and questionable activities which often led to trouble here.

Our stay will be short before we either get our pockets picked, or involved in a game of cards with money on the table.

From the Directories, Magistrates' records and licensing register, the following were innkeepers at The Sportsman:

1821 James Haston	1879 George Blaylock
1834 John Bell	1894 George Nixon
1844 Joseph Routledge	1897 F. Howland
1871 William and Isabella Railton	1901 John Tait

We have only 6 yards to walk to our next public house The Jolly Butcher at number 6 Front Street.

5

THE JOLLY BUTCHER

Those who strode off the street into the parlour of number 6 Front Street in the 1800s would be astonished to find today, their public house turned into a Chinese take-away restaurant.

Here, at the Hoi Sun, Egg Foo Yung and fried rice have replaced that *"wholesome beverage of locally brewed beer,"* that once poured from the casks, at the Jolly Butcher public house.

Although never a coaching inn, The Jolly Butcher did have a dining area that could cater for 40 people, and there was overnight accommodation for 12. On the night of the 1851 Census, there were 5 lodgers staying overnight here.

The Jolly Butcher owes its name to the butcher's shop which for many years occupied these premises at the same time as being a public house. William Edmondson had been butcher/innkeeper here from 1805 to 1829 when he died at the age of 88 years.

The premises were put up for sale together with two other lots – a shop and the Sportsman Inn as shown in the following advertisement:

FREEHOLD PROPERTY FOR SALE

To be SOLD, by AUCTION, at the House of Mr. JOHN EDMONDSON, *Pack-Horse Inn*, BRAMPTON, on WEDNESDAY the 3d Day of JUNE, 1829, (in lots,)

ALL those PUBLIC-HOUSES, MESSUAGES, or TENEMENTS, situate at BRAMPTON, in the County of Cumberland.

Lot 1.— All that PUBLIC-HOUSE, situate in the Front-Street of BRAMPTON; consisting of a Kitchen and Parlour on the Ground Floor; Dining-Room, Drawing-Rooms, and 3 Lodging Rooms above; 4 Cellars, with a large Yard behind, and lately in the Possession of Mr. Wm. Edmondson, deceased.

Lot 2.— All that DWELLING-HOUSE and SHOP adjoining Lot 1st, consisting of One Shop and Two Rooms above, and now in the Occupation of Mr. Elizabeth Proud.

Lot 3.— All that PUBLIC-HOUSE known by the Sign of the *Sportsman*, adjoining Lot 2nd, consisting of Kitchen, Back Kitchen, and Two Parlours on the Ground Floor; 4 Lodging Rooms above, and 3 Cellars, now in the Occupation of Mr. James Hasting and others.

Lot 1, Lot 2, Lot 3.

Mention of Superintendent Pearce has already been made when we visited the Sportsman Inn where he had been involved in a fracas with 3 or 4 locals. It appears that Mr Pearce was not backward in using a bit of force to deal with trouble:

"John Potts charged with committing assault on Richard Pearce – Police Superintendent. In Court James Bell "I am a butcher in Brampton and on the night of 28th February – between 11 and midnight, I was disturbed from my bed by very loud shouting from a dozen or more persons. There was a mob hurraing – they were near the Horse and Farrier public house. I saw John Potts shouting and wanting in to the Horse and Farrier but the landlord would not let him in. Potts then picked up a stone and I heard a smashing of glass." Richard Pearce – "I am a police Superintendent I heard a great noise in the street. There was a crowd of 5 or 6 near The Jolly Butcher kept by Mrs Crozier. There was a noise in the house and I complained to the innkeeper. I later returned to find Potts kicking down the door of The Jolly Butcher. Mrs Crozier is a widow and she was pleased to see me and said these men are trying to take over my house. I then went to Parker's shop (The Black Bull Inn) there were many people standing about – 12 to 15 – they surrounded me. The prisoner Potts came up to me and in front of everyone taunted me and demanded why I had turned him out of The Jolly Butcher – when clearly there were others in Parkers Inn – but I did nothing and therefore he accused me of favouring Parker's Black Bull. He told me to open Parker's door and let him in. The crowd

5. The Jolly Butcher

swore at me – they then rushed at me. We fought. I defended myself with my stick. I was greatly abused. I then went into Parker's Black Bull and desired him to clear it of company. He said that he had had a window broken. I left Parker and then saw Potts standing in Front Street opposite Peter's Lane. Potts then struck me with a heavy stick. I received blows to my head and was sorely injured and taken into The Horse and Farrier and a surgeon sent for."

Carlisle Journal, 18th April 1846

Potts went on to testify and claim that it was Superintendent Pearce who laid the first blows. The Magistrates were not convinced with Potts' story and he was later found guilty of assault of a police officer, and was given 12 months in gaol with hard labour.

Later, during 1880 – 1897 Thomas Ramshay became the owner and Mr Riddell was innkeeper. Between them, these two developed the business as a wholesale and retail wine and spirit depot under the name of Riddell's Vaults. Although both the wholesale business and the public house operated side by side, The Jolly Butcher was forced to close by The Magistrates following increased pressure from The Brampton Temperance Movement in 1901.

From the Directories and Magistrates Licence Register the following are recorded as innkeepers at The Jolly Butcher:

18??–1829 William Edmondson
1834 Robert Armstrong
1847 Mary Crozier
1851 John Hardy – 1851 Census shows Mary Hardy as innkeeper
1890 Mr. T. R. Riddell

Our next port of call is a matter of 3 yards away – The Half Moon.

6

THE HALF MOON INN

The Half Moon Health Food Shop today, stands in the very same building that was The Half Moon public house during the 1800s. This public house had already existed here for many years before the beginning of 1800, and continued to survive throughout the following century, attracting quite a different clientele from its neighbours The Jolly Butcher and The Sportsman. Farmers in particular, regularly called here and stayed, not only for their personal rest and refreshment, but also to conduct business deals, hire labourers, sell cattle and horses, and order supplies.

The entrance to The Half Moon was not through today's door from Front Street into the shop, but into a passage-way from Front Street leading into the back yard, where there were stables, haylofts and a back gate into Beck Lane. The actual entrance into the Half Moon was through a door along this passage-way. Farmers on market days would lead their horse down this passage giving the impression that they were going into the public house together.

For more than a hundred years this public house was owned by the Thompson family. One of the rooms here doubled as a barber's shop as well as a public drinking parlour. Joseph Thompson was barber/innkeeper here in 1760 as were his son Joseph junior in 1812, his grandson (also Joseph) in 1838 and his great grandson Thomas in 1881. Thomas married Rebecca Nixon, and, like his predecessors was cutting hair and shaving his farmers well into his old age. Some people were not keen on Thomas' haircuts, as he had only one style for everybody – the gaol crop, others however, felt

6. The Half Moon Inn

it was good value as the gaol crop could last a long time before they had to pay for their next haircut.

Thomas' wife Rebecca is referred to by Peter Burn as being a cheery hostess with a comfortable and spotless kitchen. Rebecca outlived her husband, carrying on both the business of innkeeping and haircutting after he died in 1894. It would be interesting to know if she adopted the same gaol crop style as her husband.

In 1900, George Nixon – possibly a relative of Rebecca Thompson is recorded as landlord.

Left at The Half Moon – one sword and a bonnet

"The Half Moon Inn was where 8 of the troopers of Bonnie Prince Charlie were quartered in 1745. One of them left behind a dress sword which may have belonged to someone of distinction. Also left behind was a bonnet – both were of French origin and suggest that this public house was the headquarters of the French Ambassador who accompanied Bonnie Prince Charlie."

Onlooker Cumberland News, 5th December 1934

The Half Moon played an important part in the politics of Brampton, serving as one of the Tory strongholds of the town. This made it the target for the opposing Liberals. (See following chapter "Brampton Public houses and Politics –Half Moon eclipsed").

Incidents continue to happen here today. The current occupiers of The Half Moon have often experienced objects moving or falling off the shelves for no apparent reason, and occasionally a "presence" is felt. The ghost appears to be friendly and frightens no-one.

The Half Moon survived to 1901, but was put out of business by pressure upon the Magistrates from The Countess of Carlisle and The Brampton Temperance Movement. From The Directories and other records, the following innkeepers are shown for the Half Moon:

1790 Joseph Thompson
1822–1829 Joseph & Sarah Thompson
1847–1861 Miss Dinah Thompson
1869–1894 Thomas Thompson
1894–1900 Rebecca Thompson
1900–1901 George Nixon

The 1892 return of Public Houses and Beer Houses describes The Half Moon as:

"2 sleep, 12 Dine, 4 Horses, Next nearest public house 20 yards."

After our experiences in the Sportsman which was very cramped with little opportunity for privacy and quiet conversation, our stay in the Half Moon would be much more satisfying. It felt clean and well managed – a place where private discussion and business deals could be carried on without being overheard or interfered with – even by a ghost.

So, a little more relaxed than before, we can now proceed to our next public house which is only 20 yards away – The Black Bull.

7

THE BLACK BULL

The Black Bull was at 20 Front Street, the site occupied today by The Conservative Club. Like The Half Moon, entry to the Black Bull was not through a door opening off the street, instead, a passage way led from Front Street into a yard at the rear where there were stables and a gate opening on to Beck Lane. It was along this passage way that a door gave entrance to the Black Bull public house.

One of the front rooms of The Black Bull was used as a shop where Edward Parker, between 1823–1834, Thomas Snaith, between 1874–1884 and Senhouse Martin Winthrop 1892–1900, were all butchers as well as innkeepers.

The Black Bull was a "Tied House" – no beer other than that supplied by the John Iredale Brewery in Carlisle could be sold here, the £30 annual licence fee being paid by the brewery.

There are some uncertainties about The Black Bull public house. The 1829 directory describes The Black Bull as being in the Market Place; however this might be explained by looking at very early photographs of Brampton which show market stalls and carts on the cobbles in Front Street, as well as the Market Place. Although the Black Bull is described in the 1892 Return of Public Houses and Beer Houses as: *"No sleepers, No diners, 5 Horses"*, there is evidence to show that social gatherings did take place here:

Much Mirth and Glee from the ladies at the Black Bull

> *"On Monday last, a number of ladies in Brampton assembled at The Black Bull Inn and with much mirth and glee, partook of tea and tansy cake – after which music struck up and the matrons nimbly tripped to the floor with "Oh the days when I was young."*
>
> Carlisle Journal, 16th May 1808

Attempted Sale of a Bay Mare at the Black Bull

> *"On Tuesday last, a man came to Robert Armstrong's Black Bull Inn at Brampton and offered a bay mare for sale. He first demanded £20 for her, but at length agreed to take £7.10s, although she was worth double that sum. Mr Armstrong, innkeeper accused him of having stolen the mare and sent for the constable. On hearing this he started up and ran off. He was pursued by some young men and overtaken a short distance out of town when he confessed to having stolen the mare out of Yorkshire, and said that he would steal another the first opportunity as he would rather be hanged than die of starvation. The young men not having a constable with them allowed him to go."*
>
> Carlisle Patriot, December 1818

We shall look at crime and punishment shortly, but this story clearly shows that for some people without work or means, survival must have been very difficult. Anyone found guilty of horse stealing was usually sentenced to death by hanging or transportation overseas. This story suggests that the horse stealer was prepared to run the risk of being hanged rather than endure a painful death by starvation. It might also suggest that the young men chose to release him out of compassion rather than take him into custody.

We have already heard about the fracas which took place outside of the Black Bull between an unruly mob led by John Potts, and the superintendent of Police Mr Pearce. 20 years later the unfortunate police continued to be victims of drink fuelled violence:

7. The Black Bull

Assaulting a Police Sergeant

"William Edgar was charged with assaulting Sergeant Birrell of the Brampton Police whilst in the execution of his duty. It appears that at about quarter past 12 on Sunday morning, Sgt. Birrell was called to The Black Bull Inn at Brampton to assist in ejecting the prisoner. Edgar refused to leave the public house and struck the officer in the face, blacking his eye. Another officer coming up, the prisoner was secured and locked up. The Bench fined the prisoner thirty shillings."

Carlisle Journal, 25th February 1868

Brampton Brewster session
In 1881, the Brampton Magistrates bench carried out a review of all licensed premises:

"Altogether there are 64 public houses and 10 beer houses in the district. They were all granted new licences with the exception of The Black Bull whose landlord Ann Snaith was convicted and fined for selling drink during prohibited hours."

Carlisle Journal, February 1881

Despite this conviction, the public house licence was renewed, however The Black Bull featured in a further damning report by Superintendent Lancaster in 1892:

"The Black Bull, where Mr Winthrop is occupier is rather peculiar. A passage leads from Front Street to Beck Lane, and 12 yards along this passage there is a door into the kitchen. Two yards further on is the door into the bar. Mr Winthrop regularly locks this door to keep the police out."

North Cumberland Reformer, September 1892

Details from the Directories, Magistrates Records and Census, show the following innkeepers for The Black Bull:

1818–1822 Mr Robert Armstrong – he was also a horse dealer
1823–1834 Edward Parker – he was also a butcher
1847–1858 Ann Parker
1861 John Oliver
1871 Margaret and John Story – he was also a grocer
1869 John Philips
1874 Ann and Thomas Snaith – he was also a butcher
1879 Christopher Harding
1892–1900 Senhouse Martin Winthrop – he was also a butcher and politician

The 1892 Return of Public Houses and Beer Houses describes the Black Bull as:

"No sleepers, No diners, 5 horses. Next nearest public house 10 yards."

It is interesting to note that the Conservative Club now occupies this site because The Black Bull had for many years, strong links with the Tory party. Peter Burn mentions this public house in his lecture about life in Brampton when he was a boy, having visited here because free refreshments were on offer as part of the canvassing and electioneering of the people of Brampton, to encourage them to vote.

Senhouse Martin Winthrop was not only a butcher and innkeeper, but also a notoriously firebrand politician, eager to recruit to and further the Tory cause. It may well be because of this that the Liberal Countess of Carlisle and leader of The Temperance Movement targeted the Black Bull to become one of the very first public houses to be forced out of business by politics and by the Abstinence Movement.

So, exactly what would we have seen going on at The Black Bull when it came to election time?

BRAMPTON PUBLIC HOUSES AND POLITICS

Today, we have a system for voting which is open to everyone, and how we vote is kept a secret, thanks to the Ballot Act. However in 1841, things in Brampton were very different during political elections.

Apart from public houses, there were very few meeting places for the public, so each political party went to great trouble to use the public houses for "gatherings" or meetings, to promote their party and encourage the local people to vote for them in particular. The Black Bull, Half Moon and The White Lion sponsored the Tory candidate (the Yellows), whilst the Earl Grey and the Howard Arms sponsored the Whigs (The Blues):

> *"At Brampton yesterday, blue predominated everywhere in the streets, in the windows of houses and in the inns, with the exception of the White Lion where an inconsiderable number of yellows exerted themselves ineffectively to keep up their spirits. Blue carriages received loud and prolonged cheers as they drove up to the Howard Arms Inn, the headquarters of the blues – it was full to overflowing with the enthusiastic gatherings of farmers who had come to declare their fidelity to the cause of Liberalism. Among the visitors to the Howard Arms were Mr George Howard and his wife."*
>
> *Carlisle Journal, 6th April 1880*

The candidates standing for election visited their public house strongholds regularly during the election campaign, not only to speak about their political beliefs, but more importantly to win voters support in any way possible.

One way was to "buy" people's votes. This could take the form of actually giving money to a person in exchange for his promised vote at election time. Other candidates would pay for refreshments, giving free drinks and free tickets to buffets, meals or drinking sessions. Voters at the same time were not always scrupulous or loyal in their acceptance of such bribes, they clearly saw this as an opportunity of getting something for nothing, and they certainly took advantage, many not voting for the person to whom they had promised – others not bothering to vote at all. Peter Burn recalls as a boy going to the Black Bull and The White Hart public houses to partake of the free refreshments that were on offer and describes the scene in his lecture notes "A fireside Crack."

Another way that the public houses contributed to the politics and voting on the day was by "Boxing" voters. This was practised equally by both of the political parties. Men who were known to be definitely voting for "The other side" were enticed into a public house with the promise of free drinks and refreshments. They were plied with drink and when they became fuddled or under the influence, they were bundled into a room and locked there until the voting had closed!

Just picture the scene in Front Street at the end of the day of election when the unfortunate locked up voters were set free, only to find that the ballot station had closed! How did they respond to and deal with their captors? How did they drown their sorrows?

Eclipse of The Half Moon!

> "An eclipse took place at The Half Moon public house during the election! The landlord of this inn was known to have voted Tory, so some of the lively spirits amongst the local Liberals resolved to revenge him. During the night one of the radicals, liberally(!) supplied with coal tar and some stepladders painted over the sign of the Half Moon with black tar so as to eclipse it, and put the whole front of the house into mourning."
>
> *North Cumberland Reformer, January 1892*

The Half Moon was the target of another practical joke in the same election:

> "The same landlord was treated to another practical joke, when one of the Radicals ordered a large number of cabs from Carlisle under the name of the landlord of The Half Moon, to convey his friends to the polls. I remember standing in Front Street when about a dozen cabs duly arrived as per order from Carlisle, and the amusement which the needless arrival of these vehicles created in the town."
>
> *Brampton Then and Now – North Cumberland Reformer, January 1892*

Another incident which caused a great sensation started with a telegram being sent by an anonymous Liberal voter to the Military Authorities at Carlisle Castle, for soldiers to be despatched immediately to Brampton to quell a riot which was taking place in the town outside the Tory headquarters.

> "I remember standing in the Market Place when the soldiers arrived. A train had conveyed the soldiers to Brampton Fell gates, and they were marched down to Craw Hall where they fixed bayonets, and then into the town centre. Nothing in particular was going on in this sleepy town to relieve the monotony of parliamentary lobbying. The soldiers were eventually

kept at the police Station should any occasion arise for them to be used– but this was all a practical joke set about by one party against the other."
North Cumberland Reformer, January 1892

After the above election had taken place, there were great celebrations by the Liberals in Brampton;

"The display of Blue favours has made it obvious that Unionism is on its last legs in Brampton. People expressed their delight by forming a procession headed by a fife and drum band and banners. On approaching the public houses of the Tories the band left off the cheerful strains and took up "The Death March." The innkeeper appeared at the front door and the inmates at the windows with an abundant supply of water. While in the act of throwing it upon the Liberals, a Gladstonian pushed the Landlord out into Front Street – he alone receiving the deluge intended for the Gladstone Band."
North Cumberland Reformer, September 1892

So, as we escape from the exhortations of politicians urging us to vote, promising a brave new world, we will just escape into the passage way and then outside to take 10 paces along Front Street towards our next public house – The Samson Inn, but keep a look-out for buckets of water and soldiers with fixed bayonets.

8

THE SAMSON INN

The Samson Inn was in Front Street and occupied the premises which are now the gallery of Castle Framing Ltd. The Samson Inn is first recorded in 1851 and had a fairly short career as a public house, closing in 1900 due to pressure from The Temperance Movement upon the Magistrates, to close it.

The naming of Public Houses was often determined by current fashion or important events taking place locally, nationally and even internationally. Since this public house came into being around 1830–1840, it is likely that the Samson is named after the locomotive which travelled the newly opened Newcastle to Carlisle railway line. Having been built by Hawthorns of Newcastle in the spring of 1836,

8. The Samson Inn

The Samson's first assignment was to demonstrate the power of steam locomotives at a grand opening ceremony of the Carlisle to Greenhead section of the Newcastle to Carlisle Railway. The problem however was how to get the locomotive from Newcastle to Carlisle for the ceremony, as the line between Haydon Bridge and Haltwhistle had not yet been built!

A team of 15 horses hauled the Samson by road for the occasion, and the locomotive was described in the newspapers as:

"A powerful and beautiful engine calculated to draw immense weight."

This statement was later well proven when the Samson hauled a train of 34 wagons laden with coal, and 12 coaches containing 180 passengers from Brampton Station to Carlisle.

The arrival of rail travel caused quite a stir in Brampton. Many business people feared the impact such high speed travel would have upon the mail coaches, blacksmiths, cart makers and menders, post houses, coaching inns – a whole industry that depended upon travel by horse on roads. Such businesses felt quite threatened by the prospect of speedy travel for large numbers of passengers and parcels at the same time – something with which a coach and four horses could never equal. The wonder of carriages travelling as fast as 30 miles per hour caused sensation in some, and fear in others that passengers would not be able to breathe at such a high speed.

The Samson Inn had no accommodation for horses and was therefore not a coaching or posting inn. In 1892 things got a little out of hand at The Samson:

Only one pint at Ramshay's

John Scott, Thomas Thompson and William Robinson were charged with being drunk and disorderly but all pleaded not guilty. Sergeant Lewis heard a disturbance at 11.40pm and found the defendants very drunk, shouting, singing, swearing and wanting to fight each other. He ordered them away but they renewed their disturbances. Robinson said that all that they had drunk was one pint of ale at Ramshay's. All were found guilty and fined 7s and 6 pence – as they had all been up before the magistrate for drunkenness on previous occasions."
North Cumberland Reformer, September 1892

Returning to the theme that many public houses were named after contemporary events, locally and internationally, we will visit the back yard of The Samson Inn later in our travels, to find The Klondike Bar. This bar was set up in the 1850s by The Brampton Old Brewery, at the rear of the Samson Inn facing into Beck Lane. Around this time there was much interest in the newspapers about investors rushing to the Yukon to join entrepreneurs prospecting for gold, hoping to become rich overnight.

Details from the Directories, licensing records etc show the following innkeepers at The Samson Inn;

1851 Robert Hutchinson
1858 James Watson
1879 Mary Watson
1892 James Patterson
1894 George Ramshay
1901 Mrs C. Carrick

The 1892 Return of Public Houses and Beer Houses describes The Samson inn as:

"4 sleep, 12 Dine, No horses. Next nearest public house 10 yards."

But why are there so many public houses so close together? I hear you ask. Well, perhaps it is the moment for us to take some time out from our public house crawl to consider exactly that question:

BUT, WHY ARE THERE SO MANY PUBLIC HOUSES AROUND?

Ale houses were established in this country as early as A.D. 721. In Restoration England, local water was too dangerous to drink because of pollution, so ale is what most people drank, it was an Olde English drinke, but quite weak. In the 16th century the idea came from Flanders to add hops in the making of ale, and as a result, "beer" became the stronger and much more acceptable drink for most people.

By 1600 beer was being manufactured in an organised way by breweries, and beer houses, taverns and inns developed where people gathered together either for business or the pleasure of each others company.

By the nineteenth century across the country, there were three types of retail outlets selling drink to the public:

Alehouses – in which beer and ale were on sale.
Taverns – where wine could be bought in addition to beer and ale.
Inns – which provided food and shelter, wine, spirits, beer, and ale.

These establishments found it a good idea to advertise their existence to passers-by, travellers and coachmen, by fixing a board outside their premises, often with a name on it.

In 1621, the Government had recognised the need to control the consumption of beer alcohol and wine, so passed laws which gave the responsibility to the local Magistrate to control the number of places where such drink could be bought, and called them "licensed" premises. Later in 1736, the Government introduced the following Act of Parliament:

37 Anno Novo Georgi II Regis 1736

"An Act for laying Duty upon the retailers of spirituous liquors and for licensing retailers thereof."

Life in Brampton with 63 Public Houses

The Government felt that it was necessary to control drunkenness in "the lower orders" since it feared that drunkenness might lead to violence and revolt against the State, and be detrimental to the economy. However philanthropic this may have been, there was perhaps a stronger motive behind the Act – an opportunity to raise income for the government by putting a tax on all drinking, and forcing taverns to pay an annual licence fee for the privilege of serving the public with drink. No tavern was allowed to stay in business unless an application was made to and approval given by the local magistrates, with an annual fee of £30 to be paid – in addition to a surety or a bond of £20 payable by each of two other people, which would be forfeited in the event of failure by the innkeeper to keep good order and discipline.

London was allowed 40 licensed houses, small country villages only one, and small towns, ten. This then was the case at the turn of the century – in 1795 Brampton's ten licensed premises were:

The Horse Head, The King's Arms, The Bush, The Howard Arms, The Crown, The Globe, The Pack Horse, The White Lion, The Shoulder of Mutton, The George and Dragon.

For the period 1800 – 1820 this number stayed the same; very strict control was exercised by the magistrates over the number of public houses allowed, their hours of opening, and their conduct. Landlords were fined if drunkenness was permitted on their premises.

In 1822 however, the first signs of dissatisfaction with the system began to appear. Breweries had become a very powerful monopoly, dictating and controlling to their own favour, all manufacture and distribution of beer. Breweries would pay the landlord's licence fee to the magistrate in return for the landlord's agreement to selling only beer made by that brewery, at risk of being evicted if this agreement was infringed. The quality of beer was poor and often diluted. Lord Brougham, a Penrith politician, felt that the public deserved a better quality beer and that it should be available in the same way as people bought their loaves of bread, at the chandler's shop. He felt that the monopoly of the brewers should be broken up and competition from other manufacturers should be introduced to improve the quality of beer:

Mr Brougham's Beer Retail Bill – Third Reading

"To enable the poor man to purchase his beer as he now does his loaf – at the chandlers shop. As the law stands, no "strong beer" is allowed to be retailed. Small beer only is sold and we know that the word "small" never was applied better than in this case. Never was there a more meagre or miserable liquid than this small beer. If we wish to put down the Gin shops which are injurious to health and morals of our community, we must give the humbler portions of the people something better than this "small beer."

Carlisle Journal, 1822

Gin had become a very cheap and popular drink – more so in London than in Brampton, but its effects upon the masses was clear for anyone to see. There was increased drunkenness, violence, theft, family break down, with men selling their wives' possessions to obtain money for gin, with accidents in the street and at work becoming a significant problem alongside the poverty caused by people's increasing dependency or addiction to gin drinking. Lord Brougham therefore believed that by encouraging more brewers to make a better quality "Strong" beer which would be cheaper, and then the social degradation caused by gin would be turned around. There was a great belief that beer was a wholesome and healthy drink whilst spirits were damaging to the human body. Lord Brougham in the meantime became Chancellor of the Exchequer and his Beer Retail Bill was put off to a later date. In his position as Chancellor he would have a greater sphere of influence, and be able to encourage others – like the Duke of Wellington to address the issue.

The Duke of Wellington's Beer Act 1830
The following report appears in the Carlisle Journal of 11th September 1830:

> *"the one measure of the last session of Parliament – the Duke of Wellington's Beer Bill is likely to prove highly beneficial to all classes by encouraging the production of a good and wholesome beverage at a very cheap price – so cheap that it is to be within the reach of almost the poorest classes and still more – by breaking up a most pernicious system of monopoly – a system of the grossest nature by which ample fortunes are being made up by breweries at the expense of the public – we mean the licensing system.*
>
> *What could be more disgraceful for a country – to see a junta of proprietors of the inns and brewers refusing to license another house unless it is their own property or where the landlord would only agree to sell their beer and no other.*
>
> *The second clause of the Bill allows any householder to apply for and obtain a licence to sell ale, beer porter or cider by retail – by paying a licence fee of now only two guineas, and a surety of £20 for their keeping an orderly house. The sole qualification is that the person licensed be a ratepayer on the Parish books. Further, it allows a licensee to brew their own beer. This in one fell swoop destroys the present monopoly."*

Politically, the Tories believed that by changing the licensing laws and making it easier to grant licences for public houses, increased sales of beer would follow – with the resulting need for more malt and therefore more wheat and barley to be produced. Farmers would gain from this increased demand, and it would set up new businesses in the brewing industry – more employment, more prosperity and therefore good for the economy.

The Whigs on the other hand believed that the new system would liberalise the manufacture of beer, by forcing competition and pressing for free trade, it would take away the stranglehold that existing brewers had on all aspects of the trade, and would provide more employment opportunities for the labouring classes.

Both sides of Parliament agreed that it would be a measure highly beneficial to all communities. The Bill had a very smooth passage through the House of Commons. In his summing up of the proposal in the House of Lords, The Duke of Wellington stated that he believed that there would be no real danger of disturbances, or of riotous behaviour – but instead the Bill would cut the price of a quart of beer from 5d to 3d and that was good enough for their Lordships. No-one even troubled to put it to parliament for a vote, and on Friday 23rd July 1830 The Duke of Wellington's Beer Act received Royal Ascent.

The passing of the Act marked a major turning point in the fortunes and history of public houses in Britain. A "Beer House Boom" took place all over the country. All that was needed was a fee of 2 Guineas, which allowed any house owner to set up in business as a public house – but could only sell beer, ale, or porter – not spirits or wines.

Many premises became beer houses overnight. The two guineas licence fee was often quickly found by relatives or friends combining together to put one of their family into business – providing them with hope of a steady second income.

Some parishes even paid the two guinea fee for some widows – to help them set themselves up in business and thereby remove them from the parish poor relief list.

Immediately the result was astonishing. Queues formed outside the Excise offices, of house owners anxious to put their two guineas on the table and go back home to begin business as a beer house keeper. Within 6 years of the passing of the Duke of Wellington's Beer Act, beer house numbers increased rapidly, blossoming in every tiny hamlet and large town of the country. Often a carpenter, butcher or tailor would set up as a beer house to supplement his income, his wife often being left to run the business during his working day. This is clearly illustrated in Brampton shortly after the Act was introduced:

1834 Robert Armstrong – innkeeper of Jolly Butcher, was also a butcher
1851 James Barker – innkeeper of The Crown, was also a plasterer
1834 Joseph Bell – innkeeper of The Board, was also a draper
1850 George Brown – innkeeper of The Odd fellows, was also a farmer
1850 John Dodd – innkeeper of White Lion, was also a cabinet maker
1850 Elizabeth Knott – innkeeper of Hare and Hounds, was also a widow
1851 Ann Parker – innkeeper Black Bull, was also a widow
1847 Margaret Ward – innkeeper of Coach and Horses, was also a widow
1840 Thomas Thompson – innkeeper of Half Moon, was also a barber
1830 Henry Story – innkeeper of The Sands House, was also a wheelwright

Some reporters claimed that it was customary for wives to run the business throughout the day whilst the husband after returning from a day's work would spend

But, why are there so many Public Houses around?

the evening "drinking the profits." Several records of inns show that, following the death of the innkeeper, the surviving widow continued the business, as shown by this amusing epitaph seen on a gravestone (not in Brampton):

"Here doth lie in hopes of Zion
the one-time landlord of the Lyon
resigned into the heavenly will
his wife doth keep the business still"

The Victorian public house

At the same time as all these changes were taking place, the Government decided to remove all taxes from beer and ale. The objective was to encourage the consumption of beer, rather than gin. Although greatly welcomed by most people, there were some voices who doubted the wisdom of such liberalisation:

"The labourer on his way home now has to run the gauntlet through three to four beer shops in each of which are his fellow labourers, carousing and beckoning him to join with them."

"Many of our readers will regret the Beer Bill. It is nothing more or less than converting all the hucksters' shops in the towns and villages of the kingdom into alehouses and without the control of the Magistrates."

"There will be a total loss of the taxes taken by the Inland Revenue."

"We observe that the arrangements fixed by the Magistrate for granting beer licences in Cumberland – it is a great pity, they are intolerable nuisances. Several of them have actually been opened in premises that were never suitable and their condition poor. They are now scenes of riot, debauchery, and many are now resorts for the idle and profligate – a shame and disgrace to a civilised country."

"The beer Emancipation Bill as it is facetiously called is most injurious to a large portion of the working classes. The disturbed state of our streets on a Saturday night and Sunday morning owing entirely to intemperance has never had a parallel."

Carlisle Patriot, 9th November 1832

Brampton Magistrates also felt the impact of the New Beer Act:

"As a result of the passing of the Beer Act, the price of beer is reduced to 4d. Late on Saturday night last, several young men were taken into custody by police constables for noisy and turbulent behaviour on the streets. They had been enjoying the fourpenny and appeared determined to let their fellow citizens hear the effects of this new potent beverage. They were liberated on Sunday morning to appear before the magistrate on Monday – when they were discharged after a suitable admonition."

Carlisle Journal, 1830

In 1833 The House of Commons held a review of the impact of the Beer Bill to determine whether the objectives were being achieved. There was acknowledgement that *"considerable evils have arisen initially from the changes in the supervision of Beer Shops"* but no change to the provisions of the Act was proposed.

We can now resume our visit to the public houses of Brampton – understanding perhaps a little more clearly why so many of them suddenly came into being. So far we have visited 10, we have another 53 on our list, and we were about to stroll the 10 yards to our next stopping place – The Shoulder of Mutton.

9

THE SHOULDER OF MUTTON

The Shoulder of Mutton stands in Front Street today, in precisely the same place that it has occupied for over 200 years. The Shoulder of Mutton was already a well established public house and coaching inn before 1800, with a busy dining room upstairs, lounges downstairs, kitchen, stables, hay barns and a large secure yard for coaches and carts at the rear, with innkeeper John James who was also a victualler. In the mid 1830s a brewing house was built as a direct result of the opportunities provided by the Duke of Wellington's Beer Act for small breweries to be set up.

Although directories refer to this public house as The Shoulder of Mutton, a record of a meeting held in October 1794 refers to The Quarter of Mutton:

> A WELL-ACCUSTOMED
> **PUBLIC HOUSE IN BRAMPTON,**
> *And TWO FIELDS, to LET.*
> To be LET, for a Term of Years, and Entered upon at May-day next,
> ALL that old-established and well-accustomed PUBLIC HOUSE, situate in the Front Street in BRAMPTON, in the County of Cumberland, called and known by the Sign of the *Quarter of Mutton*, consisting of an excellent Dwelling House, Brewhouse, large Cellar, inclosed Yard, two Stables, with Hay-lofts above the same, and other Out-offices, and now in the occupation of Mr. James Nicholson.

Carlisle Journal, January 1832.

"At the house of John Gill at the sign of The Quarter of Mutton, Brampton to set up the rules and orders of The Undaunted and Benevolent Society."

Cumberland News, 1954

An advertisement in the Carlisle Journal also names this public house as The Quarter of Mutton:

The main story to tell about the Shoulder of Mutton concerns the visit by a Lancashire man called Thomas Whittaker, later to become Sir Thomas Whittaker, an earnest enthusiast of the Total Abstinence Movement which was the forerunner of The Temperance Movement. Thomas was engaged in a tour of Cumberland, visiting various venues to speak about the folly of drinking. He had come to Brampton to try to convince people to give up drinking altogether, but as can be imagined, he was not warmly received, particularly by the innkeepers. On arriving in Brampton on his speaking tour, Thomas Whittaker found that all the chapels and public meeting halls were shut against him and he was left with no alternative but to hire a room – in a public house of all places! That room was here, upstairs at The Shoulder of Mutton.

No sooner had Thomas begun his talk, than there was a noisy interruption at the door by one of the "regulars" of The Shoulder of Mutton, rather the worse for drink interrupting the speaker and making a general nuisance of himself. After some minutes the troublesome drinker was encouraged back downstairs much to the relief of the speaker, who, picking up from where he had left off was able only to utter the next sentence before another of the regular drinkers pounded on the door wishing to add his contribution to the debate. Thomas Whittaker's meeting

9. The Shoulder of Mutton

was made very difficult by the frequent interruptions by relays of drunks from the bar downstairs which appears to have been a deliberate plan to dissuade him from his course.

This public house was used regularly as a venue for assemblies, public auctions of property and occasionally the Coroner conducted inquests here. The 1879 Cumberland Directory refers to The Shoulder of Mutton having an excellent Bagatelle Board. For such a busy public house, it seems surprising that so many of the innkeepers could find time to practice their other trade or profession:

1800 John James was also a victualler
1811 John Gill was also a nailor
1847 Robert Taylor was also a farmer
1871 Isaac Park was also a potato, poultry and manure merchant!

Other licensees were:
1832 James Nicholson
1847 George Humbrel
1851 William Richardson
1865 John Noble
1866 W. J. Burrows
1869 George Hogg

George Humbrel's recycling scheme for newspapers.
In 1847 the Carlisle Journal was the well recognised local newspaper providing most of the news for the area, as does the Cumberland News today.

Costing 7 pence, the Carlisle Journal was considered quite expensive and so was not generally taken by the less well off or poor people, most of whom could not read anyway. George Humbrel's Shoulder of Mutton took this newspaper each week and introduced an innovative scheme in "recycling." The newspaper was available for clients using the public house, but when it was a few days old, it was made available on loan to outsiders – for a charge of a half penny an hour.

Peter Burn in his talk "Brampton as I have known it" describes the scheme;

"Children were sent by their parents to the public house to hire the newspaper for an hour's reading – for which they paid a half penny – this privilege enjoyed on a paper that was 2 to 3 days old."

After leaving the Shoulder of Mutton, George Humbrel moved to Newcastle, but appears to have become involved in a rather suspicious incident when visiting Carlisle later:

George Humbrel robbed

"On the 29th October George Humbrel was in Carlisle and was proceeding down Botchergate in a quest for lodging when he met Jane Anderson (Age 21 years) and another woman. Jane Anderson asked him where he was going; when he said he wanted a bed, she recommended him to come with her and she would accommodate him. He went to her house and having seen the bed, approved of it, took out his purse and paid one shilling for it. He put his purse back in his waistcoat pocket, when Jane Anderson snatched it out again and ran off with it. In Court George Humbrel was reluctant to give other details. Jane Anderson was sentenced to 3 month's imprisonment and hard labour."

Carlisle Journal, 10th January 1851

The 1892 Return of Licensed Public houses and Beer houses describes The Shoulder of Mutton as:

"6 sleep, 30 Dine, 10 horses, next nearest public house 20 yards."

20 yards will lead us to our next port of call – Modlen's Spirit Vaults.

10

MODLEN'S SPIRIT VAULTS

Brampton News is today's resident at number 32 Front Street, but in the 1800s it was Modlen's Spirit Vaults that were in business here. The first records which identify this public house appear in 1835 under the management of a Mr Cheesebrough, who was also a parish councillor.

Thomas Modlen came next – he was married to Arabella who had inherited two dwellings in Front Street from William Edmondson; one close to the Sportsman Inn, and the other here at number 32, which Thomas ran as a hatters shop. It was Thomas' brother Robert who was the spirit merchant, renting premises in the Back Street, but he died whilst quite young, so his widow Jane and her three children moved into Thomas' house bringing their spirit business with them:

41

Life in Brampton with 63 Public Houses

Thomas Modlen sets up a Spirits Vaults in Front Street Brampton

"Thomas Modlen begs leave to respectfully inform his friends and the public generally, that he has commenced the above business on his own account in the shop next door to his house situated in Front Street, where he hopes by strict attention and keeping to hand articles of first quality only, to merit their support. Thomas Modlen also begs to intimate that he has constantly on hand a first class stock of beers wines and cordials."

Carlisle Journal, 5th February 1857

The Tithe map shows Thomas and his sister-in-law Jane living here:

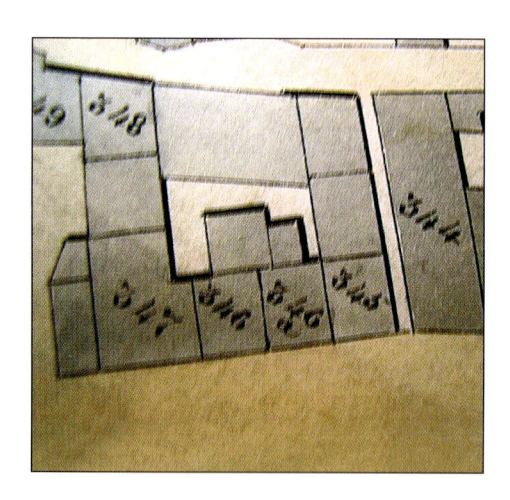

In his Shire book "The Victorian Public House" Richard Tames suggests that in the industrial midlands and the North, the public bar was often called "the vaults."

NOTICE OF REMOVAL.

ROBERT MODLEN,
WHOLESALE AND
FAMILY WINE AND SPIRIT MERCHANT,
FRONT STREET, BRAMPTON,
Begs to inform his Friends and Customers and the Public generally that he will, on THURSDAY, AUGUST 6th, REMOVE to the Premises lately known as the *STRING OF HORSES INN*, situate at the head of HIGH CROSS STREET, BRAMPTON, which has been recently Enlarged and adapted to meet the requirements of his Business, and where he trusts to be favoured with a continuance of their esteemed Orders.
Brampton, July 24th, 1868.

Carlisle Journal, 6th August 1868.

42

10. Modlen's Spirit Vaults

Modlen's, Shoulder of Mutton, Samson, Black Bull.

Modlen's was a small public house by comparison with its neighbours. There was a bar, kitchen and store on the ground floor, with overnight accommodation upstairs for 4 guests, but no dining room is mentioned. There were neither stables nor yard at the rear to park carts, so this public house was used by casual drinkers and as a stopping place for visitors travelling on foot.

In 1859 Thomas died leaving his sister in law Jane to manage the business until her own son Robert was old enough to take over. Robert, after gaining experience as an apprentice here, eventually set up business on his own in The String of Horses, taking his mother Jane and his sisters with him to live there:

Following Robert Modlen's removal to The String of Horses, the premises here at number 32 were sold and converted to a shop. After such a brief visit we will press on to our next venue, a matter of 10 yards to:

The Shepherd – or is it The Lion and The Lamb?

11

THE SHEPHERD AND THE LION AND THE LAMB

The Shepherd was at 36 Front Street in premises that are now occupied by an Indian take away Restaurant, and on the corner of Shepherds Lane. Old photographs identify the Shepherd as being at that location in the 1860s–1870s.

However the history of these premises is a puzzle. Peter Burn, historian and poet in his lecture notes about Brampton presents the puzzle:

11. The Shepherd and The Lion and the Lamb

"Two or three public houses have changed their names. The Crown Inn in my day was known as The Horse and Farrier. The Shepherd as the Lion and the Lamb; the Anchor as the Shepherd and also The Lord Nelson. Sammy Smith ran that public house as The Lord Nelson – he was succeeded by Peggie Hetherington who gave it name of Shepherd. Peggie on her removal to The Lion and the Lamb took her sign board with her. Her husband had been a shepherd and it would seem the good woman sought to perpetuate the departed's memory in the usage of the Shepherd sign."

The Lion and the Lamb

The first records of The Lion and The Lamb show Thomas and Jane Bell as innkeepers in 1816. In 1830 a notice was placed in the Carlisle Patriot about a bankrupt person called John Robson and asked anyone who was owed money by John Robson to attend a creditors meeting at the:

"Public House of Thomas Bell at the sign of the Lion and The Lamb."

Five years later, the innkeeper here was a Mr Loftus, as shown in the accounts book of a Brampton butcher:

In 1850, The Lion and the Lamb was advertised for sale:

"To be sold by public auction on Wednesday 15th May 1850, at 6 o'clock in the evening, at The Lion and The Lamb inn at Brampton: all that well accustomed and old established INN known by the sign of The Lion And The Lamb in the Front Street Brampton with stabling, slaughter house and enclosed yard adjoining, now occupied by Mr and Mrs Groves, owners thereof."

Carlisle Journal, May 1850

Life in Brampton with 63 Public Houses

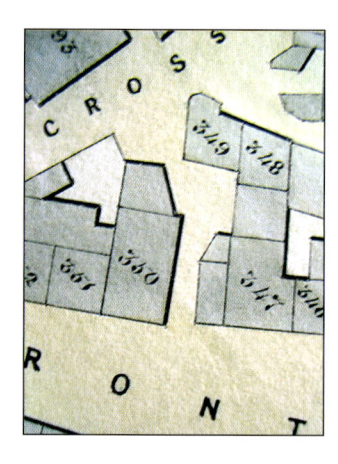

Robert Smith	178
Elizabeth Hope	231
Anne Parker	341
Joseph Parker	342
Margaret Hetherington	350
James Millican	351
William Hind	352

These are the only records to confirm the existence of The Lion and The Lamb public house, which had a fairly short career of only 34 years. No Magistrate's Court reports have been seen of untoward incidents here, so we can assume that it was a well run establishment managing to keep out of trouble. The inn was small but enjoyed a central position in the town so was well used by people travelling to and from the market. There was room for 6 overnight guests and stabling for three horses with a lock up yard at the rear for carts, but this was never a stopping place for coaches.

The Shepherd Inn
Without moving an inch, we can now move one month to June 1850 when The Lion and The Lamb had been bought and renamed "The Shepherd" by Peggie Hetherington the new innkeeper and owner. Peggie Hetherington's husband had been a shepherd and was possibly alive when they managed a different public house further up the street at number 25. The 1851 Census records Margaret Hetherington (Peggie) a widow aged 47, as landlady living here with James Little her brother. The Tithe Map also records her as owner of these premises:

In 1861 The Shepherd was advertised to let, perhaps Peggie Hetherington had grown tired of running the public house herself, preferring to remain the owner of the premises but letting it out to someone else to manage it:

The Shepherd public house – To Let

"To be let and entered upon at Whitsuntide next, or sooner if agreed upon.
All that well accustomed PUBLIC HOUSE with good stabling situate in the Front Street of Brampton known by the sign of THE SHEPHERD successively carried on by the owner for a number of years. Proposals will be received up to the first day of April."
Carlisle Journal, 22nd March 1861

11. The Shepherd and The Lion and the Lamb

    Resulting from this advertisement, Henry Taylor became the new tenant, staying here until 1881 when Christopher Harding took over the licence.

    In 1884 The Countess of Carlisle, had gained a fair head of steam in her campaign to fight the demon drink, and in her efforts to support the Temperance Movement in Brampton. Rosalind Howard saw the ailing Shepherd Inn as an excellent target, so brought pressure to bear on the Magistrates to close it, claiming that there were already too many public houses in Brampton. Immediately upon its' closure, Rosalind herself took out a lease on the Shepherd and re-opened it as The Shepherd Coffee Tavern providing a meeting place where people who did not want to drink intoxicating drinks could meet to read newspapers and books, and have discussions with like-minded people. The Shepherd became a popular meeting place for families. It was managed by Mr Hamilton Harding, and served as the venue for band practice for the Brampton Temperance Movement Brass Band, of which Rosalind was president.

    Our next port of call is The Blue Bell Inn at 56 Front Street – a stroll of 30 yards.

12

THE BLUE BELL

The Blue Bell was in Front Street, opposite the entrance to Church Lane. The 1892 Return of Licensed Public houses describes the Blue Bell as:

"4 Sleep; 15 dine; 2 horses. Next nearest public house 30 yards."

The first record appears in 1813 when Mrs Wallace was licensee, and throughout its career from 1813 through to 1900 when it was closed by the Magistrates following pressure from the Temperance Movement, the Carlisle and District Bank were owners. This was a "tied" house – no ale, beer or porter other than that manufactured by the Brampton Old Brewery Company could be sold here.

12. The Blue Bell

What was Porter? Was it different from beer?

"The wholesome and excellent beverage of porter obtained its name in 1730, from the following circumstances: Prior to the above mentioned period, the malt liquors in general use were ale, beer, and twopenny; and it was customary for drinkers to call for a pint of half-and-half, i.e. a half of ale and half of beer, or a half of ale and a half of twopenny. In course of time, it also became practice to call for a pint of three threads, meaning a third of ale, beer and twopenny. Thus the publican had the trouble to go to three casks, turn three cocks, for a pint of liquor. To avoid this trouble and waste, a brewer of the name of Harwood, conceived of the idea of making liquor which should partake of the united flavours of ale, beer and twopenny. He did so and succeeded, calling it entire, meaning that it was drawn entirely from one cask. It was a very nourishing liquor and was very suitable for porters and other working class people, hence the name of porter."

Carlisle Journal, 2nd January 1802

A Stolen coat re-appears at The Blue Bell

"John Boyle age 28 was indicted for having stolen a coat valued at two shillings belonging to John Charters of Stapleton. John Charters lives at Luckens, 9 miles from Brampton..
"On the 13th January I went into a field to work. I took off my coat and placed it under the hedge on the road leading to Nicholforest. I was working 60 yards away from it. I went to dinner, left the coat under the hedge, and when I got back it was gone." Archibald Goodfellow said "I live at Boltonfellend 3 miles from John Charters told me of his losing his coat. Two days later, I was in Brampton at The Blue Bell public house. I saw the prisoner begging and later saw him with the coat on and I told him that I thought it had been stolen. I told him that he was my prisoner – but he ran away. I cried "stop thief." Joseph little, constable of Brampton arrested John Boyle. He was found guilty and given 6 months in prison with hard labour."

Carlisle Patriot, 1840

Six months in prison with hard labour seems a very high price to pay for stealing a coat worth two shillings. Later, we shall be looking at crime and punishment, but here is a report of another incident which took place in The Blue Bell – this time with a remarkably light sentence for quite a serious crime.

Landlady assaulted at The Blue Bell

"Robert Elsdon landlord of The Blue Bell complained in court of James Jackson for an assault. James Jackson went into the Blue Bell Inn and abused the landlady, and insisted upon being supplied with drink – which was refused. A row ensued and James Jackson

struck the landlord on his head and kicked him and then took possession of the house. The family wisely deeming discretion the better part of valour withdrew to a more peaceful place in a neighbour's house and sent for the constable. James Jackson was found guilty and fined five shillings and costs or 14 days in confinement."

Carlisle Journal, May 4th 1844

Landlord waters down his rum

"Thomas Parker, landlord at Brampton's Blue Bell Inn, was charged with selling adulterated rum on the 27th February. Supt. Parks bought a gill of rum and sent it to the County Analyst who certified that it was diluted with one third of water. Parker was fined five shillings."

Carlisle Journal, 16th April 1880

In 1891, the Temperance Movement worked hard to convince the licensing Authority that there were too many public houses in Brampton, and persuaded the Magistrates to carry out a 6 month inspection and assessment of the condition of all public houses in the town. When the report was completed, the evidence was put forward by the police to the magistrates, with an eager Lady Rosalind in the public gallery. In respect of the Blue Bell, Police Sergeant Fisher reported:

"I have regularly seen half a dozen women in the Blue Bell, of the class which come from the common lodging houses."

North Cumberland Reformer, 1892

The Blue Bell was amongst seven other public houses closed by the Magistrates as a direct result of this survey.

The Directories, and Magistrates Court reports, show the following innkeepers at The Blue Bell:

1811 William and Mrs Wallace	1879–1884 James and Annie Graham
1823–1829 W. Turpin	1881 Thomas Parker
1834 John Elliot	1882 David Phillips
1844 Robert Elsdon	1892 George Taylor
1847–1851 James Watson	1894 John Richardson/M. Laidlow
1855 William Jackson	1897 Daniel Lawson
1858–1879 Mrs Ann Crozier	1900 Hannah Allen

30 yards along Front Street will take us to The Nursery Arms.

13

THE NURSERY ARMS

Number 88 Main Street was demolished almost 50 years ago, and now the statue of Emperor Hadrian stands guard over the spot that once was The Nursery Arms – at the junction of Main Street with Front Street:

Very few records exist of the Nursery Arms; the first appears as late as 1841 when William Pearson is shown on the tithe map and census of that year as owner/innkeeper:

William Pearson moved out to 87 Main Street to become owner/occupier of The Coach and Horses, with his daughter Sarah, and so, in 1879 the new licensee here at the Nursery Arms became John Armstrong who was the well known Brampton character "Jack the Pack." How he earned this name is not certain, but since he had previously been landlord at the Pack Horse Inn in the Market Place for 30 years this might offer some way of explanation. John was married to Margaret and they had a son called William who worked as a tinner and brazier in a blacksmith shop at the rear of the public house. Despite there being a blacksmith shop so close, there was no accommodation here for horses so this public house never featured as a coaching or posting inn or a stopping place for merchants.

Life in Brampton with 63 Public Houses

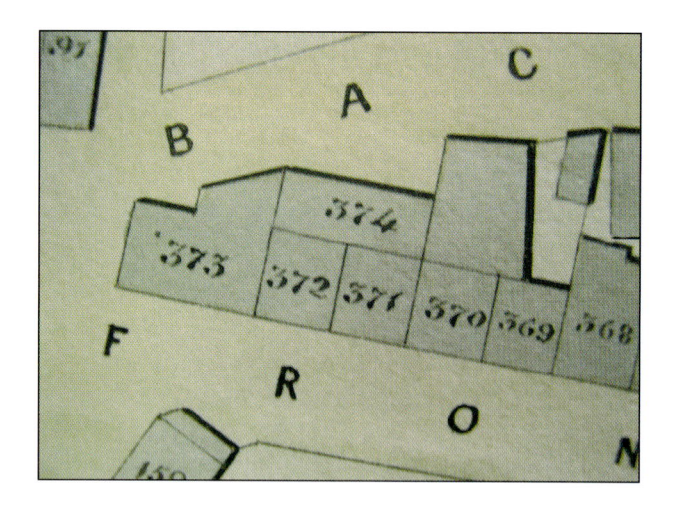

Whitfield Dickinson 371, John Slack 372, William Pearson 373, James Cornell 374.

Although the Return of 1892 records a dining room for 20 people, no records have been found in the newspapers of events, assemblies or meetings having taken place here. In 1899 the Nursery Arms was advertised for sale, the property at that time was one of 19 public houses owned by The Wigton Brewery, all of which, including the brewery were being offered for sale as one lot:

"The Nursery Arms Inn (Beer Licence) including 3 cottages adjoining let separately, is a well accustomed house in the famous old market town of Brampton, now in the occupation of Mrs Batey."

From the Licence register the following innkeepers are shown for The Nursery Arms:

1858 William Pearson
1879–1884 John Armstrong
1900 James Batey
1901 closed by Brampton Magistrates

The 1892 Return of Public Houses and Beer Houses describes the Nursery Arms as:

"6 sleep, 20 dine, no horses. Next nearest public house 80 yards."

80 yards will take us to the Barley Stack – or is it The Barley Mow?

14
THE BARLEY STACK
OR THE BARLEY MOW

The Barley Stack public house was at number 9. Carlisle Road often called Town Foot, although the Jackson Directory records it as Front Street. Today, the same premises exist, but have been restored to a private house and the owners have respectfully named it "The Barley Stack."

The Barley Stack (left).

Life in Brampton with 63 Public Houses

In 1817 and 1847 this public house was known as the Barley Mow, but in 1822 and 1900 it is recorded as The Barley Stack. In 1825, one Directory shows The Barley Stack whilst another records it as The Barley Mow. William Clark is shown as innkeeper in 1833:

The Barley Stack had a career of more than 175 years as a public house and had a very regular and loyal clientele.

During the 1840s – because of worries about increasing poverty, and loss of work, a number of Friendly Societies were formed throughout the country and Brampton was no exception. We will hear more about these societies shortly and their connections with public houses. At the Barley Stack, a Friendly Society known as The Good Samaritans formed a lodge which regularly met here to discuss ways of supporting each other in times of difficulty. Subscriptions were gathered for membership and a general fund developed from which payments could be made to members if things became dire.

> The members of the Good Samaritan Lodge held their seventh anniversary at the house of Mr. William Slack, Barley Stack Inn, Brampton. After the business was concluded, the members partook of an excellent supper, which was served up in a style that reflected great credit upon the worthy host and hostess. Mr. Thomas Tinling presided, and Mr. Isaac Barnes officiated as vice-chairman, and the duties of both offices were discharged in a creditable manner. After the removal of the cloth, the Queen and the rest of the royal family was given from the chair, accompanied by suitable addresses. The health of Lord Morpeth was received with very great enthusiasm by the company. The conviviality of the night was considerably enlivened by the vocal powers of Messrs. Sewell, Davison, Whitfell, Bell, and others; and the evening was spent in the enjoyment of that true sociality which has reason for its guide and good feeling for its support.

Carlisle Journal, 28th December 1844.

The 1851 Census records William Mounsey horse breaker, age 38 years living at the inn with Elisabeth his wife age 29. In 1864 William Mounsey came close to trouble when he was summoned to appear in court accused of having sold a horse that had not been broken in adequately.

14. The Barley Stack or The Barley Mow

The capers of a mare – Bainbridge v Dodd

"Mr Bainbridge of Alston wanted a horse, and hearing that Mr Dodd of Brampton had one, so they arranged to meet at Halton-lea-Gate. William Mounsey the horse breaker was riding the mare when they arrived. Mr Bainbridge the prospective buyer mounted and rode the mare for a mile. He said that he wanted the mare to run in a Phaeton and to ride. Mr Dodd said that the mare would suit these purposes and William Mounsey backed up Mr Dodd by saying "Yes she will do that, for we have driven her over all sorts of road, the roughest roads we could find and she was perfectly quiet. After purchase Bainbridge the next day put the mare in the Phaeton but he did not like the look of her and thought that she was meditating mischief. She refused to start at first and when she did she bounded forward and crashed through the garden hedge. Bainbridge led her down the lane to try to soothe her but in Alston she was very prancy and fiery. After much debate, the magistrate found Dodd and Mounsey not guilty."

Carlisle Journal, 18th October 1864

This public house is not mentioned in the 1892 Returns of Public houses and Beer houses, but it certainly did exist in 1892 and survived well into the next century despite efforts by The Temperance movement to have it closed.

Details from the Directories, Magistrates Licensing Registers show the following Innkeepers at The Barley Stack:

1822–1847 William Slack
1845–1855 William Mounsey
1855–1861 Thomas Mitchinson – he was also a brewer
1869–1873 William Mounsey he was also a horse breaker
1879–1884 Elisabeth Mounsey – wife of William
1894–John Grindley
1897–Elisabeth Graham

We have now reached the Western limits of the town of Brampton of the 1800s. We will therefore now return to the town centre by way of the south side of Front Street to find The Greyhound public house – or is it The Hare and Hounds?

15

THE GREYHOUND AND
THE HARE AND HOUNDS

The Greyhound was at 47 Front Street, Brampton, in part of the premises now occupied by the Furness Building Society.

The first record of The Greyhound appears in 1822 when the licensee was a Margaret Graham. The premises were quite small and there was no accommodation for horses, so it never functioned as a coaching inn, post house, or stopping place for travellers on horseback. This public house was almost opposite the Blue Bell and therefore there must have been some competition between these two.

15. The Greyhound and The Hare and Hounds

Peter Burn refers to The Greyhound Inn where, in the 1830s Mrs Leonard was innkeeper, but from 1847 there is no mention of the Greyhound in any records – but there is for the first time, a record of a public house by the name of The Hare and Hounds at exactly the same address.

The Greyhound and the Hare and Hounds enjoyed a 60 year life without getting a mention in any of the newspapers or into the Magistrates Court.

David McGregor is recorded in the directories as landlord of The Hare and Hounds, and the Tithe Map of 1851 confirms him as occupier of the premises:

Landlords at these two public houses are recorded as:

1822–1829 Margaret Graham
1830 Mrs Leonard   – The Greyhound
1834 William Wallace

1847–1855 David and Mary McGregor   – The Hare and Hounds

There are no records of either of these two public houses after 1882, and there are no reports of their closure, but clearly their demise took place around the time when the Temperance Movement was in the ascendancy.

A stroll of 30 yards takes us to The Horse and Farrier where Professor Scott from Longtown and his assistant Jammie McKenny are waiting for us.

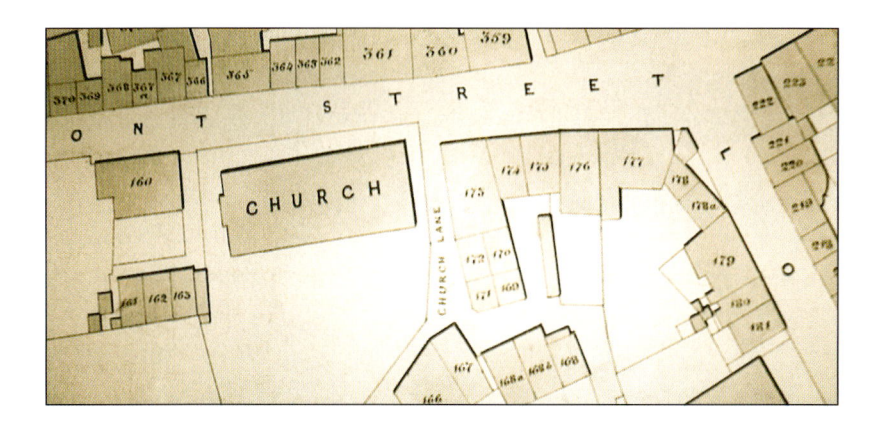

Tithe Map: Occupiers, Thomas Richardson 173, Dorothy Sibson 174, David McGregor 175.

16

THE HORSE AND FARRIER AND THE CROWN

The Horse and Farrier was at the junction of Gelt Road with Front Street. Gelt Road was called The Lonning and The Horse and Farrier was on the South-Eastern corner of the cross roads there. This was the Lonning Foot. A small open space with a flower bed and a waste bin now occupy the site of the one-time Horse and Farrier.

Accommodation at the Horse and Farrier was cramped, but it was a well frequented public house, holding dinners and providing entertainment. There was no room for coaches or horses, however, a stable and a yard *are* mentioned by Peter Burn, historian and poet, when describing life in Brampton in the 1830s:

> *"A word about pleasures, and entertainments of the past. Our fairs and hirings were lively occasions – festivities running the round of the week. We were honoured at such times with*

16. The Horse and Farrier and The Crown

the presence of Professor Scott, the Longtown fire eater and conjuror, with his confederate Jammie McKenny. A better drummer than Jammie was not to be met in the North of England. A few beats on his drum would bring people to the show. The ground of operation was the Lonning Foot.

The wall of the stable yard of The Horse and Farrier – now The Crown Inn, was the spot chosen by the Professor for eating his fire dish. Having partaken of it and surfeiting, he would set about delivering himself of it – then untold yards of coloured ribbons drawn from between his teeth with amazing rapidity to the delight and astonishment of the gazing multitude."

The Horse and Farrier therefore, changed its name to The Crown Inn, which must have been before 1813 as the following notice in the Carlisle Journal refers to The Crown:

J. Bird moves from The Crown Inn

"J. Bird, wine and spirit merchant of The Crown Inn, Brampton respectfully begs leave to return his sincere thanks to his friends and the public for the favours which they have been pleased to confer upon him during his continuance at the above inn. Also, to inform them that he has removed from the above inn to an elegant shop nearly opposite the end of the White Lion Inn – lately occupied by Mr Miller wine and spirit merchant wholesale and retail."

Carlisle Journal, 1813

The Horse and Farrier and The Crown Inn present us with a puzzle to solve: What facts or records exist?

1. There is no Horse and Farrier mentioned in Peter Burn's list of public houses, in his lecture "A Fireside Crack", nor in the Directories at the turn of the century 1790–1800 – but there *is* a Crown Inn listed.
2. The Horse and Farrier existed between 1830 and 1850 as shown in reports in the Carlisle Journal and in Directories for the years of 1842 and 1847.
3. Peter Burn refers to The Crown Inn of the 1890s as having previously been The Horse and Farrier when he was a boy in the 1830s.
4. The Crown Inn features regularly throughout the 19th Century in Front Street, The Carlisle Journal records it in 1790 and 1813 and the directories record it in 1851, 1869, 1879, 1884, 1894 and 1901.
5. In 1892 a Crown Inn is recorded in The Return of Public Houses and Beer Houses – but there is no record of a Horse and Farrier.
6. A Crown and Anchor, a Crown and Thistle, and a Crown and Cushion are all recorded between 1800 and 1850 in Front Street.

When all of this information is presented in diagram form, the picture becomes a little clearer:

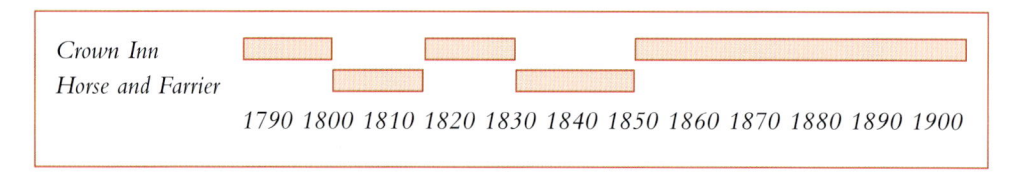

Crown Inn
Horse and Farrier
1790 1800 1810 1820 1830 1840 1850 1860 1870 1880 1890 1900

From the diagram above it seems that over the century, the names of The Horse and Farrier and The Crown Inn never appear simultaneously, which suggests that they were one and the same place. The Crown and Anchor; The Crown and Cushion; and The Crown and Thistle Inn must have all been separate public houses from The Crown as their names are recorded in the directories of the same year, each with different landlords.

Before we leave The Horse and Farrier/The Crown Inn and Professor Scott the conjuror, what other events took place here?

Nailor dies from Excessive drinking at The Horse and Farrier

"An inquest at Brampton was held on the body of Thomas Aitken age 28 years – he had been at the division of Friendly Society funds, on which occasion the members dined together at The Horse and Farrier public house. He drank a bottle of rum in a very short time and sank into an insensible state and was put to bed and died at 3 o'clock in the morning. Verdict death by excessive drinking."

Carlisle Journal, 1st January 1842

Suicide at The Horse and Farrier

"On Friday 4th Dec 1846 at Brampton, Miss Elisabeth Johnstone age 29 years of The Horse and Farrier Inn was found hanging in the club room of the public house. She had resided in Carlisle until 2 months ago, when she removed to Brampton with her mother who had married a Mr Whitfield Dickinson. Whilst at Carlisle she had formed an intimacy with a man William Proud. Proud had cajoled her out of her £22 savings under the promise of buying furniture preparatory to their being married. Thereafter he discontinued his visits and correspondence to her. She told her story to her stepfather who resolved to meet with Proud the following day, but Elisabeth must have felt herself unequal to the task, and in the course of the night having left her bedroom she proceeded to the room of her mother and having taken her stepfathers neck tie, she put it through an iron loop in the ceiling of the clubroom and hanged herself. Verdict: insanity."

Carlisle Journal, 14th December 1846

16. The Horse and Farrier and The Crown

How sad to see two separate young lives brought unnecessarily to an end, and worse still to note the verdict of the coroner – labelling the unfortunate jilted young lady as "insane."

Whitfield Dickinson is recorded as landlord here during 1834–1847.

Wheels within wheels for Whitfield Dickinson

"W. Richardson summoned George Hetherington to court for the value of a wheel which the defendant had taken from his blacksmith shop, it having been his property. W. Richardson proved that he had bought the wheel from a person called Gash; that Gash had bought it from Sibson, that Sibson had bought it from Whitfield Dickinson landlord of Horse and Farrier Inn, and Dickinson claimed that he had bought it from George Hetherington 16 years ago. George Hetherington said that he had not sold it but had loaned it to Whitfield Dickinson and that he had no right to sell it."

Carlisle Journal, 17th January 1851

Several years after Whitfield Dickinson retired, a Mary Johnstone is recorded as innkeeper and may have been sister-in-law to Elisabeth who had taken her life shortly after moving into the Crown. Mary and her husband Thomas Johnstone appear to have had a poor relationship. There were frequent squabbles, and things came to blows in 1882:

Aggravated wife assault

"Thomas Johnstone keeper of the Crown Inn at Lonning Foot Brampton, was charged with aggravated assault upon his wife Mary. On Saturday night Mary Johnstone was at supper with her daughters Agnes and Mary aged 13 and 15 years. Her husband had been writing in a book and daughter Mary drew the book aside to see what he had written. Thomas shouted at his wife "She is just like you – impudent" and threw a glass of ale over her. He then knocked his wife to the ground with his fist. The older daughter attempted to get hold of him, but he kicked her. Thomas then got hold of a coal rake saying "Oh you…….. I will be your end" and struck his wife with all his might on the head with both of his hands.

Mary his wife was knocked senseless. Thomas Johnstone told the court that his hand had caught one end of the coal rake by accident causing the other end to strike her on the head. The solicitor acting for Mary Johnstone reported that there had always been a good deal of squabbling between them and a bad feeling had existed between them with many quarrels. The Bench imposed a fine on Thomas Johnstone of £6 or two months in prison. Both husband and wife agreed henceforth to live apart and that Thomas would leave the house."

Carlisle Journal, 3rd March 1882

The following year Mary Johnstone was assaulted:

Landlady of the Crown assaulted

"Joseph Mark was charged with assaulting Mary Johnstone landlady at the Crown inn. Mark ordered two penny worth of port wine, and when he was supplied with it he laid down a shilling. Mary Johnstone picked up the shilling and since the defendant already owed her 6 pence she handed him 4 pence change. He became indignant and tossed the wine in her face. She then took him by the collar and tried to push him out, when he raised a fist and struck her in the face. Superintendent Russell told the court that Mark was a crazy fellow when he got drink. Mark was fined 23 shillings."

Carlisle Journal, July 1883

Three months later Mary Johnstone was up before the Magistrate:

Too much of a good thing

"Mary Johnstone landlady of the Crown Inn Brampton was charged with unlawfully selling half a pint of adulterated whisky to inspector Russell who stated that he had had part of the whisky analysed by the public analyst who reported that it was exceedingly weak spirit 43.3 degrees below proof and heavily diluted with water. The bench replied that Brampton water was very good but the defendant should not put such an extraordinary lot of it in her whisky, and was fined 20 shillings."

Carlisle Journal, 6th July 1883

As a result of this misdemeanour, Mary Johnstone was put on a blacklist by the Licensing Magistrates and a new landlord appointed.

In contrast to the fun and entertainment of Professor Scott, the Crown Inn has seen too many sad incidents over the century.

Landlords at The Crown Inn are well recorded:

1790 Joseph James	1869–1873 Elisabeth Barker
1813 J. Bird	1879–1884 Mary Johnstone
1834–1847 Whitfield Dickinson	1884–1894 Isaac Richardson
1851–1861 James Barker	1900 Jane Richardson

The 1892 Return of Public houses and Beer Houses describes The Crown Inn as:

"4 Sleep, 15 Dine, No horses; next nearest public house 50 yards."

This will take us to The Red Lion but before that, we have to search for The Alma.

17

THE ALMA

"Excuse me, can you tell me where the Alma public house is?"

The only reference that has been found to a public house called The Alma is in the 1858 directory which records it as being in Front Street with a William Walker as landlord.

The war in Crimea (1854–1856) was a major European conflict involving the British army and was the first to be reported by journalists using the telegraph, thus raising the awareness of bravery, horror, injury, and suffering, upon the popular imagination, almost as it happened, via the newspapers.

The river Alma was the site of one of the preliminary engagements prior to the main battle in the Crimea. It was here that the Anglo-French attack broke through enemy defences allowing a swift advance towards the Russian stronghold of Sebastopol, thanks to the resolution of the British Infantry.

Since the only record of this public house appears in 1858 it is highly likely that "The Alma" was a name temporarily adopted by one of the many public houses that already existed on Front Street at that time, but for the moment this must remain the subject of further research.

Shepherd. Red Lion. Greyhound. Lion and the Lamb. Modlen's. Shoulder of Mutton.

18

THE RED LION

The Red Lion was in Front Street; the original building still stands, and is occupied by Pristine Laundry Services.

The Red Lion is not included in Peter Burn's list in his lecture notes "A Fireside Crack", nor is it recorded in the directories for the turn of the century 1790–1800. The first mention is in 1822 when John Thompson was in charge.

18. The Red Lion

However, the Red Lion certainly existed before this – in the 1700s during the time of the Jacobite rebellion. When Bonnie Prince Charlie rode triumphantly into Brampton with his retinue of soldiers and pipers, they occupied a building in High Cross Street as their headquarters. A paper contributed to the Cumberland and Westmorland Antiquarian and Archaeological Society claims that on the 10th March 1746, Leonard Deane declared that at his brother's house in Cross Street, Brampton, the mayor of Carlisle and two aldermen of the City visited Prince Charlie to hand over the keys of Carlisle Castle. It was at that meeting that Alderman Graham asked the Prince to go with them:

"To the Red Lyon to drink a glass of wine."

Whether the Red Lyon referred to in 1746 is the same as The Red Lion of 1822 remains to be determined.

Being in the centre of the town, this public house managed to attract its fair share of business. There were lodging rooms for 8 people overnight and stabling for 20 horses as indicated in the advertisement when the premises were sold in 1847:

> **FREEHOLD PUBLIC HOUSE, FOR SALE.**
>
> TO be SOLD, by AUCTION, upon the Premises, on WEDNESDAY, the 4th day of AUGUST, 1847, all that old-established and well-accustomed PUBLIC HOUSE, the Property of Mrs. ARABELLA DAWSON, called and known by the Sign of the *RED LION INN*, situate in the FRONT-STREET, BRAMPTON, in the Parish of Brampton, in the County of Cumberland; now in the occupation of the Owner, and is well adapted for carrying on a large business, having four apartments on the Ground Floor; a good Cellar; and Stabling for Twenty Horses. There is a right of Peat Moss belongs to the House. The Owner will show the Premises.
>
> The Sale to commence at Seven o'Clock in the Evening.
>
> CAIRNS, Auctioneer.

Carlisle Journal, 31st July 1847.

William Armstrong became the new innkeeper, and the following bill for 86 stones of hay suggests that the stables were well used:

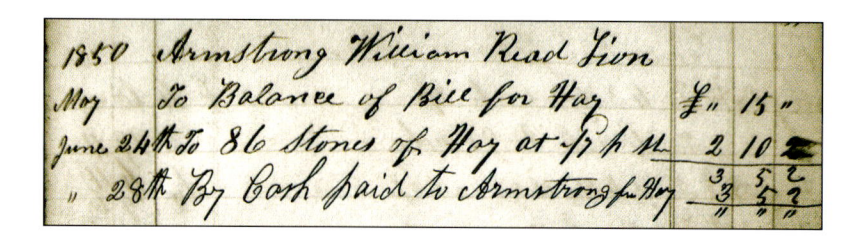

Loaded pistols at The Red Lion

"Mr James Lyon – formerly a surgeon at Longtown was charged with threatening to shoot his wife and father-in-law, a Mr Pears of Kirkhouse. Lyon had married Mr Pears' daughter 5 years ago, but in consequence of family quarrels, his wife left him to return to her parents. Lyon joined the army and fought at Crimea.

On his return to Cumberland he bought a brace of pistols, and whilst resting at The Red Lion, he loaded them, saying to the landlord: "now I am off to Kirkhouse." At Kirkhouse he carried off his wife to Wetheral where he took lodgings, telling his wife that one pistol was for her and one for him. Lyon was eventually brought before the Court and was bailed to keep the peace."

Carlisle Journal, January 1856

The Red Lion appears to have enjoyed an 80 year career as a public house, which finished around 1901, obviously as with so many others – due to the mounting pressures of the Temperance Movement upon the Magistrates.

Although Mr Crouch is shown as landlord of The Red Lion in 1901, the 1892 Return of Licensed Public Houses and Beer Houses makes no mention of it.

The following landlords are recorded at The Red Lion:

1811–1841 John Thompson – he died in 1841 aged 84 years
1844 Thomas Watson
1847 Arabella Dawson
1851 William Armstrong
1855–1861 William Mounsey – he was also a horse breaker and a grocer
1901 Mr Crouch

The 1851 census records William Armstrong age 50, widower living at the inn with his 5 daughters.

Next stop? 30 yards to The Lord Nelson – or is it The Admiral Nelson – or is it The Shepherd – or perhaps The Anchor – or maybe The Crown and Anchor, or possibly The Crown and Cushion?

19
THE LORD NELSON

At 25 Front Street today is the Discount Warehouse, where a public house existed for much of the 19th century, and possibly earlier.

A clue lies in the first record of this public house which is as The Admiral Nelson in 1804 – but all later references are as The Lord Nelson.

Horatio Nelson at first appears an unlikely hero. He was thin, narrow chested and had spindly legs, and during his childhood he encountered illnesses which left him with life long poor health. Despite these hardships Nelson became greatly admired as a leader. He believed in leading from the front, personally leading boarding parties and often in the thick of action. As a commander he was warm and friendly with his men whom he treated as his equals and made it clear that he trusted them. Following a spectacular victory over the French at the battle of The Nile in 1798, Admiral Nelson was rewarded with the title of Lord Nelson, and went on to gain further victory at Copenhagen in 1801. The victory for which he is greatly admired is the Battle of Trafalgar where against formidable odds he out-manoeuvred and out witted the combined French and Spanish fleets, sadly losing his own life in the process.

Since the first record of this public house is as The Admiral Nelson it is highly likely therefore that it was in existence in 1799 before Horatio Nelson gained his ennoblement. The Lord Nelson is the next record to appear for this site, from 1822 to 1829 under the management of Samuel Smith. Peter Burn refers to this public house:

"Two or three houses have changed their names – The Shepherd was the Lion and the Lamb, The Anchor as The Shepherd and also as the Lord Nelson. Sammy Smith ran this public house – he was succeeded by Peggie Hetherington who gave it the name of Shepherd."

This public house therefore began as The Admiral Nelson then became The Lord Nelson, then The Shepherd, and then The Anchor. Very few records have been found of The Lord Nelson. No advertisements for its sale or to be let have been seen in the newspapers, nor have any reports from the Magistrates Court of untoward incidents having taken place here.

In the late 1830s, the Lord Nelson changed its name to The Shepherd Inn:

The Shepherd Inn
Margaret Hetherington, a widow known locally as Peggie, set up business here, changing the public house name to The Shepherd, in remembrance of her husband. She stayed here for thirteen years, but when another public house called The Lion and The Lamb at 36 Front Street became vacant, she decided to move there, taking her signboard with her. Again, without moving a limb, we shall move in time to 1851 to our next public house here at 25 Front Street:

The Anchor – Or the Crown and Anchor?
Peter Burn refers to The Anchor public house in the 1850s at 25 Front Street, after Peggie Hetherington moved out to number 36. The Anchor presents us though with another puzzle – but there is an answer waiting for us: So, what pieces of the puzzle do we have already?

1. In 1851 Elizabeth Hope is recorded as Innkeeper of the Lord Nelson whilst the census records for the same year show her as innkeeper of The Crown and Anchor. The Tithe Map shows her as occupying 25 Front Street.

2. The dates recorded below for both The Anchor and The Crown and Anchor are exactly the same:

3. A further clue is provided by the names of the landlords recorded for these two public houses:

19. The Lord Nelson

The Anchor
The Crown and Anchor
                1790 1800 1810 1820 1830 1840 1850 1860 1870 1880 1890 1900

Date	The Anchor	The Crown and Anchor
1851	E. Hope	E. Hope
1858	E. Hope	E. Hope
1867	E. Hope	No record
1869	No record	W. Richards
1873	No record	G. Hewitt
1876	A. Ferguson	No record
1880	No record	E. Dodd

Throughout the thirty years of these two public houses, no record has been seen showing landlords at each of them other than when Elizabeth Hope is shown at both. It can be concluded therefore that The Crown and Anchor and The Anchor could have been one and the same place, "The Anchor" possibly being an abbreviation of the name "Crown and Anchor."

Despite all of the changes of public house names for number 25 Front Street, no reports have been seen in the newspapers or Magistrates Court Reports of untoward events here.

Now that we have put in place some more pieces of the puzzle of 25 Front Street the picture is much more clear, but not complete. There are two pieces either missing – or surplus, or possibly from a different puzzle!

20/21

THE CROWN AND CUSHION
THE CROWN AND THISTLE

From 1822 to 1829 a Crown and Cushion public house is recorded in Front Street managed by a Mr Bulman but no location given. Also in 1822, a Crown and Thistle is recorded in Front Street managed by a Mr J. Halliburton but no location given. No other record of either of these two public houses has been seen, so for the moment, their stories remain a mystery.

Our next stopping place will be a matter of 5 yards to The Howard Arms.

22

THE HOWARD ARMS

For over 220 years, the Howard Arms Inn has stood proudly in Front Street watching over the many changes that have taken place here in Brampton.

Long before 1800, this public house was already a successful coaching and posting inn; a place where travellers could stay overnight, where coaches called every day to drop off or pick up passengers and parcels, and where fresh horses could be hired to continue a journey.

Until 1869, The Howard Arms is referred to as being in the Market Place, not Front Street, because at that time, on the cobbled area in front of the Howard Arms, stood the butchers stalls and carts every Wednesday market day.

Peter Burn historian and poet of Brampton recorded his regret about the falling off of trade in Brampton's market:

"Change has come to our market day in Brampton. Once stalls clustered to a maze in the Market Square, and butchers shambles terraced Howard's' front. Now all is changed – there are no stalls fringing the Howard and but a few stalls pay homage to our ancient custom. There is no remedy for this – we can but take comfort in the thought that "When things reach their worst, they will mend."

Brampton's regular Wednesday market continues to struggle but Peter Burn can possibly rest in his grave – Brampton's town centre and businesses are surviving.

According to the 1892 Return of public houses and Beer houses, The Howard Arms could provide for 20 people to lodge overnight; for 200 people to sit down to dine together; and there was stabling for 40 horses and a billiards room.

In 1811 the Piggott directory refers to: *"The Howard Arms where the posting office is run by Mr Bell."* Thomas Bell, innkeeper and his wife Mary were in charge of a number of staff which included 4 servants, 3 maids, 2 ostlers – one of whom was Joseph Little, 4 Stable hands, and one "boots." The Howard Arms was also a major venue for large assemblies, celebratory dinners, social functions and important public meetings.

Dancing and cards at the Howard Arms Inn

"A dancing and card assembly was held at The Howard Arms Inn on the evening of 30th January which was numerously and respectfully attended – upwards of 80 people having been present. Dancing commenced at 8 o' clock and was kept up with great spirit until 5 next morning. The arrangements of the stewards and their attention and politeness were highly gratifying."

Carlisle Patriot, 6th February 1829

Waterloo Dinner at The Howard Arms

"The gentlemen of Brampton and neighbourhood intend to dine together at Mr Thomas Bell's Howard Arms Inn on Monday next in commemoration of the glorious battle of Waterloo."

Carlisle Patriot, 16th June 1820

Thomas Bell and his family managed this public house for over 40 years from 1790. The following report suggests that the Howard Arms was well managed with honest staff:

22. The Howard Arms

> **MONEY FOUND.**
>
> FOUND, in the *Howard's Arms Inn* BRAMPON, on WEDNESDAY, OCTOBER 25th a Sum of MONEY. The Owner may have it again on describing the sum and kind of Money; on applying to Mrs. Bell, of the above Inn.
>
> Brampton, Nov. 5th, 1832.

Carlisle Journal, 9th November 1832.

Mrs Bell – Thomas' wife died the following year *"In the prime of her life"* and very shortly after, the Howard Arms Inn was advertised to let. The new tenant appointed was a Fergus Lamb who had previously been an ostler at The Bush Inn in Carlisle – a large coaching inn and venue for important official Council meetings.

The 1851 Census records Mabel Lee, age 67, a widow, as landlady, living at the inn together with her niece Elizabeth Pearson age 24 as assistant landlady ; Hannah Routledge age 27 and Mary Bell age 25 – both servants; George Little age 22 as boots; Frances Routledge age 25 as cook, and Joseph Little age 34 as ostler. A matter of days after this census information had been collected, Mabel Lee was found dead in bed and the following week the Howard Arms was advertised to let. Mabel Lee's furniture, farm stock, crop husbandry, dairy utensils, post horses, carriages, gigs and phaeton were all sold at auction. John Hudspith from The Shaws Hotel at Gilsland became the new landlord.

Very shortly after John Hudspith took over as landlord, a very important letter arrived at The Howard Arms by messenger from Buckingham Palace:

BUCKINGHAM PALACE

"At The court of Buckingham Palace, The Queen's most Excellent Majesty has granted the following petition:

A Petition was presented from the inhabitants of Brampton stating that it would be of advantage to the public of the town that a County Court should be holden there for the Parishes and places thereunto adjacent.

And, Her Majesty, having taken the premises into consideration, was thereupon pleased by and with the advice from her Privy Council, to order that from the 31st day of

73

May 1853, a County Court should accordingly be held at Brampton aforesaid by the name of The County Court of Cumberland holden at Brampton.

Notice is hereby given that in pursuance of this order, His Honour Theophilus Hastings Ingham Esq. – the Judge of the said court has appointed his first court for general business to be holden at The Court House, Howard Arms, in Brampton on the 25th July 1853, at the hour of 10 o'clock in the morning."

Between the 1850s and the 1860s considerable developments and improvements at The Howard Arms consolidated its position as the leading hotel and coaching house in the town. Stables had been added, the bowling green had been refurbished, an armoury installed downstairs to provide secure storage for the Belted Will Rifle Volunteers which mustered upwards of 50 men for drill each week at The Howard Arms, a cottage provided for the drill sergeant, a warehouse established for the Co-operative Society, an office created for the Brampton Savings Bank and a blacksmith forge set up. The following advertisement gives an impressive description of The Howard Arms in 1860:

HOWARD ARMS FOR SALE

"All that well known and old established fully licensed Freehold hotel known as THE HOWARD ARMS. The largest and principal hotel occupying the best and most commanding site in the Market town of Brampton. It has an imposing frontage to the Market Place and its central position combined with the valuable reputation which has attached to it for such a lengthened period as being the chief and most attractive licensed premises in the neighbourhood, gives it a unique importance to those in the liquor trade and investors.

THE HOTEL

Substantially built and the interior affords in a superior and capacious form, all the accommodation usually found in first class Hotels. In addition to a Billiard Room, there is an assembly room which is extensively utilised for local meetings and gatherings of all descriptions including the monthly County Courts for the Brampton District.

THE LIVERY ESTABLISHMENT

The Livery Establishment attached to the hotel forms a very valuable and lucrative adjunct and an important contributor to the revenue of this department is now obtained from the Omnibus which the tenant runs to the Brampton Junction and by which the passenger traffic to and from the town is now worked.

22. The Howard Arms

THE STABLES/COACH HOUSES/AND OUTBUILDINGS

The stables have been specially built to accommodate a large number of horses and to provide for the extensive trade which the Hotel enjoys as a hostelry on Market days.

BOWLING GREEN

The bowling green has been laid out at considerable expense by the vendor and is now let to the Committee of the Brampton Bowling Club. It also includes:

THE ARMOURY OF THE BELTED WILL RIFLE VOLUNTEERS

With a cottage adjoining occupied by their Sergeant.

AN OFFICE

Occupied by the Brampton Savings Bank.

A WAREHOUSE

In the tenancy of The Brampton Co-Operative Society.

BLACKSMITH SHOEING FORGE, AND COTTAGE

All in the occupation of James Davidson."

Carlisle Journal, 1860

Even the highly successful Howard Arms Inn could not avoid the mounting pressures for closure from the magistrates and the Brampton Temperance Movement led by Mrs Rosalind Howard of Naworth Castle, the Countess of Carlisle. Rosalind writes in her diary of 1881 how one of the preachers of The Temperance Movement came to hold a meeting in the tiny hamlet of Lanercost:

"There I had a chance of hearing about the great work that was being done, and forthwith my children and I took the pledge. We carried on this crusade in 1882 and the following years in our small and ancient town of Brampton. The Society is now 1300 strong.... I have taken a seven year lease of The Shepherd Inn and have made that into a working men's free and easy coffee tavern. Then we expect in a few months that the landlady of The Howard Arms will give up for want of custom, and that we shall get that as a farmers' Temperance Inn."

Lady Rosalind's strategy became a reality and in 1884 the landlady Hannah Oliphant did indeed give up and The Howard Arms became a temperance inn.

From the directories, magistrates court reports, newspaper advertisements and Peter Burn's lecture notes, the following landlords are recorded at The Howard Arms:

1790 Mr Thomas Bell	1838 Joseph Lee
1811 Mr Bell	1847 Mabel Lee
1822 Thomas Bell and Samuel Smith	1858 John Hudspith
1823 Thomas Bell and James Bell	1880 Misses M. and M. Hudspith
1829 Mary Bell	1884 Hannah Oliphant
1834 Fergus Lamb	1900 Thomas Bell

The next public house on our journey is only 30 yards away, in the Market Place: The Pack Horse Inn.

23

THE PACK HORSE INN

Jopson's chemist shop now stands where in the 1800s a very different building stood, containing The Pack Horse Inn.

The Pack Horse Inn existed well before the beginning of the 1800s when James Brown was in charge as landlord. Although a small posting inn by comparison with its competitors which surrounded it, there was accommodation here for 6 overnight guests, a dining room for 20 people and stables for 4 horses.

Because travel was very slow by comparison with today, many merchants and travellers preferred to stay overnight in an inn or public house rather than run the risk of travelling at night time. Travel at night was not only physically dangerous because of the rutted surface of most roads, but also because of the fear of thieves or footpads who held up travellers for their money and were often quite violent in the process. Ruleholme bridge was a site frequently used for attacks on coaches and merchants carts:

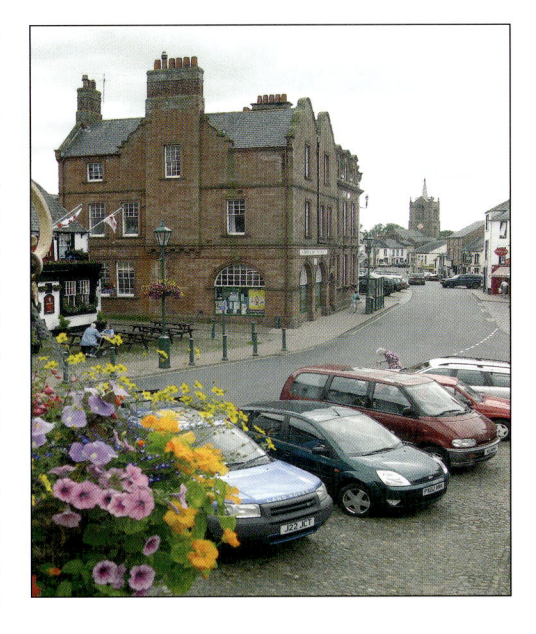

John Mason – pipe maker attacked by footpads

"On Wednesday Mr John Mason of Carlisle – a pipe maker, was very daringly attempted to be robbed by 3 footpads on the road leading from Brampton to Carlisle. Mr Mason had received a sum of money at the end of Market day at The Pack Horse Inn, Brampton – which circumstance had been observed by several persons at the time – amongst whom Mr Mason is confident was one of the villains who attacked him. On his road home he was beset by three persons at the Ruleholme Bridge, but Mr Mason

depending upon the strength of his heart of oak stick made such dexterous use of his weapon that two of his assailants soon bit the dust on which they lay during the remainder of the encounter. In the meantime, the third more sturdy than his companions, continued the engagement during which Mr Mason was severely bruised, nor did his competitor escape with a sound skin. However the man of pipes made a good and honourable retreat."

Carlisle Journal, 20…1813

And again;

Highway robbery after visiting The Pack Horse and Globe Inns

"On Wednesday January 21st 1826 – at 2 o'clock in the morning – a farmer named William Nicholson residing near Brampton was robbed on the highway of a considerable sum in bank notes by three men with whom he had been drinking a great part of the night in The Pack Horse Inn and to whom he had foolishly exhibited his pocket book full of money. Robert Robinson 38, Thomas Skelton 25, and Thomas Dawson 18 assaulted William Nicholson on the King's Highway and put him in bodily fear of his life, and stole his pocket book containing £16.

"I was at Brampton at The Pack Horse in company of others – many people were present." W. Nicholson went on to admit that he had shown others his pocket book containing money since he was looking to see if he had any change. "We all left the Pack Horse together and we then went to The Globe Inn where we stayed till early morning."

Carlisle Patriot, 21st January 1816

We shall pick up this story and see what happened next, when we visit The Globe Inn which is just 60 yards away on the other side of The Market Place, in front of The Moot Hall.

As illustrated by the two stories above, the Pack Horse Inn was regularly in trouble, either in the newspapers or at the Magistrates Court because of fights, robberies or other untoward incidents. John Edmondson is recorded as landlord in 1822–1829 and he was often in trouble:

John Edmondson – Public house still licensed whilst landlord in Gaol

"John Edmondson, late of Brampton – innkeeper and corn dealer, appeared at the Insolvency Commission. The insolvent's family live in the public house and still carry it on whilst he is in prison. The circumstances led the Commissioner to make some excellent remarks about the new Licensing Act – the provisions of which he wished there would be more attention paid. The Licensing Act cannot in this instance have been

23. The Pack Horse Inn

looked at by the Magistrates – nor the licence itself which says that the holders shall not permit drunkenness. How a man in Gaol could exercise the overance in his house so as to protect drunkenness – he knew not – but wished the Magistrates would re-consider this and always require the presence of the innkeeper when granted a licence. The Commissioner therefore requested that the license be brought in – it was sent for to Brampton. The Act said that the licence ought to be transferred to The Clerk of the Peace. The license was withdrawn."

Carlisle Journal, 2nd November 1830

John Edmondson was sent to prison for 5 years so he must have been found guilty of some serious crime, although no reports of proceedings against him have been seen. Clearly his public house was used as a meeting place for those planning robberies and thefts. After his 5 years in prison his estate had to be sold to pay off his fines and debts:

Edmondson's insolvency

Resulting from the above meeting, John Edmondson's personal property was sold off to repay his debts on Wednesday 7th May 1835.

> NOTICE is hereby Given, that a Meeting of the Creditors of JOHN EDMONDSON, late of BRAMPTON, in the County of Cumberland, Innkeeper, an Insolvent Debtor, who was lately discharged from his Majesty's Gaol of Carlisle, in the said County, under and by virtue of an Act of Parliament made and passed in the Seventh Year of the Reign of his late Majesty King George the Fourth, entituled "An Act to amend and consolidate the Laws for the Relief of Insolvent Debtors in England, will be held on WEDNESDAY the 1st day of APRIL next, at 10 o'Clock in the Forenoon precisely, at the Office of Messrs. CARRICK and LEE, Solicitors, at Brampton aforesaid, to approve and direct in what manner and at what place or places the real Estate of the said Insolvent shall be Sold by Public Auction.

Carlisle Patriot, 14th March 1835.

After John Edmondson's period at The Pack Horse things there began to improve. Messrs Reed and Routledge took over and The Pack Horse became the favoured venue and official Lodge for meetings of a Friendly Society called "The Odd fellows" of whom we will hear more shortly. Following Messrs Reed and Routledge, a Mr John Armstrong became landlord, he was known locally as "Jack the

Pack." Whether he earned this name because he was employed at The Pack Horse Inn is not known.

The rear yard of the Pack Horse Inn was very close to the Bowling Green and the following advertisement in the Carlisle Journal of 1842 and in 1854, imply that the Bowling Green was part of the Pack Horse premises:

Pack Horse Inn to let

> "*To be let and entered upon at Whitsuntide next: All that well accustomed Public house known by the sign of The Pack Horse in the Market Place Brampton, together with that large bowling green, stables and other conveniences now in the occupation of John Armstrong."*
>
> *Carlisle Journal, 1842*

The bowling green must have changed hands in the 1850s as an advertisement for the sale of The Howard Arms in 1860 also claims ownership of the Bowling Green as does the 1884 Directory, which describes the Howard Arms as a *"Posting House with a commodious Bowling Green and Billiards."*

Details from the directories, newspapers, and magistrates records show the following licensees for the Pack Horse:

1790 James Brown
1822 John Edmondson
1830 Messrs Reed/Routledge
1834 Joseph Armstrong
1869 James Reay

The Pack Horse Inn finished trading in early 1882 to make way for demolition to allow for the re-development of that area of the Market Place. The buildings currently occupied by Jopson's the chemist and the HSBC bank were completed in late 1886.

We have now arrived back in the Market Place close to The Nag's Head looking towards the stocks where we began our journey, some 23 public houses ago. We have therefore another 40 to visit!

Behind The Moot Hall is an impressive terrace of houses which has always contained shops and businesses. At the northern end of the terrace, on the corner which faces Moot Lodge and where a small lane leads to Well Meadow, we will find The Grapes. But first, we have a problem waiting for a solution:

Between 1820 and 1840, here in the Market Place, there were three other public houses – The Fat Ox, The Broom, and The Board, but where were they?

24

THE FAT OX TAVERN

The Carlisle Journal of 1841 provides the only reference seen so far of a public house called The Fat Ox Tavern:

Anniversary of Burns:
This report gives no address of the Fat Ox, but does mention "Bonnie Brampton"; and the names of Milburn and Modlin are typical Brampton surnames of that time and are of people who would probably have attended such a meeting. A similar report of the same occasion appears in the Carlisle Patriot, also naming the Fat Ox Tavern in Brampton.

Both reports mention the town clock chiming which is likely to be that of the Moot Hall, as in 1841, the St. Martin's church clock tower had not yet been built. The village of Brampton in Westmorland did not have a chiming clock, and it is unlikely that the Carlisle Patriot would report matters occurring in Westmorland, so there is much to suggest that this report refers to the Cumberland Brampton – but where was the Fat Ox Tavern?

The newspaper report implies that a Mr Sinclair was innkeeper, and a search of the 1841 census shows only one Sinclair in the whole of Brampton – a 40 year old grocer called William, living in Front Street.

> ANNIVERSARY OF BURNS.—On Monday week the admirers of Burns in "Bonnie Brampton" met to celebrate the birth-day of the bard, at the Fat Ox Tavern, where a sumptuous entertainment was provided for the occasion in Sinclair's best style,—in short, the tables literally groaned with good things, and amongst the dainties we noticed a haggis of the most delicious flavour, of which all and sundry seemed to partake with ploughman-like appetites. The duties of chairmen were humorously discharged by Messrs. Milburn and Modlin; and what with the prose effusions of the former, and the very appropriate songs of the latter, the company had a treat of no every day description. Their example was eagerly followed by a large majority of those who had the good luck to be present; and after the town clock had chimed "the wee short hour ayont the twal, he merry boys

Margaret and Sarah Parker Straw Bonnet makers. William Sinclair Grocer and family. 1841 Census.

When examining the 1841 census, it is possible to trace the eastward journey that the enumerator took along Front Street in Brampton, in order to list all of the inhabitants. William Sinclair and family are recorded after Margaret and Sarah Parker straw bonnet manufacturers living in Front Street.

Parkers the straw bonnet makers were known to live near the lane behind the George and Dragon inn, and close to The Sportsman and The Jolly Butcher.

An indenture also dated 1841, refers to a mortgage transfer for two dwellings in this area of Front Street, and records the dwellings as:

"Now in the occupation of tenant William Sinclair - bounded on the north by a rivulet called Brampton Beck, and on the south by the dwelling house of Mrs Corry ; on the west by the dwelling house of Catherine Charlton, and on the east by the dwelling house of Joseph Routledge."

The mortgage transfer shows that the new owners were Arabella and Thomas Modlin, the very name quoted in the newspaper report as one of the entertainers in the Burns night celebrations at The Fat Ox Tavern.

Applying the above information to the 1841 Tithe Map and schedule, confirms where William Sinclair, Sarah and Margaret Parker lived:

24. The Fat Ox Tavern

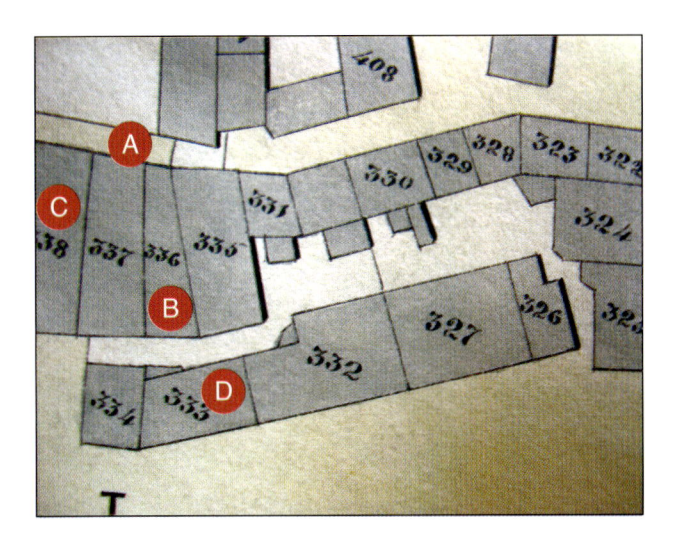

"Bounded in North by a rivulet called Brampton Beck (A). Bounded in east by dwelling of Joseph Routledge (B). Sarah and Margaret Parker Straw bonnet makers (C). Modlen's new dwellings. William Sinclair tenant. Bounded in the south by Mrs Corry's dwelling (D)."

It is reasonable to believe therefore that property number 337 may have been The Fat Ox Tavern in 1841.

25
THE BROOM

The only record of The Broom appears in the 1829 Directory, no address is given but the landlord's name is quoted as William Edmondson, the same name as the landlord given for "The Board" in the same year. Could The Broom and The Board be one and the same place? Could the Broom be an earlier name for The Jolly Butcher where William Edmondson was landlord in 1829? Further research is needed.

26
THE BOARD

Two public houses with the name of The Board are recorded in the 1822 and 1829 directories, both in the Market Place, one with a Mr Goodburn as landlord, which we shall be visiting shortly; the other with William Edmondson as landlord but its precise location is not known.

There appear to have been 29 public houses in Cumberland with the name of "The Board," which might suggest that the public house was not given an actual name, but there was a board outside which indicated that it was a public house, possibly showing the name of the licensee.

To complicate matters further, the 2nd edition of the Ordnance survey map for Brampton of 1891 shows the String of Horses public house as "The Board!" Continuing research may in the future reveal records which will help towards an answer to this puzzle.

As we cross the Market Place towards The Grapes, behind The Moot Hall, our attention is drawn to a public notice on the wall beside the stocks:

NOTICE

William Bell of Brampton – having been found guilty of stealing a woollen coat valued at 10 pence from the stable belonging to Mr Fairburn of The George and Dragon Inn – the property of a coachman, and is sentenced to be whipped in this Market Place – Saturday next.

Carlisle Journal, 1824

A public whipping for having stolen a coat worth only 10 pence! This seems to be a very severe punishment by today's standards. Perhaps this is the opportunity to take time out of our tour of public houses to look at crime and punishment in the Brampton of 1800–1900.

CRIME AND PUNISHMENT IN BRAMPTON 1800–1900

In 1830, the Assistant Commissioner for Police, in his annual report considers the principal offences of the day, and at the top of his list are:

"Drunkenness, robbery, poaching and bastardy."

There is no mention of violence and assault, both of which appear to have been very regular occurrences from the stories that we have seen so far on our journey around the public houses of Brampton. Theft of articles worth forty shillings or more could be punished by death. This could mercifully be commuted to transportation for life or a lesser period of years:

"Henry Craig of Brampton was charged with stealing from The Half Moon public house, various articles of wearing apparel and was transported for seven years beyond the seas."
"At The Hare and Hounds Inn at Low Gelt Bridge, Isaac Thompson stole a watch from Robert Fisher, and having been found guilty he was transported to Botany Bay for seven years."

Transportation and "The Hulks"
For the most serious crimes, transportation to Botany Bay or Van Dieman's Land was quite common. Convicted prisoners were sent by coach with a heavy escort to prevent escape, to "Hulks" which were old ships no longer sea-going but provided holding accommodation until such times as a prison ship arrived to load its human cargo. The following letter from a prisoner, published in the Carlisle Journal of 1844 describes life as a prisoner awaiting embarkation to Botany Bay:

"Our treatment at the hulks was dreadful. We arose at 5.30am cleaned the wards, breakfasted on a biscuit and a pint of skilly and went out to work at 7am. We worked and then dined at 12 noon on horrid beef one day, cheese and bad beer the next. Work followed at 1pm, we came in at dusk, had a pint of skilly at 6pm and went to bed at 8pm. Our

Crime and Punishment in Brampton 1800–1900

employment was carrying timber or being harnessed to a cart and with 5 others drawing the laden cart. Our hair was cut short; our whiskers all shaved off, a coarse shirt of grey and knee breeches given us. A chain weighing 6 to 8 pounds round one leg. The severity of the weather, the bad meat, thin clothing and total absence of fire nearly killed me, and when I went aboard the prison ship Isabella, I was a skeleton."

Carlisle Journal, May 1844

Stealing washing from hedges was a particular crime; the penalty would be at least a year in The House of Correction:

"David Ridley was found guilty of stealing a bed rug, in the Parish of Brampton, on 17th Nov. 1825 – the property of Sarah Gaddes of The Johnson Arms, Walton road end, Brampton, which had been hanging out to dry on a hedge. He was sentenced to seven years transportation."

We have already heard the story of the man who had stolen a bay mare and attempted to sell it at the Black Bull in Brampton. When caught, he claimed that he would prefer to die by hanging – the sentence he recognised he would face, rather than die of hunger.

Stealing handkerchiefs by pick-pocketing was also common:

"Mary Mulltender of Brampton was imprisoned for one month with hard labour for stealing a handkerchief valued at 10 pence."

Even children who were caught stealing pies and cheeses could not escape the punitive system and could be sent to prison for 3–9 months:

"Matthew Steel – a little boy was found guilty of stealing a blue coat from the house of James Scott of Brampton. The boy sold the coat to Ann Hurst for 2s and 6d – he was sentenced to 6 months in gaol in Carlisle and to hard labour."

"Robert Richardson age 14 years and Thomas Jackson age 10 years – both of Brampton were charged with stealing 12 pennies from the till in Martha Laidlaw's grocer shop in Brampton. They were both found guilty by the Magistrate and sentenced to 2 months in the House of Correction – both to be kept to hard labour and severely whipped before discharge."

Imagine these two youngsters waking up each day during their term in gaol wondering if that was the day that they were to receive their severe whipping.

Whether the threat of transportation, whipping or hard labour was an effective deterrent or not we cannot tell, but obviously many people, perhaps driven by hunger or poverty, seem to have been prepared to run the risk.

Stealing a horse was a major crime, equivalent to stealing a car today, since in the 1800s, this was the only means of transport other than on foot that was available. Horse stealing often resulted in the death sentence or transportation. There are quite lurid reports of the actual hanging in public of horse stealers.

Poaching was common but also risky. There was a shortage of jobs, hand loom weavers were being put out of business by factories with a new invention- steam driven power looms. Money for some was hard to come by and food always short, so it is not surprising that many felt it worth running the risk of getting caught in order to provide food on the table for the family.

Frequent fights developed between gamekeepers and poachers when the latter were caught in an attempt to ensure or to avoid capture and prosecution. Those found guilty of attacking a gamekeeper were sent to prison for many months. Perhaps those with scarcely any money felt it reasonable to steal from the wealthy landowners:

"Brampton Landowners have combined together to warn poachers of the dire circumstances which await them:

THE BRAMPTON ASSOCIATION

We the undersigned members of the above association at our annual meeting have agreed and resolved to use every possible means to detect and prosecute to conviction, every person found guilty of felony or other depredation upon the person or of the members of the Association. And, further, according to the articles of our agreement to cause every delinquent offending against the persons or properties of others not associated with us to be proceeded against to the utmost rigour of the law. And, whereas several robberies and other offences – stealing poultry, cabbages, turnips, carrots etc, breaking fences gates and trespassing over grounds have of late years been committed with impunity, this is to serve notice that whoever shall in future be detected stealing cabbages, potatoes, turnips or carrots or breaking gates or fences and hedges or any damage whatsoever to the persons or properties of the members of this association will be prosecuted with the utmost vigour. And, in order to detect all such offenders, notice is hereby given that proper people have been appointed to watch over fields belonging to the different members of the association.

And, for the better discovering those who shall be guilty of any offences aforesaid, the under mentioned rewards will be given to any person who shall give such information so as that the offender may be brought to justice – to be paid on conviction:

House breaking; Horse cattle or sheep stealing	5 guineas
Breaking into shops, warehouses barns & other larceny	3 guineas
Stealing potatoes, carrots, cabbages, turnips	2 guineas
Any other smaller offences	1 guinea"

Thomas Ramshay, Naworth Castle. Rev. T. Ramshay, Vicar. Simon Ewart. Charles Brough. H. B. Oliver. Rev. Lawson. Thomas Bell, Howards Arms. Thos. Foster, Grocer. John Tinniswood, Draper. Jos. Cox, Brampton Brewery. D. Tinling, Surgeon. Thos. Halliburton, Spirit Merchant. M. Maxwell, Innkeeper.

Carlisle Patriot, 1835

All of the above were wealthy and well established property owners and business people who clearly were irritated by theft from their premises. The generous rewards that they had on offer for information leading to prosecution must have been a great temptation for some to report others.

Poverty in the 1830s and 40s really became an issue, many people found themselves without work because of the introduction of new machines and steam power, and consequently resorted to stealing to obtain money or pawning their meagre belongings in order to get food – or drink to drown their sorrows.

Offences against property appear to have been taken much more seriously than attacks upon the person. Riots, fights after drinking and scraps over girl friends were frequent, but most were never brought before the Magistrate. At worst, a week in prison could result from a case of common assault coming before the Magistrate, as shown in the case we heard about at The Blue Bell Inn where the landlady was assaulted.

Fighting connected with politically motivated wage demands was taken very seriously. Damage to farmer's equipment or haystacks, and breaking machines in factories led to dire consequences.

During the first half of the 1800s, soldiers marching from their depots did not stay in barracks but "camped" overnight in public houses. It was fortunate for The White Lion as we shall see later, that when a serious fire broke out there, a number of horse soldiers – The Queens' Bays billeted there successfully got the fire under control.

Life for soldiers could be harsh. Soldiers who were found guilty of wrongdoing were whipped in front of their comrades, to show that discipline was essential. Three hundred lashes were sometimes given. One soldier – not from Brampton – died as a result of being whipped.

Apprentices were registered and completion of their full term of apprenticeship was essential. Any apprentice absconding would land up in trouble, as it was a legal contract under which the master had parental rights and duties. Apprentices who were lazy could be flogged or imprisoned.

APPRENTICE ABSCONDED

"Whereas Joseph Ferguson – Apprentice to James Johnstone shoemaker, Brampton, left his master's service on the 19th April – whoever keeps or conceals him after this public notice will be prosecuted according to the law. He had on when he went away a short tailed blue

jacket, cord vest and trousers with two pieces of new cloth on each leg. He is about 16 years of age, stout made, fair hair, thick lips, and flat soled. He was brought prisoner last Saturday from Nenthead to Brampton and on the following morning he escaped from his father."
Carlisle Journal, 14th May 1825

Before Brampton had sewers, the practice was to have a "Privy" and the contents would either be collected and taken to a cesspit or used on the garden as manure. It was an offence to dispose of it in any other way:

"On Saturday last, Peter Rush and James Machell were each fined 5 shillings for scattering night soil on the streets and Margaret Ridley and James Martin all of Brampton were fined three shillings for leaving their horses and carts at large in the town."

Sunday trading today is commonplace, but in the 1800s, opening a shop or trading on a Sunday was punished by forfeiture of the goods bought or sold. Almost anything done on a Sunday was an offence! Working on a Sunday could result in one or two hours in the stocks. Drovers driving cattle on a Sunday were fined £2. Swearing in public on a Sunday resulted in a fine of one shilling or three hours in the stocks. No record has been seen of the fine for swearing on other days of the week!

"William Armstrong of Brampton, in this County, a carrier's servant, was convicted before the Magistrates in Carlisle on the 22nd ult. In the penalty of twenty shillings for travelling on a Sunday with horses and carts in the Parish of Brampton."
Carlisle Journal, 9th March 1811

"Anthony Johnson – a Beer shop keeper in Brampton was fined five shillings together with costs, for having his house open on Sunday morning during Divine Service."
Carlisle Journal, 3rd August 1844

During much of the 19th century, Brampton had no lock-up i.e. a gaol or somewhere secure where prisoners could be locked up until investigations were complete, pending trial in the local Magistrates Court. Public houses were therefore often commandeered by the police as a lock-up for prisoners, but this was not popular with landlords:

Public houses as Lock-ups?

"John Thompson, William Johnson and Mary Stewart were found guilty of stealing 2 pork hams. Constables were able to trace their footsteps, the hams were recovered and the prisoners taken into custody. They were committed for trial at the next quarter sessions. The

want of a lock-up in Brampton was certainly exemplified in this case, the constable having to go up and down begging the publicans to take them in."

Carlisle Journal, 20th January 1854

Shortly after this article appeared in the local paper, plans were drawn up and builders sought for a lock-up for the town:

Lock-up for Brampton

"To be let by proposal, the erecting and finishing of a new lock up and Magistrates Office at Brampton. Plans and specification are lodged with Messrs Carrick and Lee solicitors who will receive tenders until 13th Feb. 1855 and the following day the contractor will be declared."

Carlisle Journal, 26th January 1855

Mrs Tamar Brown, landlady of the Oddfellows Arms, Brampton became one of the first prisoners to use this facility as we shall hear later.

At the beginning of our look at crime and punishment of the 1800s, The Assistant Commissioner mentions bastardy as a crime. The Parish Overseer was responsible for controlling this situation. Any pregnant woman who was not married was removed from the Parish of Brampton if she had not been born here. They were forcibly and legally removed to the Parish of their birth to avoid them becoming a burden upon Brampton's Poor Relief Fund. As this was the common practice across the county and country, Brampton clearly became the recipient as well as the remover of single pregnant women. The overseer would use every means possible to locate the father of the pregnant woman's child and "encourage" them to get married. Where the prospect of marriage was not forthcoming, the father was charged before the magistrate and forced to pay £40 maintenance each year. If all this failed, the father would appear before the magistrate and sentenced to pay between one shilling and sixpence and four shillings a week until the child was 14 years old. The only way the father could legally avoid paying this maintenance was by his enlisting in the army or navy for 14 years.

The Militia

The Cumberland Militia was similar to today's Territorial Army and was formed as a measure to counter the perceived threat looming from the continent. The regular army was unable to attract sufficient numbers of men, so The Militia Act was passed by government to establish a national militia with regiments in each county. Recruitment was by means of a sort of conscription – men were drawn off a list of all adult males between the ages of 18 and 45 years that each parish was required to draw up. It was the responsibility of the Parish constable to visit each house every year to obtain the details and prepare the list. A public meeting would be arranged, often at a public house, at which the constable would organise the names to be put into a ballot and the requisite number drawn out. Men whose names were drawn out were called "drawn men", who could only avoid serving their time as a soldier by finding or paying someone else to do it on their behalf, but the cost was well beyond the means of most men.

Those enlisted lived at home but spent 4 weeks each year for five years, at a training camp, for which pay, uniform and weapons were provided. All of this was a legal obligation upon the parish and upon the individual member drawn.

We saw the problems caused by Edward Atkinson the 20 year old nailor who absconded the minute he found out that his name had been drawn for the Militia, when we visited the Nag's Head. The parish would be very keen to find Edward Atkinson and bring him back to serve his time; otherwise someone else would have to be selected to take his place. The absconding of Edward Atkinson must have caused great annoyance locally and it is understandable that the Nag's Head Club was prepared to offer a reward for his capture. He certainly would not be a popular chap when he was eventually found.

Thirty years after the liberalisation of licensing laws, the profound effects of drink upon people's behaviour and peaceful co-existence in communities were becoming all too plain to see. Aggression and assaults fuelled by drink were common place; stealing of personal property, pick pocketing, shop lifting and house burglary became widespread. Money, already in short supply in most families, was often spent in the alehouse rather than on essential food and clothing. Police and Magistrates were beginning to press for changes, as the majority of their time was spent dealing with the aftermath of incidents arising from drunkenness and dependency on drink.

Something must be done!

"Something must be done ere long to remedy the present loose and reckless system by which licenses to beerhouses are granted. The evil is becoming intolerable. The gaols are becoming crowded and a great majority of apprehensions are for drunkenness. Something must be done to arrest this degeneration. The Permissive Bill before parliament must change the control of beerhouses and the granting of licenses to them to one competent and responsible authority. In 1865 the number of apprehensions for drunkenness by the constabulary was 6,000 whereas last year that number was 8,700. All committals are arising out of offences originating in beerhouses or other drinking places."

Carlisle Express, 12th March 1869

The beginning of the 1870s marks a turning point in the rise and fall of public houses in Brampton, and, nationally. The development of Friendly Societies and the commitment of a small group of Radical reformers sowed the seeds of what was to become a major campaign to bring to people's attention the destructive effects of excessive drinking upon individuals, upon families, and upon society.

27

THE GRAPES

In the northeast corner of the Market Place, The Grapes occupied a convenient stopping place, or starting place for a visit to Brampton's public houses by the many hand loom weavers who worked from their own houses in Well Meadow, locally called Shuttle Row, and the East part of the town.

The first record of The Grapes that has been found is in 1826 when Joseph Richardson Brown was in charge; it was quite a small public house, never a coaching or posting inn, but more of a drinking den with no overnight accommodation.

Peter Burn does not have much to say about The Grapes, nor does it appear to have been a significant player on the public house scene of Brampton, but it did manage to survive for 65 years without untoward incident or magistrate court proceedings. The only claim to fame of The Grapes concerns the forgetful William Tinling:

An unclaimed pony at The Grapes
A horse and cart would represent a considerable investment or asset for anyone in business, and since travel by horse was the only means of getting about and trading, it is surprising that Mr Tinling the butcher should forget about his pony.

There is no mention of The Grapes after 1894, but there are records showing

WHEREAS WILLIAM TINLING, late of BRAMPTON, in the County of Cumberland, Butcher, having left a PONY with Mr. THOS. BELL, of Grapes Inn, in Brampton aforesaid, and not calling for the same,

THIS IS TO GIVE NOTICE,

That unless the Expense for the Keep of the said Pony be paid to Mr. THOMAS BELL, on or before Wednesday, the 10th instant, it will be Sold to discharge the same.

Grapes Inn, Brampton, 4th February, 1830.

that these premises became a confectioners business in the early 1900s. The last landlord to practice here at The Grapes was a Joseph Elliot who was also a confectioner, so it is highly likely that the public house saw a brighter future in serving the public with cakes and bread rather than be closed down by The Temperance Movement.

Directories record the following landlords for The Grapes:

1826 Joseph Richardson Brown
1830 Thomas Bell
1834 Mary Bell
1867 Mrs Graham
1894 Joseph Elliot – he was also a confectioner

A matter of yards away, on the North side of the Market Place is The Joiner's Arms – that is where we are going next.

28

THE JOINER'S ARMS

At 12 Market Place today, the front door of Moot Lodge opens upon where the Joiner's Arms once stood.

The Joiner's Arms was a small and very successful public house, which enjoyed a career of a hundred years. In 1800 the innkeeper is recorded as Mr Nichol. There were five bedrooms upstairs, a small dining room for ten people, and surprisingly, accommodation for 11 horses and carts in the rear yard and stables. The Joiner's Arms was a small posting inn regularly visited by merchants and travellers by horse, and for much of its life, was managed by women. Jane Law is recorded as landlady in 1822–1829 followed by Mary Law her daughter in 1834, then Mrs Margaret Bell from 1842 to 1861; and lastly, Mary Snowball (widow of Cuthbert Snowball of Kings Arms Inn), 1869–1873.

During the 1830s and 1840s, there was increasing poverty and unemployment in the town caused by the introduction of mechanisation and factories setting up with steam driven power looms. Many home-based hand loom weavers could not compete; similarly, many farm labourers were no longer required as farms turned to more mechanised methods of working the land and harvesting crops.

Brampton clearly was not alone, such changes affected the whole country, and communities became frightened about how they were going to be able to cope in the future. At this time, Friendly Societies began to become popular country wide and The Joiner's Arms was chosen as the regular meeting place for The Ancient Order of Foresters.

Violent Assault of Landlady at the Joiner's Arms

"On Saturday night last, the police were sent for to expel a drunken man from the Joiner's Arms at Brampton. When Sgt. Mills and Constable Turner arrived they found Joseph Hetherington very drunk and in the act of striking Mrs Snowball the landlady of the house with a stick. Turner arrived just in time to seize the stick. Seeing himself defeated in his assault, Hetherington turned upon the constable taking several blows. When the prisoner was got outside, he pulled off his jacket to fight, kicking Sgt. Mills and was so violent that it was with considerable difficulty that he was handcuffed and taken to the station. Hetherington was found guilty and sentenced to two months in prison."

Carlisle Examiner, March 1869

At the same Magistrates court that day, the following case was heard, and it is interesting to compare the sentences: two months in gaol for assaulting a landlady and a policeman and for drunkenness, compared with three months in gaol with hard labour being given for stealing a milk bowl and measure worth 2 shillings:

"Pat Wyse a labourer of Brampton was convicted of having stolen a milk bowl and a milk measure value 2 shillings and was sent to prison for three months with hard labour."

Carlisle Examiner, March 1869

"Puff and Dart" at the Joiner's Arms

"Cuthbert Snowball, innkeeper at The Joiner's Arms at Brampton was summoned by the police for permitting gambling in his house after midnight. It appears that when Sgt. Mills was passing the house at 1.30am he heard someone offering to bet 2 to 1 about something. He accordingly entered the house to find nine men playing a game of "Puff and Dart" which is performed by the players projecting with their breath a small dart through a tube at a target – the player who comes nearest the bull's eye being the winner. The Landlord himself was from the house. Mrs Snowball denied any gambling taking place and said that the men were only playing for a glass of ale. All the men denied gambling. The case was dismissed."

Carlisle Journal, January 1869

Cuthbert and Mary Snowball had moved to the Joiner's Arms from the Kings Arms in Main Street, but within months, Cuthbert died leaving Mary with four children. Two years later, Mary married Joseph Bell a former landlord of the Joiner's Arms, adding later a further two children to her family.

From the Directories the landlords recorded for The Joiner's Arms were:

28. The Joiner's Arms

1800 Mr Nichol
1822–1829 Jane Law
1834 Mary Law
1842–1861 Margaret and Joseph Bell
1869–1873 Mary and Cuthbert Snowball

1878 Mary and Joseph Bell
1884 Mr Burrows
1894 Christopher Harding
1897 Isaac Richardson

The 1892 Return for Public Houses and Beer Houses records that the owner of The Joiner's Arms was John Capstick and Company Liverpool.

After 1900 Isaac Richardson changed from being innkeeper to dairyman, and the Joiner's Arms became a milking parlour, with cows being led there through the town from the fields. Daisy Richardson, one of today's Brampton characters is a direct descendant of Isaac Richardson.

The next nearest public house is 10 yards away – along the pavement past Mrs Jane Clark's milliner's shop where we have a problem:

Where exactly will we find The Salutation Inn?

29

THE SALUTATION INN

This public house is not recorded in any of the directories, or in the Magistrates Licensing Register, neither is it mentioned by Peter Burns or Rev. Arthur Penn. The only references found are in two advertisements in the Carlisle Journal:

> **Dwelling-House for Sale.**
> TO BE SOLD,
> IN PUBLIC SALE,
> On Wednesday, the 12th day of September, 1810,
> At the House of JOHN BURNS, known by the sign of the Salutation, in BRAMPTON, in the County of Cumberland,
> ALL that MESSUAGE or DWELLING-HOUSE, adjoining the above Inn, and bounded on the North by Brampton Beck, now in the occupation of John Lawrie and others, Tenants at will.
> JOHN BURNS aforesaid will shew the Premises; and further Particulars may be known by applying to Mr. JOHN ELLIOT, of Harraby; Mr. THOMAS NICHOLSON, of Crow-hall, near Brampton; or Mr. LAW, Solicitor, in Carlisle.

These premises were advertised again in September 1812, describing it as being near the Moot Hall in the Market Place:

Study of the tithe maps has revealed no information that helps to give an address. If the Salutation was bounded to the north by Brampton Beck and was near the Moot Hall, this would suggest that it was close to the Globe or the Joiner's Arms.

Since we cannot be certain of the address of this public house we are unable to pay a visit, so we shall stroll ten yards along the market square to The Globe Inn – where we have unfinished business to attend to.

30

THE GLOBE INN

The Globe Inn occupied the site where the County Library building now stands. At this place in the 1800s were two buildings each with gable ends facing towards the Moot Hall.

There was a lane behind this group of buildings called Globe Lane, part of which still exists today.

The Globe was already a well established public house at the beginning of the century under the management of Mr Graham. There was accommodation here for 6 overnight guests, 20 people could sit down to dine together and 4 horses were cared for in the two stables in the rear yard.

The Globe Inn, The Joiner's Arms.

Although small, this was a thriving posting inn for merchants and travellers and enjoyed a career of 80 years. After Mr Graham's day, Mary Armstrong became the owner and in 1813 she advertised for a tenant landlord to manage it for her:

> GLOBE INN, BRAMPTON, TO LET:-
> TO BE LET, and entered upon at Whitsuntide first, ALL that commodious and well-accustomed PUBLIC-HOUSE, known by the Sign of the GLOBE: consisting of a Kitchen, Back Kitchen, Parlour, with four good Rooms above stairs, and an excellent Cellar; likewise two Stables;—at present occupied by Mrs. Armstrong, the owner, situated in the Market place, BRAMPTON, county of Cumberland,
> Proposals in writing will be taken in by Joseph Cox, of Brampton Brewery, until the 1st day of June, when the tenant will be declared — Brampton, April 23, 1813.

Carlisle Journal, 24th April 1813.

Thomas Winthrop became the new landlord and in 1816 his wife Ann and her children had their clothes stolen:

Robbery at The Globe Inn Brampton;

"On Wednesday night being Brampton Fair, an unknown person feloniously entered the rooms of Mrs Ann Winthrop, innkeeper, and took away all the clothes of her children and several other items. Some of the clothes were later found in the home of Thomas Mc Gun a tailor in Jollie's buildings who could prove that he had bought them not knowing them to have been stolen. Francis McKenna has been charged with the theft."

Carlisle Journal, 21st September 1816

Ann Winthrop lost more than her clothes some six years later. She either became a widow or divorced from her husband and subsequently married a Mr Edward Parker who was a butcher. Both are recorded as landlords here and stayed for a further two years; they then moved to The Black Bull in Front Street.

John Hall followed as the next landlord, and it is during his tenure that we have unfinished business to resolve:

When we were at The Pack Horse Inn across the Market Place, we heard about the unfortunate William Nicholson, the farmer of Brampton who had met Thomas Dawson, Thomas Skelton, and Robert Robinson, regulars at The Pack Horse Inn. At some point in the evening William Nicholson looked in his pocket book to see if he had any change. What was seen was not change, but many pound notes and these took the interest of his three drinking companions:

"We all left The Pack Horse together and we went to The Globe Inn where we stayed till early morning" William Nicholson went on to tell the Magistrates that *"I left The Globe Inn to walk home, and soon after, two men including Dawson came alongside me. Dawson said he wanted to fight me. I refused. The other got hold of me and used me badly. Dawson and the other then kicked and punched me and made me fall to the ground – where I lay and he took my pocket book.*

Mary Armstrong was a servant at The Globe inn and was called to the Magistrates Court to testify what she had seen. John Hall landlord was also to testify. George Graham saw prisoner Robert Robinson on 12th January, who told him that a man had been robbed and that he had heard a man shout "Murder Murder" as he was going over The Sands close to The Earl Grey public house.

He went over and pulled Foster off the man.

Robert Sloan the Brampton constable apprehended the prisoners but could not find Foster. The constable found the three currently accused in a weaving shop the day after the robbery. Thomas Dawson was later discovered by Constable Sloan hiding in a chimney. Verdict: found guilty of robbery – to be transported across the seas for 15 years."

Carlisle Patriot, 1825

30. The Globe Inn

In the Magistrate Court proceedings, reference was made to *"We left The Pack Horse and went to The Globe where we stayed until early morning"* yet no action appears to have been taken against The Globe for serving drinks after closing hours. Nor was assault or violence part of the charge against the prisoners, merely robbery. This again is evidence to suggest that less emphasis was placed on crimes against the person, rather than crimes of theft and against property.

In 1854, The Globe Inn was again advertised to let, using almost the same words as the advertisement that appeared in 1813. The proprietor this time is recorded as a Mr William Richardson watchmaker. Shortly after moving into the Globe, William Richardson found that kitchen repairs were necessary:

In 1862 The Globe Inn ceased trading, to become a shop – Mr Grange's business according to Peter Burn. The buildings were demolished some time in the 1880s.

Directories show the following landlords at The Globe Inn:

1790 Mr Graham
1811 J. Graham
1813 Mrs Margaret Armstrong
1815 Thomas and Ann Winthrop
1821 Edward and Ann Parker – he was also a butcher
1823 John Hall
1829 Thomas Mulcaster
1830 Robert Armstrong
1834 Thomas Halliburton
1847 Thomas Westmoreland – he was also a farmer
1854 William Richardson – he was also a watchmaker

A matter of 5 yards leads us to our next stop – Mr Goodburn's Spirit Vaults.

31

THE BOARD AND GOODBURN'S SPIRIT VAULTS

On the very corner of the Market Place with High Cross Street once stood Good burn's Spirit Vaults. Today this site is occupied by Eric Hagan Optician.

Originally, spirit vaults were places where wines and spirits were either sold wholesale or could be bought "over the counter" but not consumed on the premises.

However, with the relaxing of the licensing laws and the breaking up of the monopoly that breweries had on the beer trade that came with the Duke of Wellington's Beer act, several former spirit vaults saw this as an opportunity to diversify and sell beer on their premises, and so becoming public houses.

The first records that can be found are for the period of 1822–1829 when this public house was called The Board, where the landlord was Christopher Goodburn who was also a grocer. Peter Burn refers to this public house in the 1830s and 1840s, when it was a spirit vault or bar, but was later changed to become part of Messrs Jackson's and Sons Draper's showrooms.

The only other reference to Goodburn's Spirit Vaults that has been found is a fleeting reference to a yeoman called Mr John Bell who lived in a rather fine house – Tree House on Tree Road. John Bell had to appear before an insolvency commission, declaring himself bankrupt. One of the people to whom John Bell owed money was:

31. The Board and Goodburn's Spirit Vaults

"A considerable sum to Mr Goodburn for spirits consumed on the premises."

There is no record seen of Mr Goodburn winding up his business, but it is generally believed that this happened some time in 1850s.

Licensees at the Board and Goodburn's Vaults are recorded as:

1822 Christopher Goodburn
1823 Joseph Bell
1826 Christopher Goodfellow
1827 James Forester
1829 Richard Dodd
1847 Ann Dodd

As we step out into the narrow "Cross Street" and look back at the building which is Goodburn's Spirit Vaults, we can imagine the scene here in 1745 when this very building was used as a barracks for Bonnie Prince Charlie's troopers. Occasionally this building is still referred to as "The Barracks."

Our next place to visit is The White Lion, a large well lit building which looks very inviting.

32

THE WHITE LION

The White Lion looks out towards the Market Place from the shelter of High Cross Street, where it has been for over 300 years.

The White Lion was already a well established busy coaching and posting inn at the turn of the century when Martha Maxwell was in charge with a staff of 4 servants, 3 maids, 2 kitchen staff, 6 stable hands and 1 "boots." This was quite a number of staff, but all no doubt kept very busy, as the White Lion was one of the busiest public houses in town. From the description of the accommodation, 20 guests could sleep overnight, two hundred could dine together in the upstairs assembly room, and 40 horses could be quartered in the stables, where there was also a lock up yard to secure coaches and carts.

32. The White Lion

In 1830 Martha Maxwell died aged 78 having been owner and manager of The White Lion for over 50 years. It appears from the advertisement in the Carlisle Journal, that following her death, Martha's daughter took over and advertised for a tenant landlord to manage the business for her:

To be Let by Proposal

> "All that old established and well accustomed Commercial Inn called and known by the sign of THE WHITE LION, situated in Main Street in Brampton, with very excellent stabling, coach housing, and other suitable offices, spacious cellars, a garden and eight acres of rich arable land in he vicinity of the town divided into 3 fields and now in the possession of Miss Maxwell (The Owner) by whose mother (The late Mrs Martha Maxwell deceased) it has been kept as the lead Commercial Inn of the town for the past 50 years."
>
> Carlisle Journal, February 1830

Although the advertisement describes the White Lion as being in Main street, there is no doubt that this public house has always been in High Cross Street.

Joseph Armstrong appears to have been the tenant appointed as landlord, having previously been innkeeper at The White Hart. A year after Joseph Armstrong moved in, The White Lion sustained great damage from a fire which broke out in the kitchens:

Clearly Brampton had no fire engines of its own in the 1830s. Fire must have been quite a problem, as this article shows that it took three hours between sending for help and help arriving! Brampton had to wait a further 30 years before plans were started to provide for a fire engine for the town.

Joseph Armstrong remained at The White Lion for 21 years during which time the public house was re-built to the building more or less that we see today. It was fortunate and foresightful for the owner that the building was insured. The

> ALARMING FIRE.—On Thursday evening last, about 5 o'clock, an alarming fire broke out on the premises of Mr. Armstrong, White Lion inn, Brampton, which, from the extent and fury of its ravages, would have proved destructive of the whole range of buildings attached to it, but for the laudable exertions of some horse soldiers at present stationed in Brampton, who, assisted by the principal inhabitants, succeeded in getting the fire under about 8 o'clock the same evening. As soon as the fire was discovered, the Rev. Mr. Ramshay, who, says our correspondent, was one of the most active in lending assistance, sent off an express to this city for the fire-engines, which were immediately despatched under the care of two police-officers, but by the time they reached Brampton (half-past eight o'clock), the fire had been got out. The house is much injured, part of the dining-room floor, where the the fire originated having fallen in ; and a quantity of the furniture is destroyed. The whole of the property, we understand, is insured.

Carlisle Journal, 12th November 1831.

During the first 50 years of the 1800s, soldiers were regularly billeted in public houses whilst they marched from one base to another and although obliged to provide overnight quarters for the military, many innkeepers did so grudgingly. Joseph Armstrong was certainly fortunate that when fire broke out in his premises, help from the soldiers was at hand.

1851 census records John Armstrong age 69 as landlord with Mary age 60, and three servants: Ann Nicholson, Mary Little, Maria Little; and a "hostler" William Foster. After Joseph Armstrong's time, John Dodd became innkeeper; he was also a cabinet maker. Unless John Dodd's wife took a very active part in the management of the public house, there would be little time left in the day for John Dodd to make cabinets, because as always, the White Lion was an exceedingly busy place. Like other large public houses in the town, The White Lion was regularly used for public meetings, assemblies, dances, coroners' court hearings and public auctions.

The White Lion was used as The Commercial and Inland Revenue Office and later as The Excise Office for the area. The Oddfellows – one of the many Friendly Societies which were formed in Brampton around the 1830s and 1840s, regularly met at The White Lion Inn which they adopted as their "Lodge":

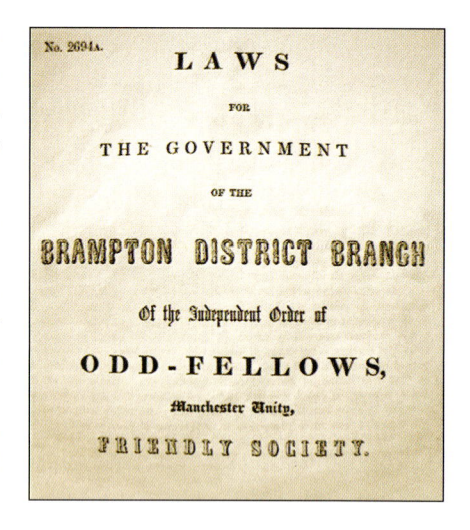

Directories and advertisements and licence records show that the following landlords at The White Lion were:

"The Oddfellows Lodge met last Wednesday at The White Lion Inn, Brampton. 80 of the most respectable and influential gentlemen of the town were assembled. Over the year they had paid out £60 towards sick and funeral expenses and there is £80 remaining in their funds. The meeting was followed by a Ball which broke up at 5am."
Carlisle Journal, 1st January 1845.

1790 Mrs Martha Maxwell
1829 Miss Margaret Maxwell
1830 Joseph Armstrong

1858 John Dodd
1882 Thomas Bell
1894 James and George Moffatt

The White Lion survived all attempts by The Temperance Movement to put it out of business. The 1892 Return for Public Houses and Beer Houses shows a Mr Thomas Ramshay as owner – he was a very significant landowner and property owner in Brampton.

Stepping out of The White Lion, we will turn left up High Cross Street. We can see The Freemasons Arms across the way, but we will leave that to later because we have heard that there will be a competition of Quoits there later on. Instead we will take a mere 6 to 7 strides to our next public house:

The Plough.

33
THE PLOUGH

At 21 High Cross Street today, The Barber Shop quietly snips away the time, but here in the 1800s a public house once stood – it was The Plough.

The only reference seen of the Plough is that by Peter Burn, who records that it existed in 1830s and was *"where Miss White was landlady."*

The Plough is not mentioned in any of the Directories, nor are there records in the newspapers advertising the premises for sale or to be let. No cases are recorded in the Magistrates Court proceedings about The Plough, so it must be assumed that this public house enjoyed a short and trouble free career.

High Cross Street in the 1800s was very different from what it is today. A conglomeration of buildings stood at the northern end at the junction with Main Street. These buildings were known as Souter How, and a narrow lane providing access from the Market Place to Main Street passed on each side.

In this complex set of buildings at one time were two shops; two businesses; dwellings, stables, and two public houses.

Our next port of call is two doors away along the pavement of High Cross Street to find The Graham Arms.

34

THE GRAHAM ARMS

At 23 High Cross Street today, is the office of Cumbrian Properties – Estate Agents, and it is here that The Graham Arms existed for thirty years.

William and Elizabeth Bell were innkeepers here at The Graham Arms in the 1830s; their public house was small but did cater for overnight guests and travellers on foot or by horse, as stables are described in the following advertisement in the Carlisle Journal:

In 1834, the local joiner carried out repairs to William Bell's cart wheel and the bill for the work shows the cost of a glass of Rum taken whilst on the job.

In the 1833 advertisement, *"Opposite to Mr George Elliot's Spirit Merchant"* helps to locate where the Graham Arms was situated as Mr Elliot's premises were on the southwest corner of Souter How buildings. The 1851 Census records Miss Elizabeth Bell age 31, as landlady here, with a 22 year old servant Mary Park, and the tithe map confirms her as occupier.

> GRAHAMS' ARMS INN, BRAMPTON,
> Opposite to Mr. Geo. Elliott, Spirit Merchant's.
> **WILLIAM BELL,**
> LATE OF THE WHEAT SHEAF INN, BRAMPTON,
>
> BEGS to announce to his Friends and the Public in general, that he has entered upon the above Inn, and assures them that no exertion on his part will be wanting to add to their comfort. W. B. feels much indebted for past favours, and respectfully solicits a continuance of the same.
> N.B.—GOOD STABLING kept.
> Brampton, Nov. 7, 1833.

109

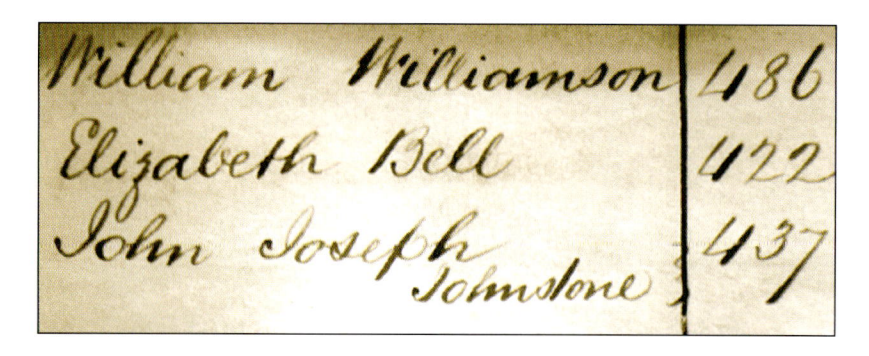

Robbery at the Graham Arms Inn Brampton

"Thomas Beetham labourer at Farlam was brought before the Magistrates at Brampton in the custody of Mr Pearce – Superintendent of Police, charged with having stolen a valuable gold brooch from the bar of The Graham Arms Inn Brampton. Elizabeth Bell, Landlady – daughter of William Bell explained that the brooch had belonged to a guest at the inn who had gone upstairs to rest. Beetham was found with the brooch and claimed that he had bought it from a hawker called Gy-neck Soglin. John Bell a yeoman of Tree House Brampton, Mr Armstrong a surgeon, and James Thompson of Kirkhouse who had employed Beetham for over 20 years all swore that Beetham was an honest and trustworthy man. It appears that The Landlady had trimmed some flowers before putting them into a vase and later threw the cuttings into the street gutter outside. Beetham later claimed to have found the brooch lying in the street. Verdict Not guilty."

Carlisle Journal, 19th July 1845

In 1853, The Graham Arms was advertised for sale showing a Mr Harrison in possession:

PUBLIC HOUSE FOR SALE

"To be sold by private contract. All that Freehold messuage or Public House known by the sign of The Graham Arms in High Cross Street Brampton, Cumberland. Now in the possession of Mr Harrison."

Carlisle Journal, 23rd December 1853

Directories provide no help with records of The Graham Arms, but articles from the newspapers have provided the only details of innkeepers.

1833–1847 William and Elizabeth Bell
1851 Miss Elizabeth Bell
1853 Mr Harrison

34. The Graham Arms

There is no record of this public house after 1853. Demolition of the Souter How buildings took place in the 1860s.

Across the dark and narrow lane and into the buildings of Souter How we will find our next public house – The White Hart.

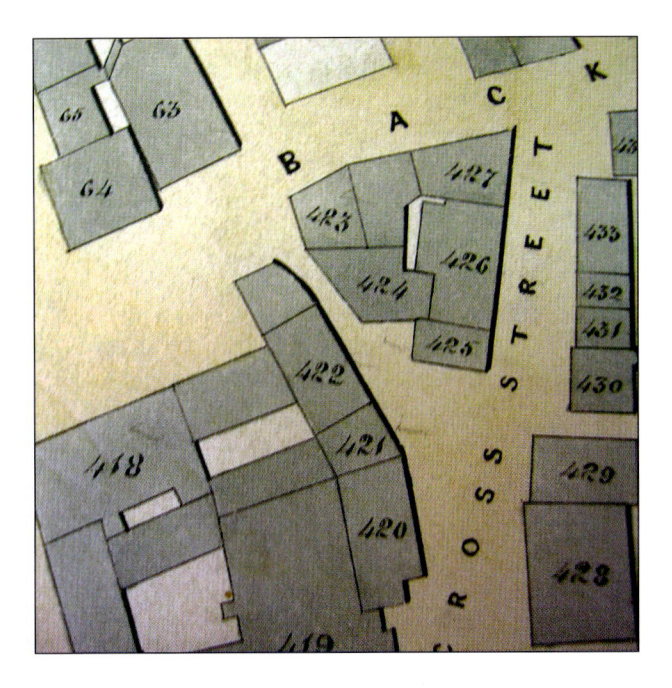

George Elliot's premises.

111

35

THE WHITE HART

In High Cross Street, in the Souter How buildings, the White Hart public house was in the east facing side of the buildings looking into High Cross Street.

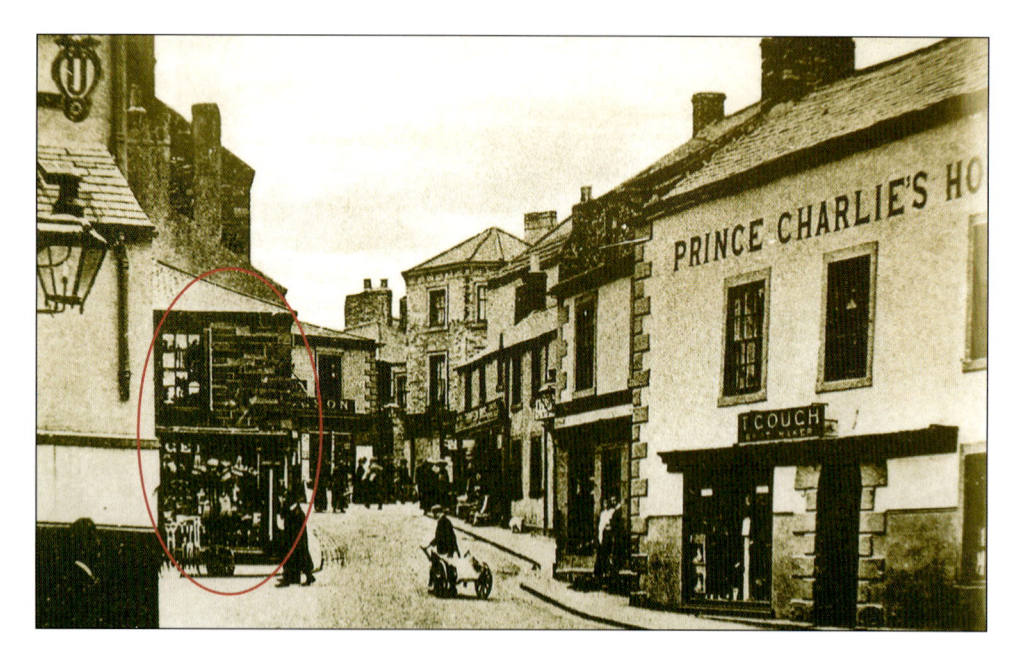

White Hart.

In 1822 Thomas Atkinson was landlord here and he was also a nailmaker. We have already come across Thomas Atkinson – at the Nags Head where he was recorded on the Militia List as being brother to Edward Atkinson the person who had absconded rather than serve in the Militia.

In 1824 Thomas Atkinson died *"in the prime of his life"* and his widow in 1825 took over, but this cannot have been a satisfactory arrangement, as William Topping took over the following year, then Thomas Marrs transferred here from The Anchor in Beck Lane, and is later shown in the Tithe map of 1841:

35. The White Hart

In 1850 a builder was called in to repair damage to the White Hart, following the collapse of a gable-end wall. The final account from the builder shows that Thomas Atkinson's brother Edward – the absconder – had become the owner of the public house.

Peter Burn refers to The White Hart and remembers the occasion when as a boy he sneaked inside to partake of the free refreshments that were on offer here as part of the canvassing of the people of Brampton by political candidates standing for election. The White Hart was a Tory stronghold and may well have been one of the public houses that enticed would-be voters for the "other side" into the bar, and when they became worse the wear for drink; they would be locked up in a room until polling stations had closed, thus denying them the opportunity of voting. This was called "boxing."

No advertisement from the newspapers has been seen for this public house; it is usually these that give good descriptions of the size and therefore the nature of the enterprise. It is not possible therefore to determine whether the White Hart took overnight guests or had stables. It must have been a reasonably busy and successful business as it survived for 40 years.

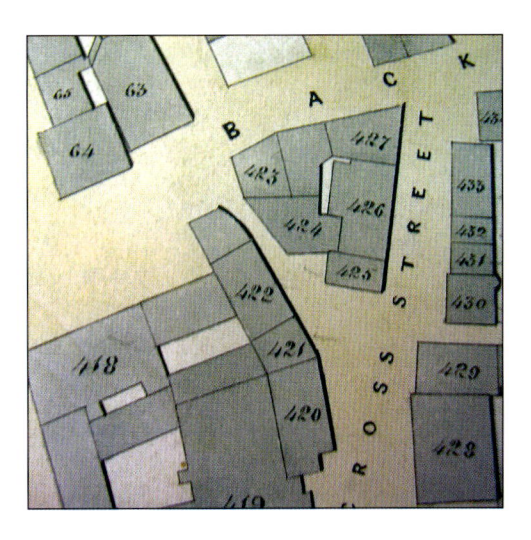

It is highly likely that The White Hart went out of business during the 1860s when the buildings were being considered for demolition. The buildings had made it increasingly more difficult for carts and coaches to pass each other with safety. Coaches travelling along Main Street were obliged to slow down considerably to negotiate the narrows caused by the Souter How buildings jutting out into Main Street.

Directories record the following landlords at The White Hart:

1822 Thomas Atkinson – he was also an ironmonger and nail maker
1825 Elizabeth Atkinson – widow
1826 William Topping
1829 Joseph Armstrong – he left to go to The White Lion
1834 Thomas Johnson
1847 Thomas Marrs
1855–1860 Joseph Mawbray – he was also a bookmaker

Last of all in this complex of buildings at Souter How, surrounded by dark narrow lanes is our next stopping place:

Mr Elliot's Spirit Vaults.

36
ELLIOT'S SPIRIT VAULTS

Mr Elliot's Spirit Vaults were at the west corner of the buildings called Souter How, at the junction of High Cross Street with Back Street.

George Elliot's premises were opposite to what is now the gable end of the Spar grocer shop. Main Street was narrow at this point as the Souter How buildings jutted out into the path of the street, hardly leaving sufficient room for two vehicles to pass each other. Mr Elliot took over this site in 1828 which had previously belonged to Mr Walter Armstrong:

After 1828, licensing laws were relaxed by The Duke of Wellington's Beer Act and Elliot's Vaults changed from being a wholesale spirit merchant to a public house where wines, spirits and beer could be consumed on the premises. Mr Elliot claimed to be the sole agent for the whole of the North of England for Glen Livet Whisky.

In 1862 George Elliot died and his business was advertised for sale. From the description in the advertisement, it seems that his business had become quite successful:

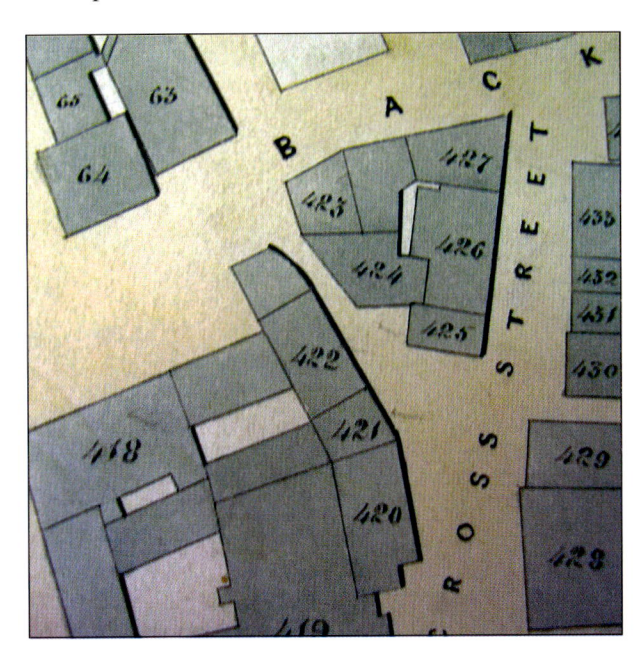

Tithe map, George Elliot 424. The buildings have been demolished, and this area is now a wide expanse of street and pavement allowing the free flow of traffic and pedestrians, and provides several parking spaces. In the 1800s this area was very crowded.

115

George Elliot's Wine and spirit Business for sale

> GEORGE ELLIOT,
> *(Successor to WALTER ARMSTRONG & Co.)*
> WINE & SPIRIT MERCHANT, BRAMPTON,
>
> BEGS to intimate that he has opened the WINE and SPIRIT ESTABLISHMENT of WALTER ARMSTRONG and Co. (formerly under his Management), and trusts, by strict attention to the Selection of his Wines and Spirits, to be found deserving of that Patronage and Support so liberally bestowed upon his predecessors.
>
> G. E. having formed a connexion with some of the most celebrated North Country Distillers, is enabled to supply the Public with WHISKEY, of superior quality, on very advantageous terms; and, in addition to his usual Stock of this Liquor, he has at present on Hand a Quantity of prime Highland Whiskey.
>
> Brampton, June 5, 1828.

"To be sold by private contract with immediate entry, all the stock in trade, fixtures and good will of this excellent old established wholesale and retail wine/spirit business lately carried on at Brampton by Mr George Elliot deceased.

The business is a very valuable one from the extent of private custom. For particulars apply to Mrs Elliot; in the meantime, the business will be kept on."

Carlisle Journal, 1862

In 1869 Elliot's Vaults are recorded as:

"*George Lowther Spirit Merchants High Cross Street (Late Elliot).*"

Shortly after George Lowther took over from George Elliot, the premises were demolished.

37

THE HIGHLAND LADDIE

Today, the Spar grocer shop looks out onto Main Street just as The Highland Laddie public house did over 175 years ago.

Peter Burn refers to the Highland Laddie of the 1830s being managed by a Miss Topping, who may have been some relative of Mr Topping, landlord of The White Hart round the corner in High Cross Street. In 1834 Mr Thomas Bell is recorded as landlord, thereafter the trail runs quiet of events until the 1860s when Mr. G.L. Carrick became the owner, and extended the business to include Carricks Spirits Vaults.

It is highly likely that the George Lowther who took over at Elliot's spirit vaults next door was the very same George Lowther Carrick of The Highland Laddie. This might explain why both Elliot's vaults and The Highland Laddie each advertised themselves as the sole agent for Glen Livet Scotch Whisky for the whole of the North of England.

This area of Brampton seems to have had a lasting Scottish connection. The building in which the Highland Laddie and Carrick's vaults were housed was sometimes called Highland House and whisky was stored here by the bottle and the barrel.

The Highland Laddie however was nothing more than a public drinking bar in the spirit vaults owned by Mr G. L. Carrick, but did manage to survive to the end of the century as the 1892 return of Beer houses records:

"No sleepers, No diners, No horses, next nearest public house 30 yards."

Two months later, following a six month detailed assessment of all public houses in Brampton, the Magistrates received the following report from the Inspector of Police:

"The Highland Spirit Vaults of G. L. Carrick is merely a drinking bar with very little accommodation for the public – no stabling, no lodging accommodation, and there are 5 other fully licensed public houses within 75 yards radius."
North Cumberland Reformer, September 1892

The Highland Laddie public house was closed down by the magistrates, but Carricks Vaults was allowed to stay in business, but only to the wholesale trade.

To continue the Scottish connection with this area of Brampton, a walk of ten yards, not 30, brings us to a house now called "The Glen" where in 1800 one of the oldest public houses in Brampton found a new home.

We are off to The Kings Arms – or is it The Old Kings Arms?

38

THE KINGS ARMS

Adjacent to the Spar Grocers shop and set back from the thoroughfare of Main Street stands a house called "The Glen."

At the turn of the century, The Glen was a private house, and The Kings Arms was a public house in High Cross Street – in the shoe shop now called Bonnie Prince Charlie's house. Around 1816 the public house in High Cross Street was sold and the new owner preferred a different landlord and a different name for his new enterprise, so David Hope, innkeeper, together with the sign of The Kings Arms were both looking for a new home. The Glen became their new home but was much smaller than that to which they had become accustomed.

The Glen.

Life in Brampton with 63 Public Houses

The 1851 Census shows John Little age 27 years as innkeeper at the Kings Arms inn with Mary his wife age 32 years, and 2 servants. The accommodation was large enough to take 6 overnight guests and had a dining room for 20 people, but it must have been quite a crush when the following event took place:

"On Wednesday evening last, The Belted Will Howard Court of Ancient Foresters met to celebrate their anniversary dinner at The Kings Arms Inn at Brampton, where Mrs Little arranged an excellent dinner for upwards of 60 brethren."

Carlisle Journal, 1850

By 1860 Cuthbert Snowball with his wife Mary, had become landlords. Cuthbert had been a boarder at Croft House Academy in Brampton, and by the age of 22 years he was married, and a public house landlord with ambition. Considerable repairs and improvements were carried out with new stables built at the rear in order to attract coaches and travellers to stay overnight, and extensions to the dining facilities. One year after these improvements had been completed, fire broke out and fortunately, only minor damage was sustained:

Fire at the Kings Arms

"Yesterday week a fire broke out in the Kings Arms Inn at Brampton, but it was extinguished before much damage was done. The fire was confined to the bedroom; the only property consumed was the washstand and bed hangings. It is supposed that the fire had been accidentally caused by one of the landlord's children while playing with matches in the bedroom."

Carlisle Journal, 24th September 1861

One month after the fire, a pigeon shoot took place in the back garden!

> PIGEON SHOOTING—OPEN TO ALL COMERS.
> A SWEEPSTAKE will be SHOT FOR at the House of Mr. C. SNOWBALL, *King's Arms Inn*, BRAMPTON, Cumberland, on THURSDAY, OCT. 10th, 1861, by an unlimited number of Shooters. Seven Birds will be allowed to each. Entry, 10s. 6d.
> Single-barrelled Guns, 21 yards rise, and 2 oz. of Shot; Double-barrelled Guns, 19 yards rise, and ¾ oz. of Shot. The Bird to be caught within 80 yards of the Trap.
> All disputes to be settled by the Stewards, and all entries to be taken and money paid by the 10th of September, or not accepted afterwards.
> Shooting to commence at 10 o'Clock.
> Post Office Orders to be made payable to Mr. C. SNOWBALL.
> Any persons having Pigeons to dispose of may communicate with Mr. C. SNOWBALL as to prices, &c.

38. The Kings Arms

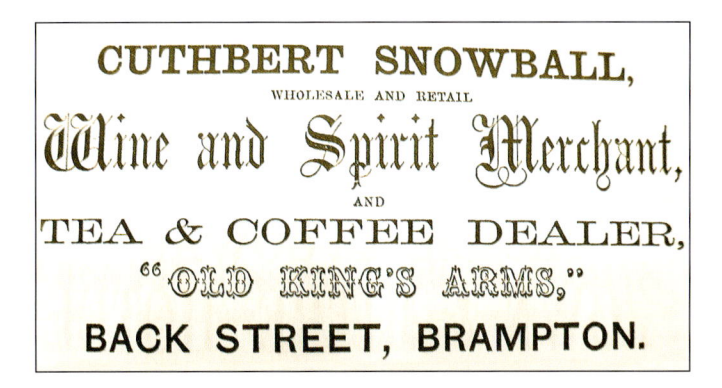

CUTHBERT SNOWBALL,
WHOLESALE AND RETAIL
Wine and Spirit Merchant,
AND
TEA & COFFEE DEALER,
"OLD KING'S ARMS,"
BACK STREET, BRAMPTON.

Moon's Directory 1862.

By 1862 Cuthbert Snowball had developed not only a wine and spirits business in the same building but also a Tea and Coffee dealership:

However, possibly because of declining health, the following year he advertised his premises for sale, as he was planning to retire:

Wine and Spirit business for sale: Public House to let

"To be sold with immediate entry, all the stock in trade, fixtures, and GOOD WILL of the wholesale and retail wine and spirit business at present carried out at Brampton by Mr Cuthbert Snowball who is retiring solely on account of other engagements. Also to let, to the purchaser of the above business all that well accustomed PUBLIC HOUSE called and known by the sign of The King's Arms adjoining the wine and spirit vaults. Further particulars from Mr Cuthbert Snowball owner."

Carlisle Journal, March 1863

Perhaps the "other engagements" were those of auctioneer:

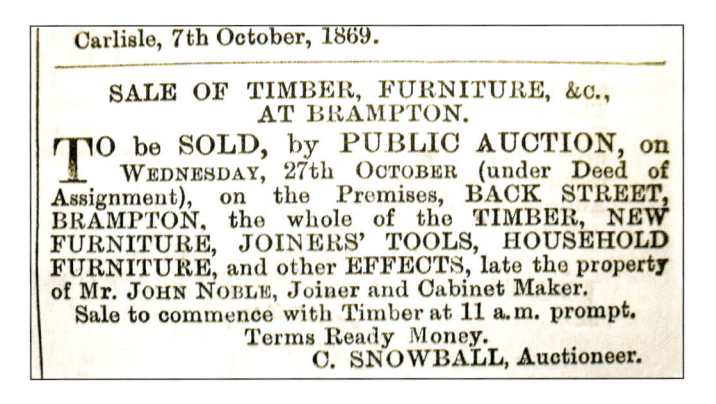

Carlisle, 7th October, 1869.

SALE OF TIMBER, FURNITURE, &c.,
AT BRAMPTON.

TO be SOLD, by PUBLIC AUCTION, on WEDNESDAY, 27th OCTOBER (under Deed of Assignment), on the Premises, BACK STREET, BRAMPTON, the whole of the TIMBER, NEW FURNITURE, JOINERS' TOOLS, HOUSEHOLD FURNITURE, and other EFFECTS, late the property of Mr. JOHN NOBLE, Joiner and Cabinet Maker.
Sale to commence with Timber at 11 a.m. prompt.
Terms Ready Money.
C. SNOWBALL, Auctioneer.

Mr George Lowther Carrick became the new owner of The Kings Arms, having recently taken over the Highland Laddie next door. Cuthbert Snowball appears to have moved to The Joiner's Arms in the Market Place from where he managed his auctioneer business, but aged only 33 years, he died in 1870, leaving Mary with four small children to look after. Two years after Cuthbert's death, Mary married Joseph Bell the former landlord of the Joiner's Arms and added a further two children to her family.

Fire again 31 years later – same cause!

"On Sunday morning, one of the bedrooms at the Kings Arms Inn, Brampton was found to be on fire, the children having set fire to the bed. The Police and others quickly extinguishing the flames."

North Cumberland Reformer, November 1892

The Kings Arms was also known as The Old Kings Arms – landlords were:

1810 David Hope	1852 Cuthbert Snowball	1880 George Bell
1816 James Bell	1860 Joseph Parker	1890 W. Armstrong
1829 John Armstrong	1869 Mary Gray	1892 Samuel Dufton
1842 Mary Rutherford	1873 William Fisher	1894 George Jamieson
1850 John Little	1879 George Dunwoodie	1901 George Errington

The next nearest public house is 30 yards away, across the road: The Wheatsheaf.

39

THE WHEATSHEAF

Elliot's Painters and Decorators stands on the north side of Main Street at number 44, and it was here that The Wheatsheaf public house served the people of Brampton for more than 80 years in the 1800s.

Although no competition to the much larger Scotch Arms nearby, there were many occasions when rooms at The Wheatsheaf would be pressed into action when the Scotch Arms was full. There was accommodation here for 8 overnight guests upstairs, 20 people could sit down to dinner, and there was space in the rear yard and stables for 6 horses and their carts and coaches. This public house relied heavily on passing trade, being on the main route between Carlisle and Newcastle.

The first record that can be found is in 1817, in a spirit merchants account book:

Wm Bell Wheatsheaf
To 1 Gallon B. Gin — 14 —

Jollie's directory confirms William Bell as landlord in 1822, after his own business as a brandy merchant had failed:

William Bell – bankrupt sets up at The Wheatsheaf

"The Commission for Bankruptcy. Hearing in 1817 awarded against William Bell of Brampton Brandy merchant will meet 28, 6, 1821 to make a final dividend of the estate and effects of the said bankrupt. Disposal of assets to include a pew at Haltwhistle Church."

Carlisle Journal, 23rd June 1821

During Mr Bell's time at The Wheatsheaf, the inn was regularly used by farmers as a base to hire farm labourers on hiring days and also to conduct business deals:

Business deal goes wrong at The Wheatsheaf Inn Brampton

"Mr Waugh – a farmer of Kirkhaugh had bought some cattle from a person called Mr Hunter at Brough Hill and they were to be paid for in Carlisle at the bank. Mr Hunter wrote to Mr Waugh asking him to pay the money into the Leith Bank in Carlisle. Mr Waugh set off on his journey to do so, but on reaching Brampton, he met a man called Goodfellow who offered to save Waugh the trouble of travelling any further as he himself was going to Carlisle. Sometime after, Mr Waugh received a letter from Mr Hunter demanding his £20. It was later found that the £20 had never been paid into the bank. Fortunately a witness proved that Waugh had handed over the money to Goodfellow at The Wheatsheaf."

Carlisle Journal, 8th March 1828

Mr Bell continued for several years, but in 1842 The Wheatsheaf was put up for sale, and the new owners appointed a William Armstrong to take over. He cannot have lasted very long because in 1847 The Wheatsheaf was advertised to let, showing a Mr Taylor and Mr Hewitt as tenants:

39. The Wheatsheaf

Wheatsheaf Inn to Let

"To be let at Whitsuntide – comprising a commodious and well adapted HOUSE for an Inn, a good garden, a roomy stable and hayloft together with a suitable and recently erected out-houses all within a closed yard in which a shed for additional horses may be erected if wished The choice situation of these premises and they are yet intended to undergo further improvements in every necessary respect – at once accounts for their having been so long and so thoroughly well-established in an every day, but more especially a Market day custom, and they will be obligingly shown by Mr Taylor and Mr Hewitt the occupying tenants."

Carlisle Journal, 10th April 1847

Joseph Nixon was next on the scene, and the 1851 Census shows him as Innkeeper, age 24 years, with his wife Jane age 27 years living here with their daughter Mabel 2 years and a servant Margaret Little age 16.

In 1857 The Wheatsheaf Inn was again advertised, but this time it was for sale as a result of a decree in the High Court of Chancery Lane in London, made in a case of Cogswell v Armstrong.

Butcher, Barber, Joiner and Landlord in trouble at the Wheatsheaf

"J. Routledge joiner, R. Armstrong butcher and John Noble barber were charged with removing the furniture out of the Wheatsheaf public house and ejecting the county Court bailiffs. Proceedings had been entered into by the County Court against Mr Thomas Graham, landlord of the Wheatsheaf for debt, and on the same day a summons was served on him. The furniture was advertised for sale by the bailiffs of the Court to raise money to pay for Mr Grahams debt, but Mr Graham meanwhile privately sold the furniture for £40 and kept the money. Jacob Dayson miller of Milton Hall was charged with assaulting a bailiff whilst in the discharge of his duty at the Wheatsheaf Inn. It appears that Dayson had called Atkinson "A bum" and then assaulted him."

Carlisle Journal, 20th February 1880

The Wheatsheaf continued trading successfully for a further 46 years, but in 1903, together with 7 other public houses in Brampton, it was struck off the Register by The Magistrates of Brampton. The meeting of the Magistrates in Brampton arranged to discuss the removal of these eight public houses almost became a riot. There was:

"a grim battle between the brewers and the licence holders on the one hand and the Police and the Magistrates on the other. The Police Station was far too small to conduct this public

125

meeting because of the large number who wished to attend. The court was transferred to the newly built St. Martin's Hall and sat for three days."

Rev. Arthur Penn

Innkeepers at The Wheatsheaf appear to have changed regularly – most staying for only 4 to 5 years:

1817 William Bell	1879 John Dunwoodie
1847 William Armstrong	1882 George Dunwoodie
1851 Joseph Nixon	1884 Isaac Richardson
1855 Isaac Holliday	1892 George Jamieson
1858 William Parker	1894 Samuel Dufton
1861 Mary Parker – widow	1897 James Batey
1873 Thomas Graham	1900 Henry Gleed

When this list is compared with the list of landlords at The Kings Arms across the road, there seems to have been much trafficking in staff between these two public houses.

40
THE SCOTCH ARMS

The traditional hooded porch over the front door of 37 Main Street has presided over the comings and goings of The Scotch Arms now for more than 180 years.

Today this street is still sometimes called the "Back" Street by many locals rather than "Main" Street, indeed on old maps it is named as Back Street, which seems a much more appropriate name for it. The Directories do not record a Scotch Arms at the turn of the century, nor does Peter Burn. The first records that have been seen are of the Brampton Presbyterian Church which shows that a Leonard Deane who owned this house, allowing it to be used as "An unlicensed meeting house" for the Presbyterian congregation. Directories first record The Scotch Arms in 1819 under the management of John Halliburton innkeeper. This very soon became a successful coaching and posting inn, with accommodation for 24 overnight guests, and where 25 people could sit down to meals in the dining room and in the stables at the rear, 25 horses could be cared for.

> SCOTCH ARMS INN, BRAMPTON.
> To be LET by PROPOSAL, for a Term of Years, and Entered upon immediately,
> ALL that extensive, commodious, and well-accustomed INN and Premises, called the SCOTCH ARMS, situate in the Market Town of BRAMPTON, in the County of Cumberland; now in the occupation of Mrs. Ann Halliburton, as tenant.
> For further Particulars inquire of Mr. James' Solicitor, Brampton, the Owner.
> 17th October, 1832.

Each Monday, Wednesday, and Friday mornings a coach and four horses called The True Briton left The Scotch Arms at 7.10am for Newcastle, carrying passengers and parcels. On the staff at The Scotch Arms were 2 servants, 2 maids, and 3 stable hands, managed by Robert and Anne Halliburton.

Death at The Scotch Arms

> "A man called Pearson – ostler at The Scotch Arms inn, on Thursday last, received a kick in the stomach from a horse which occasioned his death – almost instantly."
> Carlisle Journal, 7th July 1827

Charge of Slander between Landlord and Tenant of The Scotch Arms Brampton

Mrs Ann Halliburton was the tenant innkeeper at The Scotch Arms, her husband had died the previous year at the age of 29 years, and so she employed a Mr Reed to drive her gig whenever necessary. Mr James was owner of The Scotch Arms and he was a well established solicitor in Brampton, and it was both ambitious but reckless of Mrs Halliburton to take her employer – a solicitor of all people – to court on a charge of slander.

Mr James' office had been broken into and £65 and five gold sovereigns stolen. The thieves were thought to have been well equipped with skeleton keys, because a number of locks and safes had to be passed before the money could be touched. The thief even had the audacity to lock Mr James in his bedroom whilst carrying out the burglary.

Meanwhile, a man called Edmondson had been drinking at The Scotch Arms and having become intoxicated, had to be helped home. Mrs Halliburton arranged for her servant Mr Reed together with another person called Blake, to take the drunken Edmondson home in the Scotch Arms gig. Edmondson on waking up at home discovered that his money had been stolen from his pocket between leaving the Scotch Arms and his house, and suspicion naturally fell upon Reed and Blake. Reed was traced to Hexham by the Brampton constable and was found there with considerable money, which was traced to the James Solicitor robbery. Reed and Blake were found guilty of both offences at the Quarter Sessions in Carlisle and were transported to Botany Bay for 17 years.

Mrs Halliburton, presumably now with a grudge, decided to charge Mr James with slander. She claimed that Mr James had shouted at her in Front Street Brampton, for others to hear – that it was she who had stolen the money and that he had proof of it. Mrs Halliburton wanted significant financial compensation in the court from Mr James for loss of public respect, claiming that she was a genteel lady much respected in the town. After cross examination, the jury found that Mrs Halliburton had coached her 8 year old daughter to say in court that she witnessed the incident where Mr James was said to have shouted at Mrs Halliburton in the street accusing her of being the thief. This was repeated in court by the 8 year old child but the jury were not convinced. Mrs Halliburton lost her case, but surprisingly she did not lose her job. Her employer, the Mr James whom she had taken to court, continued to employ her as innkeeper at The Scotch Arms.

Mrs Halliburton continued for a further two years until 1834 when a Mrs Elisabeth Fisher took over, and, no sooner had Mrs Fisher been in post than another court case took place:

Fisher v Tinling 14th March 1835

"This was an action brought about by the plaintiff Mrs Elisabeth Fisher of The Scotch Arms in Brampton against Mr Benjamin Bell Tinling – a surgeon at Warwick Bridge to recover the sum of £82. 17s. 7d. for board, washing and lodging. It appeared that Mr Tinling has a surgery at Brampton in which he had an assistant of the name of Elliot whom he boarded at Mrs Fishers' and occasionally stopped there himself when he went to Brampton – and also put up his horse there. Mr Tinling claimed as a reduction to this account, a bill of £11.14s. 10d. for medical assistance to the plaintiff's sister Mrs Bell of Black Dub near Brampton. Mrs Fisher's father who is a respectable man residing upon his own property had sold the doctor two horses with the payment for which he had intended to put his two daughters into business at The Scotch Arms. There were other cross accounts between the defendant and the plaintiff to borrow the sum of £80. This brought the matter to a head and the present situation was the consequence. His Lordship on learning of the nature of the case, and after consultation, a recommendation was made."

Carlisle Patriot, 14th March 1835

This matter was settled out of court. The plans of the father of Mrs Fisher and Mrs Bell to have his two daughters set up in business at The Scotch Arms, never came to fruition, as two years later, the landlord is recorded as a John Boustead.

In his book "The Changing Face of Brampton", Iain Parsons shows a photograph belonging to Mr John Lee, of elephants parading through Brampton.

The photograph was taken in the late 1800s and this could well have been Mr Wombwell's circus which often visited small towns in Cumberland.

The following extract is most likely not about Brampton but refers to an amusing incident which befell Mr Wombwell's circus caravans whilst on the move somewhere near Carlisle:

"Whilst moving west with his circus of wild beasts, one of Mr Wombwells' caravans became overturned by accident and a number of animals – chiefly of the monkey tribe escaped. The animals of course were delighted with their restoration to liberty and many of them clambered up into trees – "mopping and mowing" at their keepers who endeavoured to reclaim them. The farmers living in the vicinity rendered their aid to join in the pursuit and with their dogs, commenced one of the most ludicrous chases ever beheld in this part of the country. The cunning monkeys proved that they had not forgotten the caperings of their wild state and one of them having taken refuge in a field containing a number of cows, and being hard pressed by his pursuers, jumped on to the back of a cow which started off at full gallop, throwing her hind legs in the air, astonished at her strange jockey. The monkey kept his seat well, but at length, was secured by one of the keepers."

Carlisle Patriot, 1832

40. The Scotch Arms

Stealing from carts parked in the rear yards of inns appears to have been common. We have already heard of cheeses having been stolen from a cart at The George and Dragon after trading at the Wednesday market day, it seems that the same thing occurred at The Scotch Arms:

Items go missing at The Scotch Arms

"On Monday last, a carriers cart belonging to a person of the name of Cowen, was robbed in The Scotch Arms Inn yard, at Brampton. Seven large hams were stolen there from. No trace of the thieves has yet been obtained."

Carlisle Journal, 14th January 1832

To help people from outlying villages on Market days, The Scotch Arms provided a "Market Room" which was a secure room in the inn rather like a cloakroom, where people could leave their bags and any bulky items bought throughout the day, for collection by them later when they were ready to return home:

Robbery from the Market Room at The Scotch Arms Inn

"Mary Angus was charged with having stolen 3 yards of wincey and 2 yards of Calico the property of Betsy Armstrong at Brampton. Both were at Brampton Hirings together and in the course of the day Betsy Armstrong purchased the materials for £1.4s.10d. which she made up into a bundle and left at the market room at the Scotch Arms till she was ready to go home. Afterwards however Mary Angus called and obtained them from the woman in charge of the market room who could not remember the identity of the prisoner. The police constable visited the house of Mary Angus who stated that she had bought the materials in Carlisle from a Mr Mitchinson. In Court Mr Mitchinson denied having sold the material to Mary Angus who was then found guilty and sentenced to 3 months imprisonment with hard labour."

Carlisle Journal, 5th July 1861

In 1862, Mr R. Cairns a valuer and auctioneer of Brampton, set up a cattle market, using pens in the rear yard of The Scotch Arms. Every two months, a mart day was held here, with cattle and sheep being driven down the streets of Brampton. This initiative brought considerable extra income to the Scotch Arms, but it was short lived, as developments in road and rail transport made it more convenient for Carlisle and Longtown to become the major cattle markets for the area.

At some stage, Mr James solicitor and owner of The Scotch Arms sold his public house as in the 1892 Return of Public Houses and Beer Houses, the owner is shown as William Routledge.

Life in Brampton with 63 Public Houses

Directories and Magistrates Records show the following landlords at The Scotch Arms:

1820 John Halliburton	1847 Robert Lawson
1828 Robert Halliburton	1851 David and Margaret Mitchinson
1831 Mrs Halliburton	1858 John Hetherington
1834 Elisabeth Fisher	1869 William Routledge
1837 John Boustead	1900 Mrs A. Phillips

As we come out of The Scotch Arms, our next port of call is The Tom and Jerry, but this is going to be complicated as there are **FOUR** public houses in the town called The Tom and Jerry!

Perhaps this is a good opportunity to take some time out from our round of public houses, to look further at what life was like in the 1800s for ordinary folk in Brampton.

POVERTY, UNEMPLOYMENT, DRUNKENNESS – POOR RELIEF AND FRIENDLY SOCIETIES

Prior to the 1830s, Brampton's community had enjoyed almost 200 years of relative calm and personal progress in people's fortunes, employment and general well-being. Following the instability caused by rieving across the border, things settled down in Brampton to a rural way of life - prosperity for some, particularly the already reasonably well off landowners and farmers – and a simple existence for the labouring classes, whose main source of income was from employment as farm labourers, servants, hand-loom weavers at home, and as tradesmen such as smiths, drapers, grocers and bakers.

Travel was entirely either on foot, horseback or by cart or coach. Carts carried parcels, market produce and bulk freight, whilst coaches and gigs provided passenger transport. To support this transportation industry a whole infrastructure existed of cart builders, smithies, stables and wheelwrights who kept things moving, employing a great number of smiths, farriers, ostlers, grooms, carters and coachmen. The public house and Inn trade also provided much employment, for innkeepers, servants, stable hands, maids and "boots." There appears to have been enough work or employment for anyone who needed it.

Hiring at the Sands

The Sands area of Brampton was regularly used in the 1800s to hold fairs and shows. Each Martinmas and Michaelmas, the area was taken over for the Hiring and general merry-making. Peter Burn refers to these occasions:

> *"Our fairs and hirings were wild occasions, festivities often running the round of the week."*

Whitsuntide Hirings Brampton

> *"The usual concomitants of a hiring were present in considerable numbers in the persons of strolling players, ballad singers, acrobats, maimed and deformed specimens of humanity,*

vendors of quack medicines said to cure all the ills that flesh has heir to. Cheap Johns all of whom did their utmost to levy contributions upon the simple and hard won earnings of the rustics."

Carlisle Journal, 5th July 1861

"The town was much thronged with persons from the country. The lads and lasses began to arrive at an early hour and by 10 o'clock the street was almost impassable near the Market Place. There were many standing "wi straws in their mouths." Known good servants obtained high wages – but some went away unhired. During the day and the evening, the dancing rooms were crowded."

Even the townsfolk of Brampton, a small market town, considered those who did not live in Brampton, as people from the country – a more commonly used phrase for such people was that they were from "oot bye." To stand with a straw in one's mouth apparently signified that that person was looking for employment.

The public houses and inns on The Sands – The Earl Grey, The Coal Waggon, The Sand House Inn and The Horse and Groom eagerly threw open their doors to this sudden and fortuitous influx of visitors, right on their doorsteps. Hiring and business deals took place downstairs, whilst upstairs, carpets were rolled back and dancing was the great attraction. Farm labourers met servant girls, and pickpockets practiced their skills upon the hapless country visitors.

Life was quite comfortable during this period for those fortunate enough to be property or landowners or professionals i.e. doctors or lawyers.

BRAMPTON ESTABLISHMENT
To commence 26th January 1824
For the education of a very limited number of
YOUNG LADIES
By Miss Nudham

"Who has been engaged for the last 11 years as a private Governess in a highly respectable family in the south of England and who is now residing with her sister Mrs Captain Moses of whose 2 daughters she has undertaken the charge. The pupils would be treated in every respect as part of the family and the plans of private instruction would be adopted as nearly as possible. Terms of Board and tuition in English, French, writing, arithmetic, history, geography and use of the globe, and needlework – forty guineas per annum. Pupils under 10 years of age 30 guineas per annum. Every young lady will be expected to provide herself with a silver dessert spoon, six towels and a pair of sheets."

Carlisle Journal, 30th December 1823

However, for many – particularly the common labourer and servant, life was not so comfortable:

Employment for labourers and servants

Agricultural labourers were usually hired for a half year. They often lived in their master's house and worked with the farmer's own family. Some were poorly treated and worked hard, and poorly paid. But, soon their master's reputation got around and few would offer themselves to that farmer at the next hiring. Honest reliable workers became valued and integrated into their master's family. Agricultural workers earned 1s. 6d a day, which was less than a miner, but they were well fed – potatoes, oatmeal, milk, and home-baked bread, bacon, beer and eggs, fruit and vegetables were quite common in addition to lodging.

Brampton was described as a well established market town serving a hinterland of local villages. The town had many tradesmen and shopkeepers, some of whom had apprentices in training working for them. Hand loom weaving was the main industry with agriculture and mining the next major employment. Certainly most people were employed – in 1830 out of the whole population of Brampton, only 110 were recorded as unemployed, and in addition, there were over 80 vagrants, all of whom depended upon the Parish for poor relief.

Trade and Employment go down: Unemployment and Poverty go up

Following the Duke of Wellington's Beer Act, most of the Government's objectives had been achieved and by the late 1850s the number of public houses and beer houses had risen dramatically, providing much employment and business. The increase in beer consumption required farmers to greatly increase production of wheat and barley for making malt and beer. The monopoly previously held by a small number of breweries was broken and hundreds of small brewing businesses produced local beers, again providing employment for anyone who wanted to work.

However welcome these changes may have been initially, they were soon found to be the harbinger of major changes in working practices resulting from new inventions and mechanisation. Because farmers needed to produce more, machines were invented for sowing and harvesting that meant these could do the job of a labourer in less than half the time. Steam power revolutionised almost everyone's way of life eventually.

Riot against reaping machines

> *"Great excitement prevailed on Monday evening in Brampton in consequence of the introduction on to one of the principal farms of the parish of a reaping machine, which*

excited a great deal of ill feeling amongst the labourers. Several farm labourers came onto the field where the work was proceeding and pulled the driver off his seat by force, stopped the horses and would not allow the work to proceed. The mob declared that by the introduction of machines, "the bread was being taken out of their mouths." On the following day the labourers and their wives caused a more serious disturbance. Whilst the reaping machine was at work, a number of persons surrounded it, assaulted Herd who was the driver. Superintendent Jefferson and Sergeant Kay had taken up a position but the labourers and women were intent upon mischief. Many stones were thrown and the policemen flung to the ground – some women pulled their whiskers so violently and consistently to lessen their quantity."

Carlisle Journal, 1866

Meanwhile in towns, large factories were being built with looms driven by steam power that would produce more cloth in one day than fifty hand loom weavers could produce in a week.

All this industrial revolution had a major impact upon the lives of the people of Brampton. Many farm labourers were no longer required and hand loom weavers became desperate to find other work:

Brampton Whitsuntide Hirings

"Amongst those offering themselves as servants this week were weavers – who had been induced by the wretched state of their business to endeavour by this means to better their condition."

Carlisle Journal

And again:

A meeting to discuss relief for the poor in Brampton:

"A meeting to discuss means of alleviating the prevailing distress of the poor of Brampton district you will be aware of the distress which now exists among the poor classes of people. The weavers are in a most distressed state in consequence of the trade being flat. Local subscriptions have been commenced and has given some relief. Now there are only three plans to be adopted:

1. To give money to the poor.
2. To give meal and potatoes.
3. To employ them in some manner.

Poverty, unemployment, drunkenness – Poor relief and friendly societies

Last week however, some poor labourers were employed in sweeping and shovelling up dirt about the town, for which they were paid one shilling a day. This sum they did not like and they wanted as much as other labourers. In Brampton, they employ the poor in breaking stones and in other kinds of service for which they are paid 18 pence a day."

Carlisle Journal

Whilst unemployment and poverty began to take a hold, so did drinking, thefts, robbery, poaching, family violence and general dissatisfaction. In towns, attempts were made to sabotage the new machinery in factories. On farms, around Brampton, several hay and corn stacks were set on fire.

Despite their falling incomes, many turned to the now numerous public houses and beer houses to seek the company of others in similar circumstances, to drown their sorrows, and to reflect upon better days. We have already seen and heard many stories as we have visited the public houses of Brampton, of cheating at cards for money, theft, burglary, robbery on the highway and violence. The larger coaching and posting inns of Brampton were increasingly used by merchants, business men, and farmers – and were places commonly used for public meetings and auctions, thus managing to maintain a respectability. The smaller inns and beer houses like The Sportsman, The Pack Horse, The Blue Bell and The Globe, on the other hand developed into drinking dens with poor reputations – such places as these were where hapless visitors to the town might be fleeced of their earnings, or robbed on the highway after they had left the premises.

Poor relief becomes a serious issue in Brampton

"On Monday last, 40 cart loads of coal were distributed to the poor housekeepers of Brampton by the agents of the Earl of Carlisle which have been afforded considerable relief. The poor housekeepers of that place who are not in receipt of Parish Poor Relief have for some time partaken of the liberality of The Rev. Ramshay who with praiseworthy benevolence has distributed at every alternate Sunday after divine service in the church, the sum of one shilling to each poor person – the number of which is seventy."

Carlisle Journal

Brampton Poor relief Board had been set up to look after the poor of the Parish – not only in the workhouse, but also to distribute money to the poor in their own homes – usually between 1s. 6d and 2 shillings per week. The criteria for home support were simple – old age, widowhood, or desertion. Widows were encouraged to take up employment as innkeepers. Fathers who deserted their families were hunted down and brought before the Magistrate:

Life in Brampton with 63 Public Houses

> **ONE GUINEA REWARD.**
>
> WHEREAS JOHN M'KNIGHT, a Pedlar, or Hawker, hath run away and left his Wife and Family chargeable to the Parish of BRAMPTON. Whoever will apprehend him and lodge him in any of his Majesty's Gaols, will receive the above Reward on application to JOHN ROUTLEDGE, Overseer, Brampton. He is about 5ft. 2in. high, Scottish Accent, red Whiskers, wears a Hose Black Coat and Worsted Cord Trowsers.

Brampton Workhouse, Carlisle Journal, 8th October 1831.

Those who were taken into the Workhouse found quite a strict regime:

05.45 Rise. Roll Call. Inspection and prayers	12.00 Lunch
06.30 Breakfast	13.00 Work
07.00 Work	18.00 Supper

The regime was well organised without being repressive. However, on one occasion the Master did exceed his authority when he took a stick to John Aydon *"a pauper of weak intellect"* who had been in the habit of singing in the back yard during the night – but after punishment caused no more trouble! Wherever possible, the inmates were put to work no matter what were their circumstances. Young children, when they became 9 years of age and were in the workhouse, were offered for apprenticeship:

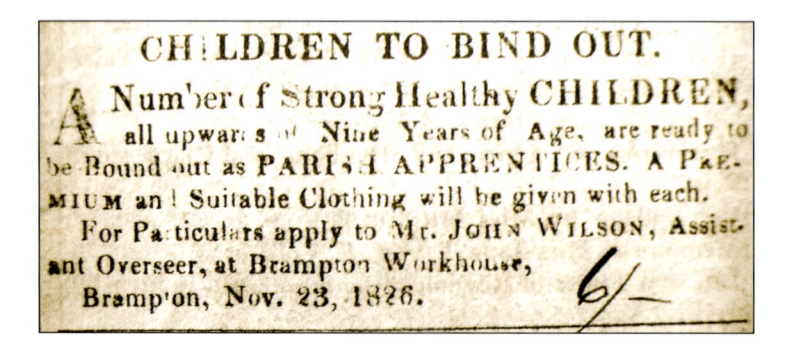

> **CHILDREN TO BIND OUT.**
>
> A Number of Strong Healthy CHILDREN, all upwards of Nine Years of Age, are ready to be Bound out as PARISH APPRENTICES. A PREMIUM and Suitable Clothing will be given with each.
> For Particulars apply to Mr. JOHN WILSON, Assistant Overseer, at Brampton Workhouse,
> Brampton, Nov. 23, 1826.

Carlisle Journal, 1826.

The parish was keen to reduce the number of people being supported on their poor relief list so offered a "golden handshake" i.e. a premium and a free set of clothing to anyone taking a child off their hands to become an apprentice.

Poverty, unemployment, drunkenness – Poor relief and friendly societies

Along the same lines, when a person was discharged from the workhouse, they were issued with a complete set of clothes and given a weekly allowance – all this to help prevent them from becoming destitute again. In 1832 June Harkness was discharged from the workhouse and given:

2 suits of clothes, 2 slips, 2 frocks, 2 pairs of stockings, 2 petticoats, 1 bonnet, 2 shirts, 1 pair of clogs.

The Poor Relief Board also helped to reduce the burden upon the parish by encouraging people to emigrate to Canada to find new employment there and to seek their fortune. In 1842, several families travelled from Brampton to Maryport to set sail in the brigantine "Jane" bound for Quebec. The journey took 64 days. Two of the families who emigrated from Brampton eventually arrived at a wooded part of Canada and literally cut down trees to make a clearing for houses. They decided to call their settlement Brampton after their home town in England. Today, the population of Brampton Ontario is 400,000.

The Poor Relief Board also helped with unemployment. In 1848, when work became difficult to find for hand-loom weavers because of the growth of factories in towns operating steam driven power looms, many weavers were encouraged to re-train or diversify. The parish of Brampton purchased 20 hammers and brought in tons of stone to employ redundant weavers in the manufacture of road stone and setts. Many of the weavers had found other work after a fortnight's stone breaking. The cost of looking after someone in the workhouse was 4 pence a day. There were very few able-bodied men in the workhouse which was usually two thirds full and could cope with 100 inmates, most of whom were unmarried mothers, widows or wives who had been deserted.

Ian McDonald – Poor Relief in Brampton Union

Although we have heard many stories of theft, cheating and robbery as we have progressed around the town it is important to recognise that there was also a great deal of compassion, with many people prepared to support and help those in need.

> ROBBERY IN BRAMPTON.—Jane Wilson, a poor but industrious widow from the village of Talkin, went to Brampton market on the 17th inst., received the price of her fat pig, and was shortly afterwards robbed of the whole sum upon the street. She was nearly broken-hearted at being so summarily deprived of her little all, and the circumstance created so much sympathy that a subscription was set on foot, which soon amounted to

Carlisle Journal, 26th December 1851.

The town of Brampton had a good record for helping the poor and unemployed. In 1832 to celebrate the passing in Parliament of The Reform Bill, great celebrations were held in the town and the poor were not to lose out:

"The spirited inhabitants of Brampton intend to celebrate the passing of The Reform Bill and glorious triumph of the people by a public dinner at The Howard Arms. Collections had been made to assist the poor to rejoice on this occasion. 350 families were assisted and partook of the bounty of the donors. There was best beef and mutton provided."

Carlisle Journal, May 1832

The Emergence of Mutual and Friendly Societies
Friendly Societies began to become popular across the Country in the 1830s and 1840s, and Brampton was no exception. Mutual and Friendly Societies were formed due to the increasing worry about poverty and people's inability to cope financially with life's sudden changes in personal circumstances e.g. illness, loss of work, injury, widowhood and death. Friendly societies like The Oddfellows, The Foresters, The Buffaloes, The Rechabites, and The Good Samaritans were each set up in Brampton to protect and care for their members at a time when there was no welfare state provision, no trades unions, or National Health Service. The aim was to provide help to members when they needed it. The Societies were non-profit making, were owned by their members, and often had a strong religious background.

How did the friendly societies start in the first place?
Friendly societies are thought to have been started in the Roman army – where Legionnaires made regular contributions of small change into a pot which was held by the most senior soldier. When one of their number was seriously injured and forced to retire, a donation was made from this fund to give him or his family a help. This philosophy continued and formed the basis of mutual societies.

But where does the name "Oddfellows" come from?
After the Romans, there was considerable growth in the economy – craftsmen and professions developed specialist skills and formed themselves into guilds. But, the philosophy of helping the wider society changed to exclusivity i.e. to protecting their unique skills and privileges – almost like a "closed shop." They set up rules, devised uniform, and regalia that non-members could not afford nor understand and adopted secret signs. These master craftsmen and professionals therefore became exclusive brethren, so the ordinary people were left excluded and had to form their own organisations. These "lower" organisations were formed of ordinary people, the unskilled, to join together to help each other. They came from an odd assortment of

Poverty, unemployment, drunkenness – Poor relief and friendly societies

backgrounds but having one thing in common – the will to help each other. These new organisations called themselves The Oddfellows, or The Foresters, or The Buffaloes.

What became of these organisations?

The Oddfellows, the Buffaloes and the Foresters survive today and are to be seen on the internet. They survive with much the same philosophy, to help one another. However these organisations have not had an easy time of it. People who club together to better themselves were often seen as a threat by kings and politicians. Because gatherings of ordinary working people were considered a threat, The Oddfellows in particular, developed elaborate schemes to protect themselves and their members and their meetings. Passwords were introduced at meetings – no password = no entry, and new members could only be introduced by existing members who knew and trusted them. The rooms where they met became "lodges" or "courts", membership involved taking oaths of allegiance to each other, secret signs etc. From these organisations the Trades Union movement began. However in 1834 – whilst lodges and courts were being set up in Brampton at The Pack Horse Inn and at The Bush, six men in Dorchester were convicted and transported overseas for being members of a secret illegal society which threatened the politics of the day. They were the Tolpuddle Martyrs.

By 1850 The Independent Order of Oddfellows had grown rapidly with a stream of people flooding into towns from the country to seek work as part of the Industrial Revolution, where the need for mutual protection in factories and welfare became even greater. Only by joining a mutual society could the ordinary person protect themselves and their families from the financial catastrophe accompanying injury, illness or sudden death.

A Friendly Institution for Brampton:

> "A Friendly Institution is to be set up in Brampton to raise by subscription and by voluntary contributions, a fund for mutual relief and maintenance of its members in infancy, old age, sickness and infirmity. Thus affording a sure source in cases of poverty, sickness in old age or misfortunes e.g. a young man industriously and economically inclined may by depositing a sum of £10, insure not only sufficient to defray the expenses of a funeral in case of death but also may secure for himself a weekly allowance in old age."
>
> Carlisle Journal

Principles of The Order of Oddfellows at Brampton

> "The principles of the Brampton Order are that we must love each other as brethren, exercise and entertain supreme affection and obedience to God. To be an Oddfellow is to be a true Christian, in faith, hope and charity, to love God and one another in prosperity and

adversity – in the sunshine of life as well as in the darkness of danger, distress and despair. It is heavenly and divine to aid one's fellow and the path leads to life immortal."

Carlisle Journal

Brampton Oddfellows meet at The Pack Horse Inn

"The Loyal Brampton Lodge of The Independent Order of Oddfellows celebrated their lodge by parading through Brampton on New Years Day. The procession created a good deal of stir in the town. The Society felt well entitled to public favour and fancying that a procession would be the best means of exciting interest in the minds of many to introduce new members. The procession started at The Pack Horse Inn near the Bowling Green and consisted of:

The Brampton Band
Flag with Arms of the Order borne by Tyler with a drawn sword
Two Guardians with White wands
President of the Lodge
Dispensation in a neatly gilded frame
Brothers of the purple degree with scarlet flag
Brothers of the scarlet degree with blue flag
Brothers of the blue degree with white flag
Two small banners with blue sashes, white leather aprons
Tyler with a drawn sword."

Carlisle Journal, 17th January 1840

This parade must have been quite a spectacle, and gives a good example of the ceremonies and regalia considered to be important by the Lodge.

Similar Lodges were springing up all over Cumberland and nationally. Another Friendly Society – The Foresters was set up at The Joiner's Arms in the Market Place. The Lodge established there was called The Belted Will Howard's Court but it is amusing to note the unfortunate type-setting error in the Carlisle Journal of 1842:

THE BELTED WILLY HOWARD'S COURT BRAMPTON

"On the first of January a court of Ancient foresters under the above title was opened at the house of Mrs Bell known by the sign of The Joiner's Arms in the Market Place Brampton. The officers of the Ancient Foresters Court no 766 from the Andrew Marvel Inn Carlisle performed the duties of opening and initiation in an impressive manner. A great number of young men were enrolled."

Carlisle Journal, 1842

Poverty, unemployment, drunkenness – Poor relief and friendly societies

Two weeks later, lodges of Ancient Foresters were opened at Gilsland and Kirkcambeck with assistance from The Belted Will Howard Court Lodge.

In 1846 The Ancient Foresters moved their Lodge to The Horse and Farrier, where the Innkeeper had become a member:

"The Anniversary dinner for the Court of Ancient Foresters will be held on 18th April 1846 at Brother Whitfield Dickinson's Horse and Farrier Inn."

Carlisle Journal

Now, to resume our journey, we were just leaving the Scotch Arms in Main Street, so our next port of call is The Tom and Jerry.

But which one?

41

THE TOM AND JERRY

Life must have been complicated for those who used Brampton's public houses for the first time, or as visitors to the town. If you had made arrangements to meet your friends in the Tom and Jerry then there would be only a one in four chance of meeting up with them.

Why? Well, because in Brampton in the 1830s and 1840s there were FOUR public houses all called The Tom and Jerry. These were:

Tom and Jerry – Main Street, near Bank House
Tom and Jerry – 17 Moatside
Tom and Jerry – Ewarts Buildings
Tom and Jerry – Central Place

The Main Street Tom and Jerry was at number 58 Main Street, this building today is a private house.

41. The Tom and Jerry

But Why Tom and Jerry – – – and why four?

The title has nothing to do with the cat and mouse cartoon characters. Tom and Jerry were two fictitious characters who regularly featured in the columns of a London newspaper called "Pierce Egan's Life in London" in the 1820s. The paper was illustrated with etchings and showed Tom and Jerry as two trend-setters of fashionable life in London. They were two "posers" or "dandies" who appeared to lead a charmed life, getting into many scrapes, rather like "Del Boy and Rodney" in today's TV series "Only Fools and Horses." The full names of these two characters were Jerry Hawthorne and Corinthian Tom. So successful was the series in the newspaper that a theatrical production of their escapades was made and this toured the country, coming to McCready's Theatre in Carlisle in 1823:

Tom and Jerry – Carlisle Theatre September 1823

> *"Our Theatre was re-opened on Wednesday evening with a piece that has everywhere produced much noise – namely "Tom and Jerry – Life in London." According to the Bills it is a: Classic, comic, operatic, didactic, moralistic, Aristophanic, localic, analytic, terpsichoric, panoramic, camera-obscuric, extravaganza, musical burlesque of fun, frolic, fashion and flash" We should only betray our folly and weakness were we to attempt any addition to what is here so luminously set forth.*
>
> *"Life in London" is replete with chaunts, rum glees, kiddy catches. An animated picture of life in London. As in a mirror, life is shown in all its varieties. Virtue, vice, the age and body of the times is furnished by the author, artist and dress maker. Tom and Jerry have a moral purpose and aim. We do not say that "Life in London" contains anything unusually offensive in a moral sense – it is free from this blemish as most other light pieces, but there are many things in it which good taste may possibly object to.*
>
> *The prime chaunts, the rum glees, and kiddy catches may not exactly suit every palate – even those smacking too strongly of the moralistic. Yet others there are who deem fun, frolic, and flash your only true classic, and to such Tom and Jerry presents numerous attractions.*
>
> *Corinthian Tom – the hero – met with a very able and vivacious representative in Mr Caldcroft. Mr Lane assumes the part of the Oxonian Bob Logic a broad brimmed castor, green spectacles, crimson frock, wide stripped trousers and silk umbrella, knowing phiz, consummate assurance, up to all things, down upon everyone, and a dash of pedantry withal. Jemmy Green a thoroughbred cockney.*
>
> *There are scenes at Almack's; quadrille dancing and waltzing, masquerade characters, life in rags and London mendicants making merry after the miseries of the day. The leading characters are Crook armed Jack, genteel Tom, Little Jemmy and Billy Walters. A scene at Tattersalls and many expressions here and there may cause some to laugh and applaud, but they cannot but make the judicious grieve."*
>
> *Carlisle Patriot, 20th September 1823*

Carlisle Theatre and Tom and Jerry

"On one occasion a play called Tom and Jerry which had drawn large houses in London, did rather poorly in Carlisle. One of the Mayor's right hand men described Tom and Jerry as "Devils of fellows – enough to upset all the old women of our holy city."
A History of theatre in Carlisle – Joanna Felc

So, Tom and Jerry came to Carlisle and appears to have been a little "risqué", causing the judicious to grieve!

The sensationalism of the characters and the kind of life portrayed must have appealed to several innkeepers for them to have named their public houses after Tom and Jerry. There are no records seen that suggest why four public houses should all have the same name at the same time. For a small town like Brampton, one would assume that landlords knew each other quite well and it seems unlikely that each did not know of the other's plans to name their public house after these two popular heroes.

Pierce Egan's Life in London 26th August 1827.

Despite the fashionable name, none of the Tom and Jerry public houses achieved great notoriety. Very few records have been found in the directories, Magistrates records and Public house returns or the newspapers.

The Main Street Tom and Jerry is referred to by Peter Burn who mentions that Mr Robert Atkinson was innkeeper, this was in the 1830s but no other record has been seen so one can assume that this public house existed for at least 7 years, but perhaps not much longer.

From the doorstep of The Tom and Jerry next to Bank house we have 30 yards to walk along and then to cross over Main Street to number 87 where we will find The Ship.

Or is it The Punchbowl or maybe The Coach and Horses Inn?

42

THE SHIP, THE PUNCHBOWL, THE COACH AND HORSES

At 87 Main Street today, is the last building before the open area where Hadrian's statue now stands, and is opposite the Bethesda Hall.

The first record of a public house at this address is in 1816, when it was advertised for sale, showing Thomas Thirlwall, a hat maker as the owner:

It is not clear as to whether the premises were in fact sold, as Thomas Thirlwall is still recorded as owner and hat maker at *"The Ship Inn in Back Street, Brampton"* in the directory and in the Public House Licence Register six years later in 1822. This is also confirmed in the Licence Register of 1822 for The Abbey Bridge Inn at Lanercost, which records:

"Thomas Thirlwall hatter and owner of The Ship Inn Brampton" as surety.

Later in 1823, a public house is recorded at this address but, this time by the name of "The Punchbowl" with a Robert Hewitt, Chelsea Pensioner as landlord. Six years later, being declared bankrupt, Robert Hewitt was ordered to forfeit £7 of his annual pension, in order to pay off the debts he had incurred:

Insolvent innkeeper loses part of his pension

"Robert Hewitt, innkeeper of the Punchbowl public house, Brampton appeared before the insolvents court. Mr Carrick applied to have part of the insolvent's pension of £27 a year from the Chelsea Hospital applied to the liquidation of his debts. The Commissioner ordered £7 a year to be paid out of it."

Carlisle Journal, 28th March 1829

In 1832, the following advertisement appeared in the Carlisle Journal:

> PUBLIC-HOUSE, &c in BRAMPTON.
> TO BE SOLD BY AUCTION,
> At the House of John Gill, Shoulder of Mutton, BRAMPTON, on Wednesday, the 29th day of May, 1816,
> ALL that well accustomed Freehold PUBLIC-HOUSE, known by the Name or Sign of the SHIP, situate in the Back-street, in BRAMPTON aforesaid, with a HOUSE, now occupied as four Dwelling-Rooms, adjoining the same, all in excellent repair, and now in the respective occupations of James Nelson, James Walker, and Elizabeth Jackson, as Tenants thereof.
> For further Particulars apply to Mr. Thomas Thirlwall, Hatter; or at the Office of Mr. Thomas James, Attorney, Brampton.

> PUBLIC HOUSE, HATTER'S SHOP, & DWELLING HOUSES,
> IN BRAMPTON, FOR SALE.
> To be SOLD by AUCTION, upon the Premises, on MONDAY, the 21st day of MAY, 1832, at Six o'Clock in the Evening,—
> ALL that well-accustomed PUBLIC HOUSE known by the Sign of the COACH and HORSES, situate in the BACK STREET of BRAMPTON, in the County of Cumberland. And also a HATTER'S SHOP, and several DWELLING ROOMS adjoining, in the respective occupations of Joseph Graham, Thomas Thirlwall, James Walker, and others, as Tenants.
> For Particulars apply to the Rev. ANTHONY LAWSON, or to Mr. JAMES, Attorney, Brampton.
> R. CAIRNS, Auctioneer.

Left: Carlisle Journal, 25th May 1816. Right: Carlisle Journal, May 1832.

The advertisement refers to this public house as "The Coach and Horses", and describes it as already well established, but no records appear to exist of it prior to that date by that name. Also, Peter Burn in his lecture notes "A Fireside Crack" does not mention a "Coach and Horses" in his list of public houses of Brampton before the 1830s.

Thomas Thirlwall mentioned in the above advertisement as owner of the hat shop was previously owner of a public house here, called "The Ship." It appears therefore that the public house at this address had changed its name for a third time by 1832.

42. The Ship, The Punchbowl, The Coach and Horses

Lifespan of The Ship, The Punchbowl, The Coach and Horses

The Ship
The Punchbowl
The Coach and Horses

1810 1820 1830 1840 1850 1860 1870 1880 1890 1900

Joseph Graham, mentioned in this advertisement became the new innkeeper for the next thirteen years, and in 1845 an accident took place on the road between Brampton and Irthington:

"Mr Dodgson – together with his manservant was driving his gig from Brampton to Irthington when the horse startled, throwing Mr Dodgson out on to the road, the left hand wheel passing over his legs and arm, causing grievous injuries from which he did not recover. The manservant was conveyed to Mr Joseph Graham's The Coach and Horses inn at Brampton where he lay for several days in a precarious state. He is however now pronounced out of danger."

Carlisle Journal, 27th December 1845

Two years later, in 1847, The Coach and Horses was once more offered for sale, and as before, the sale included the adjoining dwelling rooms, which at that time were occupied by a Joseph Foster and Robert Hewitt *(Junior)*. Robert Hewitt was a carpenter and his father – also by the same name – had lived here 25 years previously as innkeeper when it was called "The Punch Bowl."

Mrs Margaret Ward became the new owner and innkeeper. Further innkeepers came and went, and this public house quietly continued in business to the end of the century without further incidents getting into the Magistrates Court or newspapers.

William Pearson is recorded as innkeeper at The Coach and Horses between 1873 and 1892 and was also owner of the building at the end of Main Street which was The Nursery Arms.

Many local people will remember an interesting Brampton character called "Willie the Gallant" who lived here at 87 Main Street until the 1990s. It is said that Willie the Gallant came by his nick name as he was born on the day that a Greyhound of the same name won the local show. Willie the Gallant was a relative of William Pearson the landlord of 1873, and the person living at number 87 today has an interesting picture of Willie the Gallant as a young boy.

In 1903, The Coach and Horses was closed as a direct result of pressure from the Magistrates and the Brampton Branch of the Temperance Movement.

The Temperance Movement had been successful in convincing the Licensing Authority that there were too many public houses in the town, and details of a six month period of inspection and assessment of the condition of every public house in Brampton was presented to the magistrates. Of The Coach and Horses, Mr Chapman, Superintendent of Police said:

"I am not exaggerating when I say that The Coach and Horses is about as bad as it could be in every respect. There is only one entrance but several exits which make it impossible to inspect after hours, as illegal drinkers escape out of the rear doors. The rear yard is only a narrow passage used as an insanitary closet and backs onto the Blue Bell Inn."
North Cumberland Reformer

From the directories and magistrates innkeeper records, the following innkeepers are shown for The Ship, The Punchbowl, and The Coach and Horses:

The Ship	**The Coach and Horses**
1816 Thomas Thirlwall hat maker	1834 Joseph Graham
	1847 Margaret Ward
The Punchbowl	1869 Charles Harding
1822 Robert Hewitt (Senior)	1871 Thomas Wilson
1823 James Tinling	1873 William Pearson
1824–1829 Robert Hewitt (Junior)	1896 Miss Sarah Pearson

The 1892 Return for Public Houses and Beer Houses describes the Coach and Horses as:

"4 sleep, 8 dine, No horses, next nearest public house 30 yards. Owner William Pearson."

As we leave The Coach and Horses – which seems a most inappropriate name as there is room for neither coaches nor horses – we cross the road to find our second Tom and Jerry, at number 86 Main Street.

43

THE TOM AND JERRY
– EWARTS BUILDINGS

At the junction of Main Street with Longtown Road, numbers 86 to 92 Main Street look across to the police station and over to the statue of Emperor Hadrian where the Nursery Arms once stood.

No records have been found in any of the directories, Magistrates Innkeeper Register, or returns of Public Houses and Beer Houses that refer to a Tom and Jerry in this part of Main Street.

Peter Burn in his lecture notes for "A fireside crack" gives the only reference that mentions a Tom and Jerry in this part of the town:

"in Ewarts Buildings where the innkeeper was Mr David Hetherington."

According to the Tithe Map of 1851 and its schedule, this part of Main Street was the property of John Heward, and a David Hetherington is recorded as living here with his wife Mary. Some of the oldest inhabitants of Brampton today still refer to these buildings as Ewarts Buildings, and it is where John Heward himself lived:

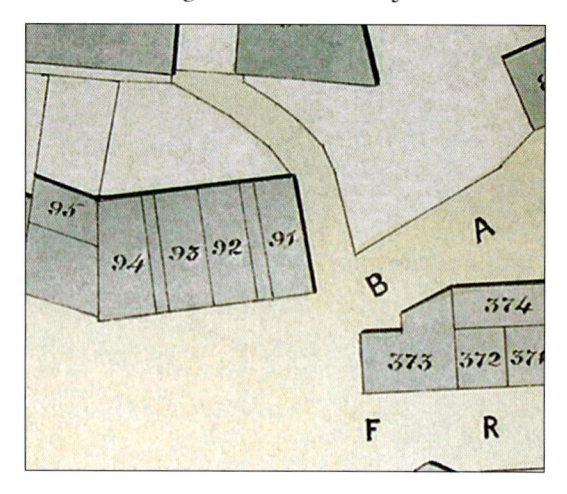

Owner: John Heward 91-94. Occupiers: Mary Hetherington 91, John Heward 92, James Fox 93, David Latimer 94.

We must therefore rely entirely on Peter Burn's memory of life in Brampton when he was a boy and assume that this public house did exist here, but did not stay in business very long – perhaps like:

"A frolic, a fashion and a flash" – just as Tom and Jerry were themselves described by the theatre critic of the Carlisle Patriot in 1823!

Our next stopping place is 100 yards back along Main Street, to find the General Wolfe.

44

THE GENERAL WOLFE

At Gill Place in Main Street Brampton are the offices of Cartmell Shepherd Solicitors.

Peter Burn mentions a public house here by the name of The General Wolfe in his lecture notes, with John Foster as landlord/shoe maker, and this is confirmed by the directories for 1822 to 1829. Arthur Hetherington is recorded as landlord in 1830, and the Rev. Arthur Penn, when he was researching the public houses of Brampton, records his discussion with a Mr Elliot who could remember a Mr Hetherington living here in Gill Place.

No records have been seen in the newspapers concerning the General Wolfe and a description of its facilities can only be imagined. The Tithe map is no help either as this public house had closed and the premises had changed owners by 1850.

Being right on the side of the busy Newcastle to Carlisle highway, with coach and cart parking facilities in front, would suggest that this public house was well placed to attract business.

Our next visit will be to The Klondyke Bar along Beck Lane.

45

THE KLONDYKE BAR

Beck Lane is a narrow passage way where Brampton Beck can be heard running underground in culverts today, but in the 1800s it was a small stream running in a ditch alongside the lane. There were regular complaints about the rubbish and foul smells here, with the local council being heavily criticised for taking no action. Along this lane were gates, doors and passage ways leading off on the right into the back yards of premises which faced on to Front Street. We are looking for the one time entrance to The Klondyke Bar.

The metal ladder fire escape is the rear access to The Picture Gallery and a disused white door marks the old entrance to the rear yard of what was The Samson Inn.

In the 1850s there was great interest in the newspapers about investors rushing to the American Yukon to join entrepreneurs selling mining rights to parcels of land in the outback to prospect for gold, and to hopefully become rich overnight.

At the price of only 2 pence a pint of beer – the cheapest in town, one would have expected this bar to have been a magnet to the town's drinkers, and consequently would have been the scene of many incidents resulting from drunken behaviour. However, despite being a cheap drinking den, The Klondyke Bar appears to have achieved a trouble free career of 40 years.

This bar was set up by Brampton Old Brewery in The Samson's back yard which looked out onto Beck Lane.

45. The Klondyke Bar

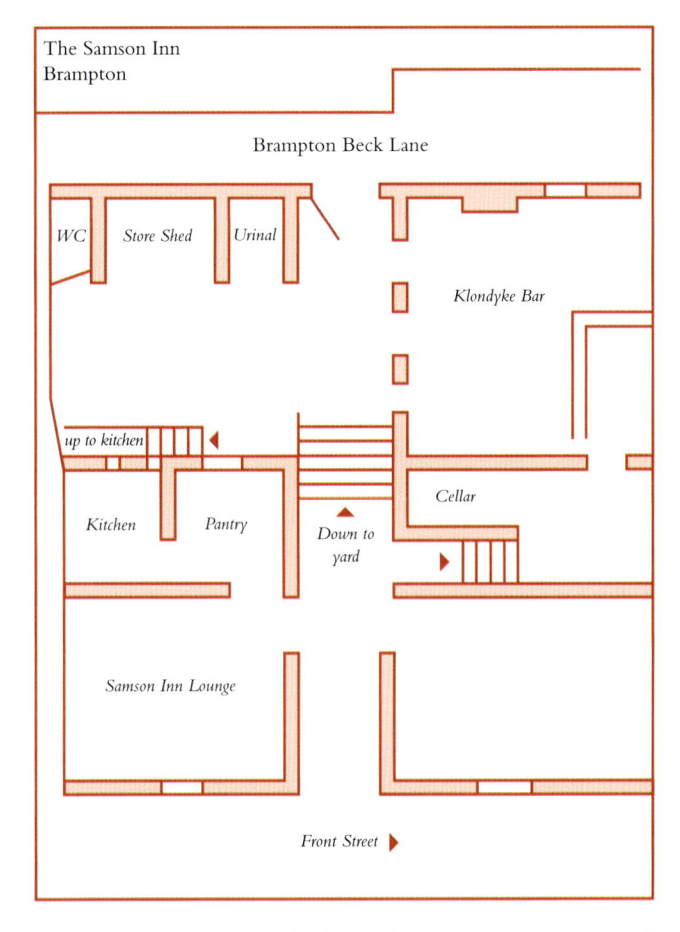

[Floor plan diagram of The Samson Inn, Brampton, showing: Brampton Beck Lane along the top; WC, Store Shed, Urinal, and Klondyke Bar in the upper portion; up to kitchen, Kitchen, Pantry, Down to yard, Cellar in the middle; Samson Inn Lounge in the lower portion; Front Street at the bottom.]

Very few records have been found about this venture; no events happening here ever reached the newspapers or the magistrate's court. The only records that have been seen are of 1851 when the licensee was a Robert Hutchinson and of 1890 when the bar was closed by the magistrates after pressure from the Temperance Movement led by Rosalind, Countess of Carlisle.

Although it may be tempting to stay a while in The Klondyke – with the price of beer only 2 pence, we are clearly not going to get rich overnight and the smell from the Beck is unpleasant. We shall visit next, The Anchor Inn, further along Beck lane.

46

THE ANCHOR INN

We have already visited one Anchor, and that was in Front Street where The Discount Warehouse is today. That public house was the Crown and Anchor and had previously been called The Shepherd, and before that The Lord Nelson. Our second Anchor rests at the bottom of Beck Lane.

The Anchor first appears in a Directory of 1818 recording a Thomas Marrs as innkeeper, and this is confirmed in a recently discovered ledger of shopkeeper Isaac Bird recording the purchase in 1818 of one gallon of gin by:

"Innkeeper Thomas Marrs of the Anchor."

The Anchor.

46. The Anchor Inn

Peter Burn in his lecture notes refers to life in the 1830s: *"The Anchor where Mr Hewetson was innkeeper"* and this is later confirmed by the Census which records a Mr Hewetson living in this area of Beck lane. This could not be a reference to the Front Street Anchor because that one did not exist until 1847.

In 1825 a Magistrate's Court heard the case of **Corry v. Blaylock** where there was a claim for trespass upon private property in this part of Brampton. The property in question was a lane which led to the rear yard of The George and Dragon Inn, and then on to Beck Lane. The Court Case was complicated, but in the description of the lanes and properties given by the solicitor, a public house with the name of The Anchor is mentioned:

Action – Trespass – Corry v. Blaylock

"There is a yard on the north side of Mrs Corry's house which fronts the south. There is a back door and a cellar window to the east of the back door. There is a road on the north side of Blaylock's house which leads into a yard with a stable – it is a private road that leads to another yard belonging to Mr Ewart. The road goes on to the back of The George and Dragon Inn – there is a gate into that yard from The George and Dragon Inn. The front of The Anchor Inn is in a lane leading to that yard. The Anchor Inn is opposite Mrs Corry's back door and there is a footway down to The Beck."

Carlisle Journal, 1825

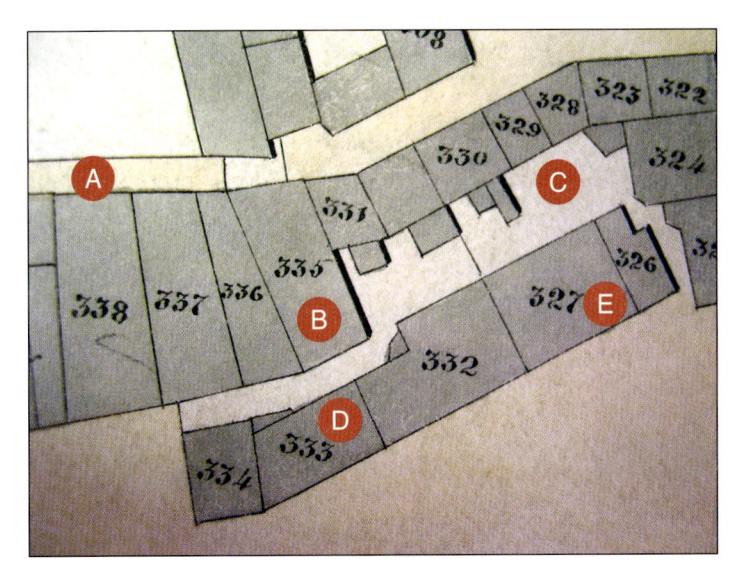

A. Brampton Beck and Beck Lane. B. The Anchor. C. Mr Ewart's yard, Mr Blaylock's house, D. Mrs Corry's house, E. George and Dragon Inn.

Life in Brampton with 63 Public Houses

The Licence Register for 1823–1825, records The Anchor with Mr Hasting as owner and this is confirmed by the Tithe Map showing him as occupant of building 335.

| Hasting George | Joseph Routledge | 335 |

The Register also shows his neighbour Thomas Modlen of The Sportsman Inn as surety for The Anchor. There are many examples in the Licence Register showing that it was regular practice for the licensee of one public house to stand as surety for another.

No records have been found of other incidents at The Anchor, and it is still recorded as being in business in 1880 with James Shaw as landlord.
The Ordnance Survey map of 1891 also shows an inn at this location and the footway to the Beck:

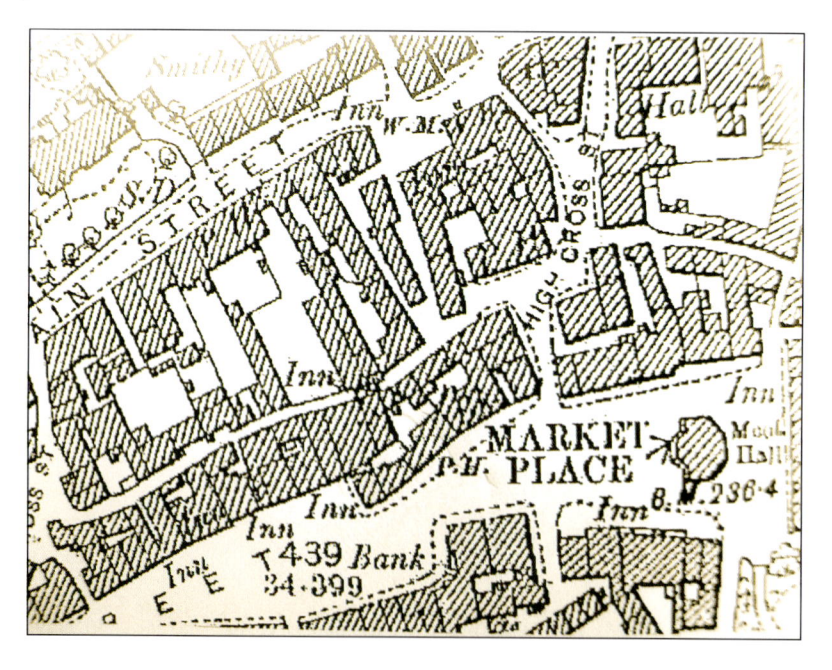

The Anchor Inn? Footway.

The 1892 Return for Public Houses and Beer Houses, however, makes no mention of The Anchor.

Standing in Beck Lane today on the site of the doorsteps of the one-time Anchor Inn, leaves us close to the Central Place car park, where we will find our next public house:

Another Tom and Jerry – or is it The Star?

158

47

THE TOM AND JERRY, OR IS IT THE STAR?

Today, a block of flats stands guard over Beck Lane and the Brampton Beck which now runs under-ground in culverts.

These flats were built in the 1990s and before them; there stood here a dilapidated store house that was used by Milburn's ironmongers shop.

The 1851 census records this dwelling and shop as being occupied by a Mr Joseph Robson, draper and innkeeper, and this is confirmed by Peter Burn who records this building as:

> *"the Tom and Jerry at Central Place with innkeeper Joseph Robson."*

The Tom and Jerry characters were popular in the 1830s being character sketches in a fashionable London newspaper called "Pierce Egan's Life in London" and which included etchings by a famous artist of the day called Cruikshank. The theatre production of Tom and Jerry caused quite a stir when it came to Carlisle in 1823, engaging the enthusiasm and excitement of some but the criticism and condemnation of others, rather like the "East Enders" TV serial of today.

JOSEPH ROBSON,
CENTRAL PLACE, BRAMPTON

SILK MERCER, LINEN DRAPER, CLOTH MERCHANT.
GENTLEMEN'S TAILOR. LADIES' COSTUMIER.
FAMILY MOURNING. FUNERALS FURNISHED.
BOOT AND SHOE WAREHOUSE.

It is highly likely therefore that this public house was named after these two characters and would therefore be in business in the mid 1820s and 1830s. No reference other than Peter Burn's has been seen. The directories and magistrate records all remain blank about this Tom and Jerry which must have been in business for at least 15 years. Peter Burn does mention that several public houses which existed when he was a boy in the 1830s had ceased trading later in the century to become shops and businesses. Mr Robson is recorded as a Draper at this location again later, so it is reasonable to assume that The Tom and Jerry became a drapers shop, and then later still the store of Milburn's ironmongers shop.

But now, a further complication: Where is The Star?

The Star

Rev. Arthur Penn in his study of Brampton's public houses mentions "The Star" in 1860. Although no other record has been seen of The Star, and Arthur Penn does not give the origin of his reference, he is certain that such a public house did exist. Arthur Penn's reference reads:

> "The Tom and Jerry Central Place was later Mr Joseph Robson's premises – but may have been "The Star" where Mary Marrs was innkeeper in 1860."

The 1851 census shows that a dwelling in the same location as the dilapidated store was occupied by a Thomas Marrs innkeeper Age 71 years, his wife Mary age 61 years, living with their daughter and grandson.

47. The Tom and Jerry, or is it The Star?

We have already come across Mr Thomas Marrs in 1822 when he was landlord at The Anchor, close by in Beck Lane.

To summarise our facts:
1. Peter Burn records a Tom and Jerry in Central Place during the 1830s with Joseph Robson as innkeeper/draper at this location.
2. The 1851 census shows Thomas Marrs innkeeper, living with his wife Mary, their daughter Mary and grandson Thomas somewhere in this area.
3. Rev. Arthur Penn records The Star in Central Place with a Mary Marrs – Thomas' widow as innkeeper.

It is therefore reasonable to conclude that The Tom and Jerry and The Star each occupied the same premises here in Central Place at different times, and which had been Robson's draper shop; much later to become a cement store, and today is a block of flats.

Occupation of Central Place 1820–1870

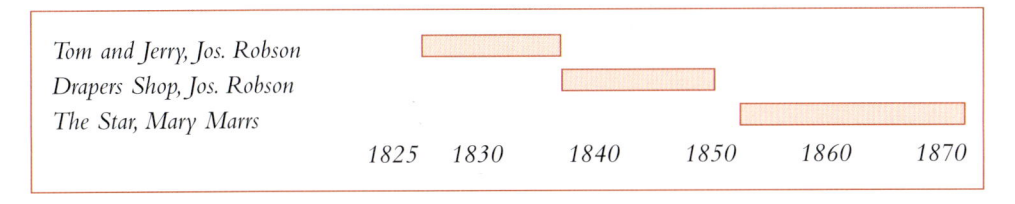

Tom and Jerry, Jos. Robson		▬▬▬				
Drapers Shop, Jos. Robson			▬▬▬▬			
The Star, Mary Marrs					▬▬▬▬▬	
	1825	1830	1840	1850	1860	1870

Stepping out of The Tom and Jerry/The Star, back into Beck lane we can see High Cross Street beckoning. We have already been to The White Lion, but across the street we are off to The Freemasons Arms where there is going to be a quoits match tonight.

48

THE FREEMASONS ARMS

In High Cross Street stands Bonnie Prince Charlie's house, now Hamilton's shoe shop. It was in this house that Bonnie Prince Charlie set up his headquarters and later received aldermen from the City of Carlisle who had been summoned here to hand over the keys of Carlisle Castle.

At the turn of the century, this building was already a well established inn, but not by the name of The Freemasons Arms. In 1798 the house belonged to John Gill who sold it to John Longrigg, and in the conveyance, the house is described as:

"Two dwelling houses with stables, yard and garden lately kept as an inn called The Kings Arms."

48. The Freemasons Arms

In 1800 The Kings Arms was owned and managed by David Hope who made big changes – adding new lodging rooms upstairs and additional stables, but in 1810, The Kings Arms was put up for sale:

TO BE SOLD

"Upon the premises on the 8th February 1810.

All that commodious and well accustomed freehold Public house called and known by the sign of The Kings Arms situated in the town of Brampton. Consisting of a large kitchen, a good parlour, a large cellar, 2 pantries below stairs, 5 good lodging rooms above stairs one brew house, 2 back yards and an excellent pump, 2 new built stables with stalls for 10 horses, 2 hay lofts now occupied by David Hope – also 2 other freehold dwelling houses adjoining the same with a good kitchen, parlour, back kitchen and two rooms above."

Carlisle Journal, 20th January 1810

The Kings Arms was again advertised in 1816. The new owner at Bonnie Prince Charlie's house preferred to name his new venture "The Masons Arms", so David Hope moved out, taking his Kings Arms sign board with him to a private house in Main Street called "The Glen", to set up a new business there.

The name Mason's Arms is recorded in the directories for 1829 and 1847 – but thereafter, the name is recorded consistently as The Freemasons Arms.

The Pretender in Brampton

"– – The Prince, who is said to have expressed an aversion to staying at an inn, took up his residence at the house of Mr Joseph Deane – whose family now extinct, possessed considerable property. This house which stands in Upper Cross Street was afterwards converted to an inn with the loyal sign of "The Kings Arms" – it is now known as "The Freemasons Arms" kept by a Mr Swallow."

"Onlooker", Carlisle Journal

This house has had a long history of being associated with the shoe trade; today it is Hamilton's shoe shop, before that it was Couch's shoe shop, and in 1823, Thomas Corbett was shoe maker here whilst Mary his wife was innkeeper, as the account from the spirits dealer shows;

Strangely, Thomas Corbett died whilst he was having his hair cut across the road at the barbers. William Edmondson, innkeeper here in the 1840s is also recorded as a shoe maker.

The Black Attic

"In 1825, Mary and Thomas Corbett spoke of "The black attic." At this time, the house was called The Masons Arms – and considerable alterations had recently been made to the house. The third floor windows had been removed, stables added and re-organisation of the lodging rooms upstairs had caused much disturbance to the old house, the Corbetts often referring to the house thereafter as being haunted. The area that gave concern was the stairs leading to the previous third floor which had been turned into an attic. It was said that as a direct result of the changes to the top floor, a ghost had become displaced and was often experienced at the top of the stairs searching for its previous bedroom haunt. Mrs Corbett was frightened of this part of the house and always took another person with her to sit on the stairs when she had anything to do in that area. Since those days this part of the house is still to this day referred to as "The Black Attic."

Mr Graham Hamilton, Proprietor

> We understand a quoit match is on the tapis between two players of Carlisle and two belonging to Brampton; to come off on Monday week at the Freemason's Arms, Brampton.

Carlisle Journal, 2nd October 1830.

Quoits Match at The Freemasons Arms

Quoits was a popular game in many northern public houses in the 19th century. To play, you need plenty of space, for a quoiting alley or a pitch. The game is played with iron rings weighing up to 7 pounds, these have to be thrown or pitched towards a target 21 yards away fixed to the ground. The target was usually a peg or

48. The Freemasons Arms

a stake in the ground. No signs remain of the old quoits alley, but one can still be seen today at The Cumberland Hotel, a public house in Alston. In Steven Davidson's book "Carlisle Brewing and Public Houses" he mentions that in 1830, 500 people assembled to play and watch a quoits match and that prizes were given to the winners.

From the Directories, records show the following landlords at The Kings Arms/The Masons Arms/The Freemasons Arms:

1800–1810 David Hope – Kings Arms
1813–1823 Mrs Graham – Masons Arms
1823–1829 Mary &Thomas Corbett – Masons Arms – was also a shoe maker
1829–1841 William Edmondson – Freemasons Arms – was also a shoe maker
1841–1858 George Lawson Swallow – Freemasons Arms
1861–1862 Sarah Swallow

We have already heard about "Swallows Corner" when we visited The Sportsman Inn where there had been a fight in 1844 between Police Superintendent Pearce and two hardened drinkers. The 1851 Census records George Lawson Swallow age 67 as landlord with Sarah age 60 his wife, living here with their three children Ann 25, Sarah 23, and Joseph 15 whose occupation is recorded as a "pupil teacher."

In 1860, George Swallow died leaving his wife Sarah to stay on as Publican, but this arrangement lasted only two years, as The Freemasons Arms ceased trading in the late 1860s. This public house was large, commodious, had good stables, the only quoits pitch in town, well situated on a busy coaching route, plenty of secure overnight parking place for carts and coaches, and a fine heritage of being associated with Bonnie Prince Charlie. These would all have been good features for a very successful business, yet this public house gave up trading. There is no record attributing closure to the pressures from the magistrates or the Temperance Movement ; it may be that the owners saw more prospect in the shoe business rather than the public house trade which was becoming seriously concerned about the growing threat from the Temperance Movement.

Our next public house to visit, is over 100 yards away, across the Main Street and into The String of Horses Yard to find The String of Horses.

Or is it The Board?

49

THE STRING OF HORSES AND THE BOARD

On the north side of Main Street today, between Mitchelson's newsagents shop and the fish and chip shop, there is The String of Horses Yard, and in the north west corner of the yard is a substantial dwelling that once was The String of Horses public house.

The first mention of The String of Horses Inn is in 1825, with Robert Armstrong as innkeeper. The String of Horses Inn was an appropriate name as there were stables for several horses, yards in which to park carts and coaches, and there was room upstairs for 6 overnight guests;

String of Horses to let

"To be let, all that well accustomed PUBLIC HOUSE known by the name of String of Horses situated in Brampton in the county of Cumberland and now occupied by Robert Armstrong horse dealer. The premises consist of a good front and back kitchen, two front

49. The String of Horses and The Board

parlours, and six rooms above with good cellars, an extensive range of stabling, a good close yard and garden with various other conveniences."

Carlisle Patriot, 17th January 1828

George Hudspith became the new landlord as a result of this advertisement and he stayed at The String of Horses for 13 years turning it into a well used and popular inn, and like others in Brampton, was often used as overnight barracks for soldiers and their horses whilst on the march and also for important public meetings and auctions. Robert Taylor took over as landlord in 1847:

Hat saves Innkeeper in attack

"Mr Robert Taylor innkeeper of The String of Horses Inn at Brampton, was on his way to Carlisle Market at 6 o' clock in the morning, sitting in the front of his cart, a man came out of the Park Barns lonning and struck him with a heavy stick. Fortunately his hat broke the force of the blow and the fellow took off."

Carlisle Journal, 1st December 1848

The 1851 Census and the tithe map, record Robert Taylor age 60 as landlord with his wife Margaret living here with their son Robert age 10 and a 20 year old servant Hannah Bell. The following year Robert died leaving his widow Margaret to manage the business.

Robert Modlen moved here in 1868 and may have been the person to change the name of the public house to "The Board Inn" as shown on the 1891 Ordnance Survey map;

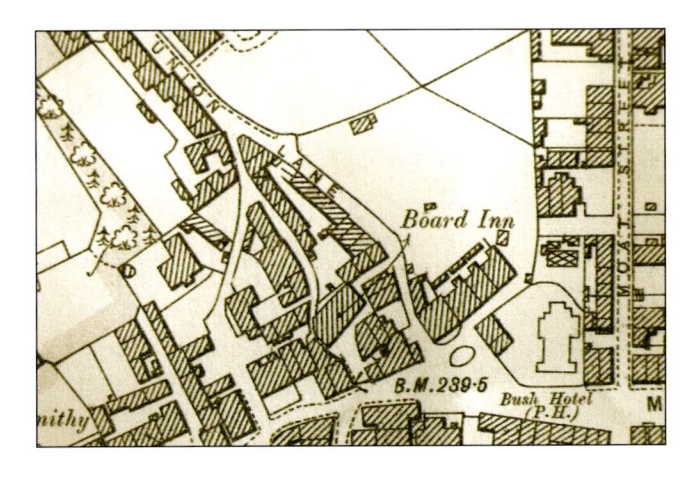

Ordnance Survey 2nd Edition 1891.

John J. Hetherington was the next landlord – a farmer at Hemblesgate. It was during the time of John J Hetherington that a serious decline in the fortunes of The String of Horses must have taken place as it appears to have stopped taking overnight guests, horses or coaches – as shown in the 1892 description in the Return of Public Houses and Beer Houses:

"String of Horses – No diners, no sleepers, no horses. Next nearest public house 100 yards."

J. J. Hetherington, feeling that the days of horse drawn travel and transport were coming to an end with the emergence of rail and steam powered travel, decided to close down the coaching side of the business and develop more of a walk-in bar and a wholesale business. These changes left The String of Horses as nothing more than a drinking house, and in 1903, it was closed by the Magistrates following a survey of all public houses in the town. Evidence submitted to the magistrates from that survey mentions:

"A most insanitary closet at the entrance, this is a working class public house which cannot be inspected adequately due to the many escape doors at the rear."

Following an appeal against the closure, the owner was successful in convincing the magistrates, that appropriate changes would be made and the String of Horses once more opened its doors to the public in 1903 for a further 60 years.

The following Landlords are recorded at The String of Horses:

1811 Robert Harding
1825–1829 Robert Armstrong
1834 George Hudspith
1847 Robert Taylor
1858 Margaret Taylor
1868 Robert Modlen
1870 John Hetherington

Our next public house to visit is 40 yards away; across the Main Street where we will find "The Bush."

50
THE BUSH

Today, opposite the Methodist church, it is the sign of the "Oddfellows Arms" that is above the door of the building which was formerly The Bush Inn.

One of the oldest public houses of Brampton, The Bush certainly existed many years before 1790 when the innkeeper is recorded as Thomas Bell, who was also a carter or carrier. Being virtually right on the roadside of the busy coach route between Carlisle and Newcastle, it is not surprising that this public house has had a long history as a busy and successful coaching and posting inn. Here there was accommodation for 7 horses, parking in the rear yard for merchant's carts and coaches, six lodging rooms for overnight guests, and where gigs, carts and horses could all be hired. Later in addition to all of these horse–based services, Mr William Bell innkeeper, also provided a full funeral service with black hearse and black horses.

In the dining room, up to 60 people could sit down to dinner together, so this public house was regularly used for public meetings, assemblies, auctions, funerals and celebratory dinners:

Brampton Hunt

"This hunt will take place on Thursday 28th inst. Mr Bowman's hounds will cast off at The Hollinstone at 9 o'clock. Dinner at Mr John Halliburton's Bush Inn at Brampton at 3 o'clock in the afternoon."

Carlisle Patriot

John Halliburton was innkeeper at The Bush from 1810–1820 after which he went to The Scotch Arms to join his brother Robert.

The Bush was regularly used by the Militia as an overnight billet for soldiers and their horses whilst on the march. Another interesting use of The Bush was as a temporary gaol. On one occasion, things went badly wrong:

Reward

This paper lately contained an advertisement offering a reward of 50 guineas for the apprehension of John Laidler and William Edger who had been charged with firing at and wounding one of the gamekeepers of William Ord Esquire of Northumberland. From the information contained in our newspaper, the delinquents were recognised at an Inn in Lockerbie, and they were taken into custody. A party of constables on horseback was despatched to return them to Newcastle for trial. It was nightfall when the party of constables and prisoners approached Brampton and the Bush Inn was chosen as the overnight stop and temporary gaol.

Escape from Gaol at The Bush

"The prisoners were put into a room in The Bush Inn, 3 storeys high, and being handcuffed, the constables did not dream of the possibility of escape.

Their astonishment however was not small when the next morning, they discovered that their captives had fled, and it was evident from the window's being open and from other

circumstances, that the prisoners had been assisted by accomplices in descending from their place of confinement by means of a ladder. No trace of them since has been obtained."
Carlisle Journal, 24th February 1816

To escape down a ladder whilst handcuffed to another person must have required agility as well as courage. No doubt the prisoners had considered the risks as well worth taking rather than face the inevitable sentence awaiting them at their trial in Northumberland – transportation to Botany Bay with hard labour.

Imagine the scene at the Northumberland Constabulary when the superintendent found that the prisoners had escaped from captivity whilst the constables were comfortably installed in the bar of a public house!

The height of the 3 storeys of The Bush Inn features in another incident which took place here, again with an amazing and narrow escape.

A narrow escape at The Bush Inn

"Early in the morning of Thursday last, whilst Moses Hodgson of Hallguards was asleep at The Bush Inn, Brampton, he arose from his bed and precipitated himself out of the window – three storeys high. Some persons returning soon after the Methodists' Chapel discovered the unfortunate man lying in the pavement in a helpless state, and immediately gave the alarm, when he was removed to his quarters and medical assistance promptly procured. On examination it was found that he was not much bruised and that none of his bones was fractured. A few hours after the incident he was taken to his own residence and it is expected that he will recover."
Carlisle Journal, 3rd January 1824

How a person could survive a fall onto the hard pavement below from the third floor window above without breaking a bone, and being *"not much bruised"* is difficult to understand, and further, we can only ponder as to why this man should *"precipitate himself."* Was it a deliberate attempt at suicide? Was drink involved? It is not surprising that the innkeeper arranged for Moses Hodgson to be carted off to his own residence before there were any further incidents.

Despite these upsets, The Bush enjoyed a long and successful career as a public house throughout the 19th century. The 1851 Census records Walter Dodd age 58 as innkeeper living with his wife Isabella age 51, two children, and 24 year old servant Ellen Armstrong. In 1861, when Nathan Charlton was innkeeper, the Bush Inn was advertised for sale because of the requirements in the will of the deceased owner, Mr Joseph Marks also the owner of The Commercial Inn across the road.

Because of its prime position on the side of the busy highway between Carlisle and Newcastle and its facilities for horses and coaches, The Bush was heavily used, contributing much to Brampton's economy, thus being able to survive, despite the efforts of the Temperance Movement to close all public houses in the district.

Yet another narrow escape at The Bush Inn

"An alarming fire occurred at 1 o'clock on Sunday morning at the Bush Hotel in Brampton. It appears that the household had retired to rest about midnight on Saturday but Mrs Dufton was roused by a commotion in the room above and voices calling loudly for help. Mr and Mrs Dufton rushed upstairs and were met on the landing by a volume of smoke from the room occupied by two guests. It was at once seen that the bed was in flames and a man seemed half suffocated with smoke. Mr Dufton immediately left to warn Supt. Simons and to summon the Fire Brigade. Bugler Edgar raised the alarm around the town within a few minutes. Mrs Dufton dragged the man down the stairs to safety and then went on to rouse all the guests who made good their escape – one of which was a young woman who, through fright, fainted. Mrs Dufton and her sons brought buckets of water. The fire had been caused by one of the guests leaving a lighted pipe in his waistcoat pocket."

Carlisle Journal, 15th September 1899

This report shows that the means of summoning the Fire Brigade was by blasts on a bugle from the steps of the Moot Hall. Mr Edgar was bugler to the Fire Brigade for over 20 years.

The Bush continues to trade today, but under the different name of "The Odd fellows." No records have been seen of this public house having been associated with The Oddfellows Friendly Society.

From the directories, Magistrates licensing records and from Peter Burn's lecture notes, the following Landlords are recorded at The Bush Inn:

1782 Thomas Bell	1861 Nathan Charlton
1810 John Hewson	1864 Thomas and Jane Bell
1811–1820 John Halliburton	1880 William Bell
1820–1822 Joseph Richardson Brown	1892 Joseph Wilson
1827–1847 Walter Dodd	1894 Samuel Dufton
1847–1850 William Dodd	

1855–1861 Thomas Moses he was also a farmer, but died at 33 years of age

On the pavement outside the Bush, as we look up towards the third floor windows, we can imagine the dramatic incidents which have taken place here.

Our next port of call is across the Main Street at Oval House – once called The Commercial – or was it Mark's Spirit Vaults?

51

THE COMMERCIAL INN

The impressive Oval House is set back from the Carlisle to Newcastle road with a traditional cobbled yard in front containing an attractive and appropriate oval design in the stones.

Today's Oval House is yesterday's Commercial Inn, the first reference of which is in 1829 when James Forester was innkeeper. Later in 1834, The Commercial Inn is recorded with the innkeeper as Mrs Dinah Forester, and in the same year, Dinah's marriage to a Mr Joseph Mark is recorded in the newspaper, so Dinah must have been widowed hence her name as licensee in 1834, and later re-married to Joseph Mark. The business continued, and in 1847, in addition to The Commercial Inn public house, "Mark's Wine and Spirit Vaults" is also recorded that year as a business here. The two businesses continued to 1861 when Mr Joseph Mark died; although the Grigg's Directory of 1865 shows both Mark's Spirit Vaults and The Commercial Inn still with Joseph Mark as owner.

In 1862 The Commercial Inn was the venue chosen for the public auction sale of The Coach and Horses Inn, and the advertisement describes The Commercial Inn as "the house of Mr Joseph Cullen." In 1869 Joseph Cullen appears to have had domestic problems:

Joseph Cullen – a violent fellow

"Joseph Cullen, innkeeper at Brampton, was charged with disturbing the public peace by shouting and using threatening language. Not only had he annoyed the public but he also threatened to take his wife's life. A summons was taken out against him but in order to prevent it being served, he locked himself up in the house. He ultimately put his head out of the window and so disturbed the peace again that a warrant was obtained. An entrance was forced into his house and he was arrested. He was found guilty but bound over to keep the peace."

Carlisle Express, 1st October 1869

The Commercial Inn had accommodation for overnight guests with stables for horses and a yard in front for loading and discharging passengers and parcels, with a further secure yard at the rear for overnight parking for carts and coaches. The name "Commercial" implies that this public house was regularly used by traders and merchants as an overnight stop over, possibly following a day's trading at the Wednesday market in town, or whilst en route between Carlisle and Newcastle. The Commercial Inn was therefore well placed, and contained appropriate and adequate accommodation, but surprisingly, it failed to survive.

In 1883 The Commercial Inn became the focus of attention of Lady Rosalind and members of the Brampton Temperance Movement. Their plan was to purchase the inn and turn it into a temperance hotel, but after close examination it was found that the premises were in very poor condition requiring considerable expenditure and were not worth the £1,550 asking price.

The Countess was a shrewd business person and decided to look elsewhere for property to take over, leaving the Commercial inn to fail on its own account. The very poor state of repair, together with increasing competition for customers by neighbouring public houses, led the Commercial to finally close its doors to the public in 1885, just as Lady Rosalind had hoped.

The premises were taken over by William Routledge watch maker and over ten years, he carried out considerable repairs and then sold it as a dwelling house with the name of "Oval House":

51. The Commercial Inn

Oval House For Sale

"Lot 1. Dwelling house known as Townhead – otherwise Oval House with yard, warehouse, gardens and a croft of about 1 acre. In the occupation of William Routledge. There is a two stall stable, loft, gig house and warehouse adjoining, and cottage in the occupation of Miss Routledge."

Carlisle Journal, September 1895

From the directories and Peter Burn's lecture notes the following innkeepers are recorded at The Commercial Inn:

1829 James Forester
1834 Dinah Forester
1847 Joseph Mark
1861 Isaac and Joseph Cullen

Stepping out of the front door of the Commercial Inn, our path will take us across the cobbles, 50 yards along Main Street towards The Mote where we will find our next public house:
The Three Crowns – or is it The Three Lions?

52
THE THREE CROWNS

At 4 Main Street stands a pair of fine houses just east of the Methodist church. Peter Burn gives us the first clue as to the location of the Three Crowns:

"Starting at The Sands we have Councillor Jackson inhabiting the Bay horse; Messrs Warwick, Barker and Ruddick in the Earl Grey; Mr Thomas Pratt in the Moatside Tom and Jerry; Mrs Stobbart the Willie Brewed; Mr John Reed in the Three Crowns; Mr Routledge at Mark's Spirit vaults – – –"

So the Three Crowns must have been further down the hill than "The Willie Brewed" at number 17 Moatside – but before "Marks Spirit Vaults" at Oval House.

The Three Crowns / Three Lions.

52. The Three Crowns

The occupier of 4 Main Street in the 1841 census and the Tithe Map is shown as a William Armstrong:

William Armstrong is recorded as innkeeper at The Three Crowns in the 1834 directory, and since most landlords lived as tenants in the premises of which they were innkeepers, it is reasonable to assume therefore, that The Three Crowns was here at 4 Main Street. The accounts ledger of Isaac Bird lists William Armstrong of the Three Crowns as a customer in 1838:

There is some uncertainty about this theory however, as the Three Crowns is first mentioned in the directories of 1822, with innkeeper Thomas Pearson, but with an address of The Sands.

The 1892 Return of Public Houses and Beer Houses does not mention The Three Crowns, so this public house must have ceased trading some time in the 1860s or 1870s.

No records have been found of untoward incidents or Magistrate Court proceedings, nor are there any advertisements "For Sale" or "To Let", which usually give some indication of the extent of the premises and the business.

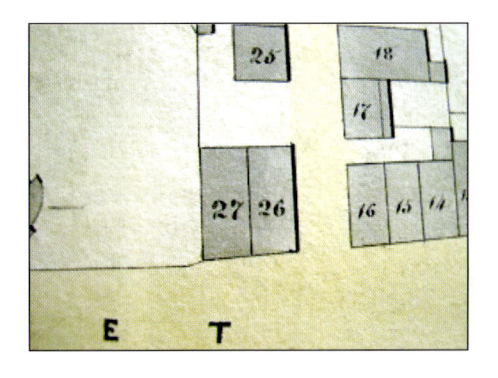

Landlords recorded at The Three Crowns are:

1821 Thomas Pearson Three Crowns at "the Sands"
1830 John Reed Three Crowns at Main Street
1834 William Armstrong Three Crowns at Main Street

Stepping out of The Three Crowns, directly into the highway with coaches, carriages and carts getting ready for the pull up the slope of Pickering's Hill by the side of The Moat, we will keep to the North side of Main Street for 20 yards to find our next public house The Willie Brewed.

53

THE WILLIE BREWED

Our visit to The Willie Brewed will also be short, since very little is recorded of this public house. Peter Burn in his lecture "A fireside Crack" gives it just a fleeting mention:

> "– – – starting at The Sands we had Councillor Jackson inhabiting The Bay Horse; Messrs Warwick, Barker and Ruddick at The Earl Grey; Mr Thomas Pratt at The Moatside Tom and Jerry; Mrs Stobbart at The Willie Brewed – – –"

This record suggests that The Willie Brewed was on the road leading from the Sands into town, and came after the Moatside Tom and Jerry, which was at 17 Moatside, and before the Three Crowns which was at 4 Main Street. Rev. Arthur Penn confirms in his notes, that a Mrs. Stobbart innkeeper, lived in the second house east of Moat Street.

Although we can be certain that this is where The Willie Brewed plied its trade as a licensed beer house, we cannot be certain of when it existed during the 1800s, as no records exist in any of the directories, nor does this public house feature in the 1892 Return of Public houses and Beer houses, and no reports have been seen in the newspapers of incidents taking place here at The Willie Brewed.

Our next public house is only a matter of 10 yards away, on the same side of the street.

Yes, it's another Tom and Jerry – our fourth!

54

THE TOM AND JERRY – MOATSIDE

Our fourth public house with the name of Tom and Jerry is at 17 Moatside. The building still stands today on the east side of a cobbled entrance to the Moat. In the 1800s this was a three storey building, but in the 1980s the top floor was removed.

The Moatside Tom and Jerry must have existed some time from the 1820s to 1830s because it was during that time that these two characters appeared in Pierce Egan's newspaper "Life in London" in a series of articles reflecting fashionable life in the metropolis. So popular were these two characters that a theatre production was made of their exploits and toured the country, coming to McCready's Theatre Carlisle, in 1823. The 1851 Census shows a Mrs Crozier, innkeeper living at Moatside, and 4 years later the following advertisement appears in the Carlisle Journal:

The extent and cost of these repairs is shown in the bill that Mary Crozier received from her builder.

> TO be SOLD, by AUCTION, at the *Blue Bell Inn*, BRAMPTON, Cumberland, on WEDNESDAY, the 27th of JUNE, 1855, at 6 o'Clock in the evening, (if not previously disposed of by private contract), all that DWELLING HOUSE, containing 5 Rooms, with a large Yard behind and a spacious frontage to the Main Street, situate at MOATSIDE, BRAMPTON, and lately occupied by Mrs. Crozier as an Ale-house. The premises have recently undergone thorough repair. For particulars apply to Messrs. CARRICK and LEE.
> Brampton, 2nd June, 1855.

Peter Burn refers to the Moatside Tom and Jerry where the licensee was Thomas Pratt, and this is confirmed by the 1880 directory, living at 17 Moatside where he was not only innkeeper but also "postman." i.e. he looked after horses that were for hire.

There are no records seen of the earlier days of The Tom and Jerry, and there appear to be no mention of untoward incidents at this public house. The Tom and Jerry closed its doors on the public house trade some time between 1880 and 1892.

Note the costs per day for: A mason - 3s 6d, A horse - 3s 0d, A labourer - 2s 3d, A boy - 1s 6d.

Coming out of The Tom and Jerry we have quite a long stroll of 180 yards to our next public house, The Wellington. As we walk along the side of the road to the Wellington which is just over the brow of Pickering's Hill at the Sands, we might remember that it was here that William Nicholson the farmer who had been drinking at the Pack horse Inn and later at the Globe Inn, was attacked by his drinking companions, he having earlier, inadvertently shown them his wallet full of banknotes whilst looking for change. On this very path, as he was being attacked on the ground and relieved of his wallet, he shouted:

"Murder – Murder – Murder!"

55

THE WELLINGTON AND THE EARL GREY

At The Sands, where the road divides into three, there is a row of terraced cottages on the left side at the very foot of the Moat. These are the Earl Grey cottages, one of which was The Wellington public house.

The Wellington is recorded here in 1822 but it is generally believed that a public house had existed here long before that. The name of Wellington is thought to have been given to this public house by the licensee Mr Story who was a veteran of the Napoleonic war.

The Duke of Wellington was a highly successful soldier defeating Napoleon at Waterloo. He was much revered as a hero and subsequently became a politician,

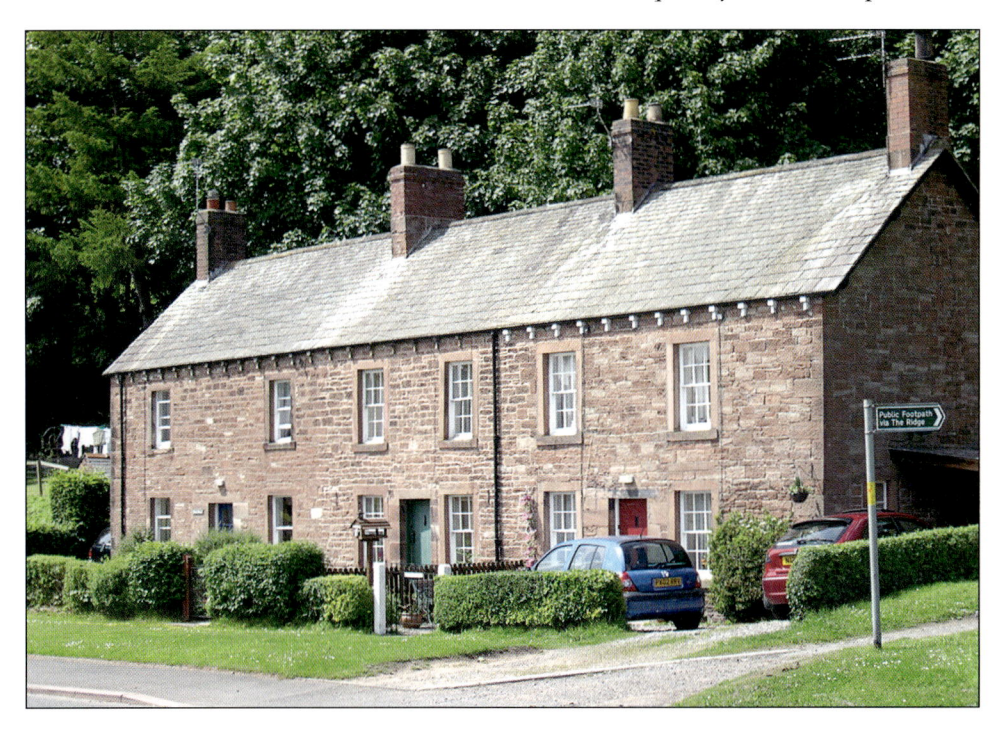

181

responsible for, amongst other things, The Duke of Wellington's Beer Act. Wellington argued the case for introducing competition in the brewery trade, for reducing the price of beer by removing beer taxes, and improving the quality and strength of beer. These changes brought benefits to farmers who had to cultivate more fields for wheat and barley; prosperity to the working class because of more employment opportunities, and benefits to business men who set up new businesses associated with the increased trade.

Popular as he may have been as a soldier and later as a politician who introduced cheaper and better quality beer for the "lower orders", The Duke of Wellington did not enjoy sustained popularity as a politician. Earl Grey became Prime Minister and it was under his guidance that The Reform Bill was passed giving more people the right to vote. Hitherto it had been only very restricted classes of people who could vote and The Duke of Wellington was not in favour of extending the vote to commoners. In 1832 The Duke of Wellington fell rapidly out of favour:

"There has been great excitement in the City of Carlisle this week and the utmost anxiety manifested to learn the news from the Metropolis – from almost every lip, the name of Wellington receives a curse."

Carlisle Journal, 19th May 1832

The passing of The Reform Bill under Earl Grey brought great excitement and satisfaction to the ordinary people of Brampton and a celebratory dinner was organised at The Howard Arms.

"On Friday, the spirited inhabitants of Brampton and neighbourhood celebrated the triumph of the people over the Boroughmongers i.e. the success of the Reform Bill. Collections have been made to assist the poor to rejoice on this great occasion. 350 families assisted, so 1200 individuals partook of the bounty of the donors. Spacious tents were erected and an excellent dinner of best beef and mutton provided."

Carlisle Journal, May 1832

With Earl Grey becoming so popular, and The Duke of Wellington falling out of favour, many people of Brampton felt that their political loyalties lay with the Whigs rather than the Tories, and as a direct result, the name of this public house was changed from The Wellington to The Earl Grey.

> On Thursday morning the cheering intelligence arrived that Earl Grey had been restored to office, and that the Duke of Wellington had been compelled to retire from the face of an indignant nation defeated, disgraced, and despised. This gratifying news was immediately circulated through the town, and in every quarter men met to congratulate each other on this most auspicious event.

Carlisle Journal, 19th May 1832.

55. The Wellington and The Earl Grey

From the directories and Peter Burn's lecture notes; the following landlords are recorded at The Wellington/The Earl Grey:

1822 William Irving – The Wellington	1853 Thomas Calvert
1829 Henry Story	1858 1861 Samuel Stephenson
1834 William Irving – The Earl Grey	1861 George Blaylock
1841–1851 John Simpson	1884 Messrs Warwick/Baker/Riddick

The Directories, census and the Tithe map of 1841 show John Simpson as landlord and occupier of The Earl Grey and identify the premises as being at the eastern end of the terrace, but with this building as having only two dwellings.

In 1856 the Earl Grey was advertised to let, and was described as having good stabling and hay lofts, so clearly was used by travellers as well as locals.

The 1892 Return of Public Houses and Beer Houses does not record The Earl Grey, so this public house must have ceased trading some time between 1884 and 1892.

It was around this time that The Sands began to lose its importance as a recreation space for public meetings, farm labour hirings and cattle markets. Changes in trading, together with increased mechanisation on farms required fewer labourers and cattle markets became centralised in large towns like Carlisle. Great improvements in travel brought about by the railway saw Carlisle becoming more of a focus for hiring farm labour, selling and showing cattle and trading in general. Brampton's annual Agricultural show moved its venue to a field behind the Howard Arms, and the Sands therefore became much less used for public gatherings. This change had a major impact upon the three public houses that had flourished upon this hitherto busy part of the town.

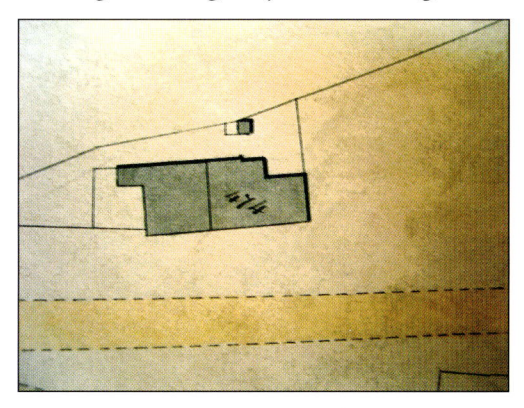

Across the roads and opposite The Earl Grey our next stopping place is The Sand House Inn.

56

THE SAND HOUSE INN
AND THE THREE LIONS

Below the Moat, where the road divides into three, stands Sand House, now a bed and breakfast establishment, but before that for many years, was The Sand House Inn, and possibly, The Three Lions.

The wide expanse of grass across which pass the three roads to Lanercost, Newcastle and Alston, was in the 1800s the prime site for fairs, hirings, cattle markets, circuses, shows and any other open air public meetings. Fairs and hirings for farm labourers and maidservants were held here each Candlemas and Michaelmas and were well attended.

56. The Sand House Inn and The Three Lions

Peter Burn recalls them:

"Our fairs and hirings were lively occasions – festivities running the round of the week."

Whitsuntide hirings at Brampton

"The usual concomitants of a hiring were present in considerable numbers in the persons of strolling players, ballad singers, acrobats, maimed and deformed specimens of humanity, vendors of quack medicines said to cure all the ills that flesh has heir to. Cheap Johns, all of whom did their utmost to levy contributions upon the simplicity and hard won earnings of the rustics."

Carlisle Journal, 24th May 1861

It is not surprising therefore that there were so many public houses close to The Sands. There would be great demand for venues for people to meet, farmers to settle deals, places to meet labourers and maidservants for hire, rooms for travelling performers, visiting merchants, rooms for dances and merry-making.

At The Sand House Inn there were stables, hay lofts and yards to cope with 30 horses, carts and coaches, whilst inside 20 overnight guests could be accommodated and 50 people could sit down to dinner together. The Sand House Inn therefore was a busy coaching and posting inn well placed at the entrance to Brampton on the busy Newcastle and Alston roads.

The first record of a public house here is in the 1822 and 1823 directory which mentions The Three Lions with an address of *"The Sands"* and a landlord Mr William Armstrong. Thereafter there is no further mention of The Three Lions but there is the first record of *The Sand House Inn* in 1824 again with William Armstrong as innkeeper. Sand House Inn may therefore have previously been called The Three Lions.

Three Lions (Landlord William Armstrong)					
Sand House Inn (Landlord William Armstrong)					
	1822	1823	1824	1825	1826

In 1826 Henry Story is recorded as innkeeper as this announcement reveals:

A whole family baptised

"Mr Henry Story – innkeeper at The Sand House Inn at Brampton. The whole of his family – six sons and two daughters were baptised by Rev. A. Lawson of Brampton on Wednesday last."

Carlisle Patriot, 14th November 1826

In 1828 although no directory records this, the innkeeper of The Sand House Inn may have been a Mr W. Batey as the following announcement suggests:

A singed pig at Brampton

"On Friday last, during the thunderstorm, a pig belonging to Mr W. Batey of The Sand House Inn Brampton, had a handful of bristles singed from its side by lightning."
Carlisle Journal, 23rd August 1828

After William Batey, came Thomas Knott in 1832 – who was also a farmer with fields at Low Gelt Bridge:

Money goes missing at The Sands

"William Crozier age 53 and Richard Skelton age 44 were charged with carrying away from the house of Thomas Knott – innkeeper at The Sands Inn at Brampton, 15 sovereigns, two half sovereigns and a purse. Thomas Knott was doing his accounts in the kitchen when a traveller came to the door. He put the purse with the sovereigns for the moment on the window sill and attended to the traveller. He then went off to his farm at Low Gelt Bridge where he remembered leaving his purse unattended and returned immediately home. He went for a constable and went to Skelton's house and found him in bed at two in the afternoon. He was searched but nothing was found. They then went to The Horse and Farrier and found Crozier who said that he had no money on him but after a search he was found to have 7 sovereigns. They went back to Skelton's house to search further and Skelton's wife admitted to having the sovereigns. The jury found both guilty, but instead of being transported, they were both given 6 months imprisonment with hard labour and the tread mill."
Carlisle Patriot, 20th March 1836

Hard labour and the tread mill are graphically described in this letter from a prisoner to the Carlisle Journal in 1845:

"The wheel consists of 24 steps which revolve round twice each minute and at each revolution a particular step strikes a bell with a wire. The tread mill is rotated by prisoners walking on the steps therefore producing motion which drives shafts of the factory. Prisoners work 15 minutes followed by 5 minutes rest."

In the 1851 census, Elizabeth Knott is recorded as a widow and Innkeeper at The Sand House Inn, she is described as a farmer, living with her two daughters, two sons, and employing 4 servants, while the 1861 census records Sarah Knott, Elizabeth's daughter as innkeeper.

56. The Sand House Inn and The Three Lions

Sand House Inn for Sale

"All that well accustomed and old established LICENSED HOUSE known as The Sandhouse Hotel along with the excellent stabling for over thirty horses.

The Hotel is substantially built of stone with slated roof, is in fair tenantable repair, occupying a commanding position on the main road, is in a most healthy part of the town and is roomy and spacious inside, comprising 2 kitchens, 2 sitting rooms, dining hall, bar, parlour, on the ground floor with 6 good sleeping apartments above.

The increasing popularity of Brampton as a health and Summer resort, the close proximity of the Sands upon which all fairs are held and travelling shows, and theatres pitch their tents along with the annual sales conducted upon the land at the rear of the hotel, combined with the steady trade of the house, makes this sale a golden opportunity for the trade or general public to secure Licensed Premises where a high class Hotel business may be carried on and vastly extended and increased under judicious management."

Carlisle Journal, 5th August 1898

From the directories, Magistrates court records and Peter Burn's lecture notes, the following landlords are recorded at the Three Lions and the Sand House Inn:

The Sand House Inn
1824 William Armstrong
1869 John Hudspith
1826 Henry Story
1829 William Batey
1832 Thomas Knott
1851 Elizabeth Knott
1861 Sarah Knott

1873 Elisabeth Ord
1879 Elizabeth Hetherington
1892 Richard Watkins
1894 John Head

The Three Lions
1822–1823 William Armstrong

The Sand House Inn was a "tied" house, the only beer that could be sold here was from the Maryport Brewery. The cost of transporting beer from Maryport to Brampton must have put The Sand House at some financial disadvantage whilst neighbouring public houses were sourcing their beer from the local Brampton Brewery.

Despite this, the Sand House Inn continued, and survived well, prevailing against the pressures from the Brampton Temperance Movement. The 1892 Return for Public Houses and Beer Houses records the owner as a Miss Waugh of London, and the next nearest public house at 500 yards.

Our next port of call is not 500 yards, but a mere 100 yards across the Sands to The Bay Horse, or is it The Horse and Groom, or probably the Ridge House Inn? But, before we march off to The Bay Horse, we have another problem to consider:

Where is the Coal Waggon public house?

57

THE COAL WAGGON

In the Magistrates Licence Register and the directories, there is a record for the years 1822–1829 of a public house called "The Coal Waggon" with an innkeeper Mr Richard Rutherford, but no address is given other than "The Sands."

So where was The Coal Waggon?

In the accounts ledger of Isaac Bird, Spirit merchant of Brampton, for the year 1817, Richard Rutherford is shown as an innkeeper at Sandhouse.

It is unlikely that The Coal Waggon was a former name for The Sand house Inn, as both of these public houses are recorded for the years 1824–1829, each with separate landlords. Perhaps Richard Rutherford may have worked at The Sandhouse Inn in 1818 but transferred to The Coal Waggon four years later.

Study of the Ordnance Survey map shows the only buildings on The Sands as being The Earl Grey cottages, The Sand House Inn, Ridge House and the Coal Staithes. Apart from the coal staithes, each of these buildings is recorded in the Directories and the Licence Register as a public house under their own name. The Coal Waggon is therefore unlikely to have been an earlier name for The Wellington, The Bay Horse, or The Sand house Inn.

There is no evidence to suggest that The Coal Waggon was part of the Coal Staithes, so the question must remain unanswered for the moment.

After weaving and agriculture, mining was the next most important industry for the Brampton area, and it is surprising that no other public houses have names associated with mining. Charles Roberts, in his biography of The countess of Carlisle, refers to a public house in Brampton used by miners which may well have been The Coal Waggon:

57. The Coal Waggon

"the colliers are a strange, rough, drinking population and the licensee keeps a public house which pays him immense rents, through which he gets back much of the men's wages."

"The Radical Countess", C. Roberts

In mining communities like West Cumberland, wealthy mine owners would buy a public house and lease it out to a landlord who would provide a room every fortnight where the colliers would assemble to receive their wages. The mine manager would often deliberately arrive much later than promised, forcing colliers to occupy their waiting time by drinking. Wages were often deliberately paid in high currency notes so that miners would need to spend money at the bar in order to get small change, and to pay their bills for beer purchased on the slate whilst waiting for the paymaster to arrive:

Pay day for miners

"On Sunday morning a number of disgraceful riots occurred. The day before being a fortnight's pay, the night was as usual spent in debauchery. How long is this abominable nuisance to continue? What a mockery it is to read about the proclamation against vice and immorality when labouring men are sent to the public house on Saturday evening to divide a fortnight's wages."

Whitehaven Herald

The Mines Registration Bill

"The Mines Registration Bill will this year put a stop to the payment of wages to miners in public houses."

Carlisle Express and Advertiser, March 1869

58

THE BAY HORSE, THE HORSE AND GROOM AND THE RIDGE HOUSE

On the north side of the road which leads to Lanercost is a sandstone house now called Ridge Valley, but in the 1800s was The Bay Horse public house.

A study of the Directories gives a confusing picture. The first record seen appears in 1827 with a Robert James as innkeeper, and the name of the public house is The Bay Horse. The following year Robert James appears as landlord of The Horse and Groom on The Sands, but he is also shown in a different directory for the same year as innkeeper at The Bay Horse.

In 1847 Robert James is recorded as innkeeper at The Ridge House Inn on The Sands. In 1858 a Mr T. Bell is recorded as innkeeper at The Bay Horse, also at The

58. The Bay Horse, The Horse and Groom and The Ridge House

Horse and Groom and also at The Ridge Inn. Similarly in 1869, a Mr Routledge is quoted as innkeeper at each of these three public houses, in different directories. It is therefore reasonable to believe that The Bay Horse, The Horse and Groom and The Ridge Inn were all one and the same place. But why should a public house be known as and called three different names at the same time?

Peter Burn in his lecture notes records:

"Starting at The Sands, we have Councillor Jackson at The Bay Horse."

but, none of the Directories mention a Mr Jackson as innkeeper! In 1824, workmen were demolishing part of a public house on the Sands in order to make improvements, and new facilities:

A mysterious discovery

"A few days ago, while workmen were engaged in pulling down an old public house on the Sands near Brampton, one of them, on moving some flags in the parlour floor, experienced considerable annoyance by a nauseous smell issuing from the earth, and soon after at the depth of one yard from the surface, struck his spade against a hard object which on being taken up, proved to be part of a human skeleton supposed from the size of the bones, to be that of a man. How the remains came to be deposited there has occasioned a great sensation in the public mind, and has given rise to much conjecture."

Carlisle Journal, 18th September 1824

No major alterations took place at either The Sand House Inn or the Earl Grey during 1824, but at present it is not possible to say for sure that it was the Bay Horse that had a skeleton under the floor – but it is highly likely it was!

In 1831 The Horse and Groom was advertised for sale in the Carlisle Journal:

Horse and Groom for Sale

This advertisement gives no detail of the accommodation at The Horse and Groom, and seems to be more concerned with the farm and land rather than the public house part of the business. In 1861 The Ridge House Inn was advertised to let, and similarly, this advertisement offers no help with a description of the accommodation:

> **PUBLIC-HOUSE AND FIELDS, NEAR BRAMPTON, FOR SALE.**
>
> To be SOLD by PUBLIC AUCTION, on WEDNESDAY the 17th day of AUGUST next, at the *Howards' Arms Inn*, at BRAMPTON,—
>
> ALL that Well-Accustomed PUBLIC-HOUSE, situate on the SANDS, at Brampton, known by the Sign of the *Horse and Groom*, and now in the Occupation of Robert James, as Tenant; together with a GARDEN, and 3 CLOSES of excellent LAND, adjoining thereto, containing together 9 Acres, more or less.
>
> Also all those 2 Freehold CLOSES of excellent LAND, called CLAYEY BANKS; containing together 11 Acres, (or thereabouts) situate within a short distance of the Town of Brampton.

191

Ridge House to Let

To be let at Candlemas next:

All that well accustomed Public House situated at Brampton Sands and known as RIDGE HOUSE together with 3 fields to let and now in the occupation of Thomas Bell. Full particulars from Mr Routledge, Carrier Brampton."

Carlisle Journal, 1st November 1861

Mr Hartley became the new tenant, but for some reason he did not stay long, the Inn was again advertised to let the following year.

Highway robbery at Brampton

"William Telford a hawker, and Mary Telford his wife were charged with stealing from the person of William Scaife, 4 sovereigns, one half sovereign, and 14 shillings and did at the same time, beat, strike and cause personal violence to the said William Scaife at Brampton.

Scaife is a farm bailiff at Warren House and he had been to Brampton market to sell corn and left Brampton at 4.30pm, and had at that time in his pocket, 4 sovereigns, a half sovereign, 14 shillings and a three penny bit, when some 50 yards from the gateway to Warren Bank the female prisoner accosted him and asked him where he was going. He replied "not far" she added "perhaps a mile or two in company." At this time the male prisoner came up from the opposite side. The woman but her right arm around the waist of Scaife, and her left hand into his trouser pocket where he had his money. The male prisoner then struck Scaife several blows with some weapon. The woman went off in the direction of Brampton, the male continued to abuse Scaife.

Ann Norman innkeeper between Brampton and Warren House said that on the day, a man and a woman came into her public house. They sat at a window which commands a view of the road. The prisoners at the court were those two people. They had entered the house together, but the woman left first and the man shortly after.

A weaver E. Wilson saw the two prisoners in the market and later at 4.25pm on the Brampton Sands at the same time he saw Mr Scaife returning home passing the Ridge House Inn. He saw the prisoners follow Scaife, who was drunkish.

Margaret Noble saw Scaife going in the direction of his house and saw 2 strangers, one man and one woman leave the inn and take the direction of Warren House. Superintendent Fowler apprehended the 2 prisoners in Brampton and after searching them, found on William Telford 4 Sovereigns, one half sovereign, 14 shillings and a 3 penny bit. Both the prisoners were found guilty, William Telford sentenced to 10 years penal servitude and two years hard labour for his wife."

Carlisle Journal, 1866

58. The Bay Horse, The Horse and Groom and The Ridge House

From the Directories and Peter Burn's lecture notes, the landlords at this public house with the three names were:

???? Councillor Jackson	1862 N. Hartley	1876 John Bell
1827–1847 Robert James	1866 Ann Norman	
1858 Thomas & Jane Bell	1869 William Routledge	

We have almost arrived at the end of our visit to Brampton's public houses of the 19th century, but we still have more to do. Obviously most of Brampton's public houses were within the built-up area of the town, where there was plenty of people within a short stroll, and most people would not own a horse.

Several public houses on the outskirts of the town were within the area presided over by the Licensing Magistrates of Brampton so we shall include these in our visit to complete the picture. To visit these outliers we will need to hire a gig from one of the posting inns as our next port of call is 1 mile north of Brampton on the road to Lanercost.

The following extract from an accounts ledger, shows the cost of hire of a gig:

At The Howard Arms a gig will cost us six shillings for an evening's hire, whilst at The Scotch Arms it will only cost four shillings. But, remember the report of the ostler at The Scotch Arms who was kicked by a horse and died almost instantly from the blow?

59

THE BLACK BULL INN, LANERCOST

The rural scene here at Lanercost bridge could easily have been the subject of a Constable painting of the nineteenth century. Cows graze peacefully in the grounds of the ruined priory whilst the waterwheel of the corn mill turns gracefully and relentlessly, powered by the waters of the mill race. The miller and his hired hand hoist sacks of corn up to the granary from a heavily laden cart, the horses, exhausted by the strain of hauling their load over the steep arch of the bridge, quench their thirst at the roadside trough whilst their driver calls for a glass of ale at the door of the Black Bull Inn.

It is difficult to believe that such a pleasant rural scene as this could have been the stage for the worst murder that ever took place in this area:

59. The Black Bull Inn, Lanercost

Amongst the regulars at The Black Bull on the evening of 13th October 1834, was 40 year old John Pearson and Jane – his new wife of 6 weeks. Pearson had spent a childhood in poverty; no father to give guidance and no school to provide education; leaving him from an early age to survive and live off his wits. Poaching, burglary, cheating at cards, heavy drinking and womanising were Pearson's strong points. Periods in prison, hard labour and fines had had little effect upon his behaviour, and he had deserted his first wife and five children to total neglect.

Pearson and his new wife had taken rooms in a common lodging house at Randylands some hundred yards west of Lanercost Bridge, and this autumn evening, John drank steadily whilst his wife obediently sat by him but "did not partake of the drink." When the time came to close the public house, Pearson begged to be allowed to continue, but his wife suggested that they purchase a bottle of Rum to finish off his drinking at home. Already unsteady on his feet and becoming argumentative Pearson stumbled across Lanercost Bridge, supported by his wife clutching the bottle of Rum.

Rachel Whitehead also occupied a room in the lodging house at Randylands next to the Pearsons and since there was no ceiling in the accommodation, all conversation could be easily overheard. Soon after they had entered their room, Rachel Whitehead heard John shouting at his wife Jane, accusing her of infidelity, to the accompaniment of many blows and cries for help. Rachel was much too frightened to intervene, fearing that she might also become the victim of Pearson's wrath. The beating continued for two hours. Later in the morning, Pearson had left to return to The Black Bull to replenish his bottle of Rum, when a feeble voice called out to Rachel Whitehead for a cup of tea. The scene confronting Rachel on entry was described in Court. Jane was lying naked on the bed, her body covered in bruises, with blood everywhere. John Pearson was heard to return and threatened to finish his wife off with a broom handle and anyone else who dared to interfere.

Eventually a constable was sent for but arrived too late to be of any assistance. Jane lay dead with a heavily bloodstained broom handle by her side and a drunken husband claiming that someone else had committed the offence.

Pearson even feigned madness and epilepsy to avoid being questioned but the jury at Carlisle Court found no difficulty in arriving at a guilty verdict, from the overwhelming evidence from Ralph Dodgson, innkeeper at The Black Bull and Rachel Whitehead of Randylands. On mounting the gallows, Pearson begged forgiveness for himself muttering religious platitudes in a selfish last attempt to seek release from his own immediate fate rather than for any concern for the five children he had neglected, or the defenceless woman he had so brutally killed.

Anyone searching for a story to illustrate the degradation that can accompany the indulgent use of drink, to serve as a cautionary tale need look no further than that which happened here at The Abbey bridge Inn. The Temperance Movement at their local meetings and during speeches often made reference to *"The Beast of Randylands."*

The Black Bull was also known as The Abbey Bridge Inn and various Directories alternate between the two names.

From the directories and records of Magistrates Court, the following innkeepers are shown for the Black Bull/Abbey Bridge Inn:

1818 Isabella Heward, Abbey Bridge Inn
1828 Isabella Miller, Black Bull
1829 Ralph Dodgson, Black Bull
1841 Thomas Esther, Abbey Bridge inn
1858 Mrs Esther Heward, Abbey Bridge Inn
1858 Mr Hugh Heward, Abbey Bridge Inn
1879 James Barker, Black Bull
1882 Henry Barker, Black Bull

Returning to our gig, we need to trot over Lanercost Bridge, go swiftly past the few remaining wall stones of Randylands, to the village of Walton, to find The Johnson Arms.

60

THE JOHNSON ARMS

A fine sandstone building marks the limit of the Brampton Parish boundary by the bridge over the river Cambeck, on the road from Brampton to Longtown. This building shows little sign of its' former life as The Johnson Arms.

The Johnsons were owners of the Castlesteads estate, from which this public house derives its' name. The first record appears in 1825 when a newly washed bed rug went missing whilst drying on the hedge:

> *"David Ridley was found guilty of stealing a bed rug, in the Parish of Brampton, on the 17th November 1825 – the property of Sarah Gaddes of the Johnson Arms Brampton, which had been hanging out to dry on a hedge. He was sentenced to seven years transportation."*

The Register of Public houses records Sarah Gaddes as innkeeper for the years 1827–1829. The Johnson Arms was never a coaching inn, but did cater for travellers on foot and on horseback, with room for four overnight guests, a yard at the rear for carts and stables for two horses. Being on the main route between Brampton and Scotland, this public house gained much from passing trade, and it was this passing trade that gave rise to an unfortunate set of circumstances resulting in the vicar of Walton being ousted by his congregation.

After settling some business deals in Brampton, William Pearson a 38 year old farmer from across the border was intent on getting home to his wife and children even though it seemed quite late in the evening. On passing the Johnson Arms at Walton Road end, and tempted by the sounds of merry making coming from within, Pearson decided to stop for a quick drink to warm him up for the journey.

At 11pm, it now being dark, Pearson resumed his journey a little unsteady in the saddle, and headed off for the village of Walton on his way to Bewcastle and Scotland.

At 11.15pm, Reverend Joseph Smith, a man of nervous disposition, was locking up his vicarage in Walton village, before retiring to bed. The good vicar had been anxious about the increasing number of burglaries and assaults particularly in the countryside, and, being the only male in a household of 3 women and 5 children, he had, without telling anyone, equipped himself with a revolver, thinking that it would be useful to warn anyone off who threatened their safety!

Making unsteady progress with his horse, and his judgement a little impaired by his drinks at The Johnson Arms, farmer Armstrong found himself near to the vicarage where he remembered that a friend called Ann Glendinning had recently taken a job as maid to the vicar.

Soon after bolting the doors and about to climb the stairs to bed, the vicar heard a gentle scratching at the window. Grabbing his revolver and opening the door, the frightened vicar fired a few warning shots blindly into the darkness and hurriedly slammed the door closed and turned the key.

Early in the morning, the body of William Armstrong was found shot three times, and his horse grazing close by. Reverend Smith never attempted to deny guilt, believing that a man had the right to defend his property. The trial judge found the vicar not guilty, much to the anger and despair of the local community who felt that he had been dealt with lightly, merely because he was a vicar. Smith was no longer a welcome person in the village, and shortly after, he left the region.

From the Directories and the register of Public Houses, the following innkeepers are recorded at The Johnson Arms:

1829 Sarah Gaddes	1879 John Laidlow
1847 James Hetherington	1900 Miss June Laidlow
1873 Miss Elizabeth Hetherington	

60. The Johnson Arms

The Johnson Arms appears to have survived as a public house well into the twentieth century losing trade only with the reduction in horse drawn traffic and development of motor vehicles.

Our gig awaits to take us to our next public house. We shall avoid following in the steps of the unfortunate farmer Pearson to Walton vicarage, but instead we shall head back to Brampton and to Low Gelt Bridge, where we will find The Hare and Hounds Inn, and where hopefully, we will not be given a bath.

61

THE HARE AND HOUNDS

At Low Gelt Bridge, a farm and its buildings at the road junction face toward the River Gelt and the entrance to Gelt Woods. Here, the river beneath the bridge is a series of narrow rapids and deep pools. The house facing the bridge during much of the 1800s was a public house called The Hare and Hounds.

The first record of this public house is in 1822 when Thomas Knott was innkeeper.

Bath at The Hare and Hounds

"One of the leading Brampton radicals has been anticipating "The General Uprising" by taking his share of a neighbour's property without leave. On Monday last, the annual Christmas Merry Night was holden at Low Gelt Bridge Inn where the person alluded to attended along with a number of others. In the course of the night, he took an opportunity of stealing 2 bottles of rum which he conveyed out and secreted in an outhouse. Some

61. The Hare and Hounds

suspicion having arisen, the gentleman's motions were watched and he was detected in the act of endeavouring to remove the bottles, and was dragged into the house.

The party was so indignant at the delinquent conduct that they determined to "swim him" in the pool at the bridge which is about ten feet deep. For that purpose, a cart rope was procured and tied around his middle. Some of the party however, begged that the punishment be deferred until daylight, and the culprit was in the meantime fastly tied up in the stable – but in the course of the night, he contrived to extricate himself and make his escape, and has not since been heard of."

Carlisle Patriot, January 1822

Thomas Knott and his brother Robert were farmers as well as innkeepers and these two businesses continued until 1847, when Thomas moved out to take over at The Sand House Inn, Brampton, whilst continuing to farm at Low Gelt, leaving Robert in charge of The Hare and Hounds:

Robbing a Master at Low Gelt Bridge Public House

"Ann Heslop absconded on Friday from the service of Robert Knott of Low Gelt Bridge public house, stealing and taking with her about £4 and a quantity of wearing apparel. Mr Sym, police officer was applied to, and on Sunday afternoon he found her at Corby Hill. She was taken into custody and is committed for trial."

Carlisle Journal, 10th November 1848

The Hare and Hounds, a popular public house because of its pleasant location by the River Gelt and Gelt Woods, was often used as a venue for celebratory dinners and meetings, where up to 40 people could sit down together to dine. There were stables for 5 horses and accommodation for overnight guests.

At this time, (1848) a new bridge at Geltside had been built to take a new road straight across the fields to Brampton by way of West Hill. This road was easier – more direct, shorter, and less of an incline than the narrow Low Gelt Bridge and Capon Tree Road into Brampton. As a consequence of the new road being built, plans were published for the closure of the Capon Tree Road, but Mr Brown, owner of The Hare and Hounds objected to the plans, on the grounds that his public house business would lose trade. The objection was supported by many others and the proposal remained just that – a proposal. 160 years later Brampton's by-pass was built, and as a consequence the Capon Tree Road was stopped up.

In 1884 the innkeeper at The Hare and Hounds was a Ridley Mewse – husband of Elizabeth, landlady of The Graham Arms at Middle Gelt Bridge. In 1888 George Grainger married Isabella Beattie the former licensee and took over as landlord until the end of the century.

From the Directories and Public house Licence register, the following landlords are recorded at The Hare and Hounds:

1822 Thomas Knott	1884 Ridley Mewse
1829 Jacob Brown	1888 George Grainger
1858 Thomas Hetherington	1901 John Little
1879 Isabella Beattie	

The Hare and Hounds enjoyed a career of at least a hundred years, no records have been seen that explain why and when this public house ceased trading. The 1892 return for Public Houses and Beer Houses records Margaret Brown of Great Corby as owner.

A journey of nearly three miles in our gig will take us around Gelt woods to find our next public house The Graham Arms where we will find Elizabeth, Ridley Mewse' wife, and possibly, – – – a dancing bear!

62

THE GRAHAM ARMS

At the road junction with Greenwell, by the banks of the River Gelt, and in the shadow of the tall railway viaduct, is a sandstone dwelling at Middle Gelt. Here at the edge of Gelt Woods, The Graham Arms was for many years a quiet country public house, relying largely upon passing trade.

The first record of The Graham Arms is quite late in the century, in 1884 with an innkeeper Elizabeth Mewse. Elizabeth's husband Ridley Mewse is recorded in the same year as being landlord at The Hare and Hounds public house at Low Gelt Bridge.

For a public house to survive at such a location, it would clearly be essential to have facilities for horses, carts and coaches. Accommodation at The Graham Arms was limited but obviously adequate: there was room for two overnight guests, 20 people could sit down to dine, and there were stables and a secure yard for 8 horses.

It would be easy to imagine that The Graham Arms was a small quiet respectable country public house, very different from the noisy town centre drinking dens like The Sportsman Inn and The Jolly Butcher. However, in the Magistrates Licensing Record, there is only one record ever of a landlord being fined, and it was right here at the Graham Arms:

Innkeeper fined

> "Police Sergeant Lowis stated in Court that at 5 minutes past three, he entered the licensed premises of The Graham Arms, to find 3 men: Andrew Forest, George Sproat, and Joseph Hetherington to be intoxicated. The innkeeper James Hetherington attempted to say that these three had been drunk when they arrived and were just trying to sleep it off on his premises. The Magistrate was not convinced by the story. James Hetherington was fined £2.10. shillings."
>
> Carlisle Journal, 1892

The Graham Arms survived well into the 20th century, despite pressures for closure from The Brampton Temperance Movement. The 1892 Return for Public Houses and Beer houses records the owners of The Graham Arms as Mr R. L. Graham of Edmond Castle, and it was let to the Brampton Old Brewery.

Although the first record that has been seen of The Graham Arms is as late as 1884, it is doubtful that this is when this public house started its career. It was around this time that many public houses were going out of business because of the Temperance Movement. It is highly likely therefore that The Graham Arms existed long before 1884 but no records of it at that time have yet been seen.

From the Directories and Magistrate Licensing records, the following landlords are recorded:

1884 Elizabeth Mewse
1888 James Hetherington
1900 Margaret Hetherington

Lost – a dancing bear from The Graham Arms

A story told by an elderly gentleman Mr H. Snowdon of Hill Garth Brampton cannot be corroborated by any records but does bear telling:

Apparently some time near the close of the 19th century, a travelling performer on his way to Carlisle after having attended the Brampton Michaelmas hirings, called in to The Graham Arms late one afternoon, accompanied by his dancing bear on a chain. The performer regularly stayed at public houses where he would draw crowds with his bear, in exchange for overnight accommodation and a few beers. On this

62. The Graham Arms

occasion, the performer had taken a beer too many and fell asleep, allowing his bear to escape – which it did – and it was last seen running free in Gelt Woods.

So, next time you take your dog for a walk in Gelt Woods – – – be careful!

As we prepare our horse and gig to leave The Graham Arms there are no signs of a dancing bear, so we shall move off, to our final public house – The Oddfellows on the road into Brampton from Castle Carrock.

63

THE ODDFELLOWS AND THE PAVIER

One mile from the centre of Brampton, a ten minute journey by gig brings us to an impressive sandstone house by the side of the road at a sharp bend close to the new bridge which now carries the Brampton by-pass. Moss House was once a public house called The Oddfellows, but it did not start its career as a public house with this name.

The first reference to a public house here at Beck Brows is in an advertisement of 1819 showing Edward Pickering as landlord, and the name of the public house as The Pavier.

63. The Oddfellows and The Pavier

> PUBLIC-HOUSE and FIELD, &c. for SALE.
> TO BE PEREMPTORILY SOLD, BY PUBLIC AUCTION, at the House of ROBERT ARMSTRONG, known by the sign of the Black Bull, in BRAMPTON, in the County of Cumberland, on WEDNESDAY, the 12th Day of JANUARY next, at Six o'Clock in the Evening;—all that old established PUBLIC-HOUSE, known by the sign of the PAVIER, with a Stable, Byer, Garden, and a small Field adjoining thereto; situate at BECK BROWS, in the Parish of Brampton, in the County of Cumberland; now in the Occupation of EDWARD PICKERING.—For further Particulars apply to Mr. HOLME, Solicitor, Carlisle.
> Carlisle, 28th Dec. 1819.

Edward and Margaret Pickering are recorded as licensees in 1821, and later records show that one of the Pickering family was a pavier by trade. In 1826 the Directories record John Pickering – Edward and Margaret's son also as innkeeper.

Riot and Affray at Brampton

"James Hogg, Jonathan Thornthwaite, John Skelton and John Dixon were arraigned on a charge of having been concerned in a riot and affray to the annoyance of the people of Brampton.

Margaret Pickering who lives at Beck Brows near Brampton said in court that on a Sunday, being the last day of the month, the prisoners were drinking in the afternoon at her public house, and after drinking, they went outside to begin fighting. She saw William Colman and Jonathan Thornthwaite stripped to the skin down to the waist and saw them strike several blows. She then barred the door they made such a noise. John Franks a constable from Brampton was returning home on horseback and saw the prisoners stripped and fighting. Skelton was sitting at the edge of the road but was not stripped. They were all in the public road. He got off his horse, demanded assistance from Skelton to help him part them and told him that he was a police officer, and would have no such work on a Sunday. Skelton abused him and said that he did not care for him or for Mr Ramshay the Magistrate. The prisoners were found guilty and sent to prison for nine months with hard labour."

Carlisle Journal, 28th April 1827

In 1832, Margaret Pickering died age 73, and three years later her husband Edward died at the age of 78, leaving John Pickering in charge of the public house. In 1835, The Pavier was advertised for sale in the Carlisle Journal:

Public House and premises for sale

To be sold by Public Auction at The Scotch Arms Inn Brampton;
On Wednesday 23 Dec 1835 – All that messuage and tenement and Public House and premises situated at Beck Brows, Beck Side near Brampton and now in the occupation of Mr John Pickering who will show the same.

Thomas Pickering was the pavier after whom the public house was named; both he and his brother John continued to live at Beck Brows.

Insolvency claim – Mark Bell hides furniture at The Pickerings

"Mark Bell – a carrier in Brampton, declared himself bankrupt and his case was heard this week by the Magistrates. I am Thomas Pickering of Beck Brows a pavier in Brampton. In November last, Mark Bell a carrier and carter in Brampton now insolvent, brought a chest of drawers, a bed, a clock and case, a tea tray, bed hangings and a table to my house – worth £15. The insolvent said that he was in danger of becoming bankrupt and wished that I would preserve these things."

Carlisle Patriot, 1837

John Pickering died at Beck Brows in 1841 age 56 years, leaving his brother Thomas the pavier the sole survivor of the family. Thomas continued living here, carrying on the family business as a public house for a further 4 years, until in 1845 when the following advertisement appeared in the Carlisle Journal:

House and Land to let

"To be let, and may be entered into immediately; All that commodious dwelling house, now used as a public house, situated at Beck Brow in the Parish of Brampton, with stables, barns, gig house, and other suitable out-offices, a large garden and 14 acres or thereabouts of land adjoining. The dwelling house stands in a healthy sheltered and pleasant situation about 1 mile distant from Brampton, and a half mile from the Milton railway station. Comprising 3 large rooms on the ground floor, 3 commodious rooms above, excellent cellarage, well adapted as a private residence for a genteel family and will be let either as such or as a public house. Mr Thomas Pickering of Beck Brow will show the premises."

Carlisle Journal, 3rd May 1845

Thomas moved out to Low Cross Street and Slater's directory of 1847 shows the new licensee as Thomas Foster who changed the name of the public house to "The Odd Fellows Arms." 1847 coincides with the height of the growth of Friendly Societies

63. The Oddfellows and The Pavier

across the country, and in Brampton, lodges of The Ancient Order of Foresters, The Good Samaritans, The Antedeluvian Order of Buffaloes, The Odd Fellows and The Rechabites were each set up and met in public houses. No records have been seen however of meetings of The Odd Fellows at the Beck Brow public house.

The very first Ordnance survey map that was published for the Brampton area was in 1862 and this clearly shows the bend in the road to Talkin Tarn with the buildings now known as Moss House. The map labels this building, not as Moss House, but as Becksides and The Odd Fellows' Arms (P. H.)

In the same year as this map was published, Mrs Tamar Brown landlady at The Odd Fellows found herself in the lock-up!

Landlady lands up – in the lock-up

"On Wednesday last, between 5 and 6 o'clock in the evening, Mr William Holliday farmer at Tarn Lodge, his sister in law Mrs Holliday, accompanied by Mr Wilkinson of The Flatt and his daughter, were returning home in a cart from Brampton Hiring. Whilst on the road, they had been jesting about who had the most money, and on reaching Beckside, they drew up for the purpose of having something to drink. Mr Holliday was the only person to leave the cart and on getting down he pulled out his pocket book saying "– – look here now, there's plenty of money." He went into the public house with the pocket book in his hand. The book contained several £10 notes and £5 notes. Mr Holliday was rather the worse for drink and after he had been in the house about 7 minutes, Mr Wilkinson got out of the cart to look after him. He could not see him in the house and went to the back door where he found him. They both returned to the kitchen when Mr Holliday missed his pocket book but could not tell how he had lost it. He could not recollect whether he had put it in his pocket or had dropped it on the floor. There was no other person in the house at the time except for Mrs Tamar Brown, landlady, who was shortly afterwards seen to go out into the barn behind the house and close the door after her – being absent for about 5 minutes. Information was sent

to Supt Fowler at Brampton Police Station and he immediately came to Beckside to make enquiries. The landlady was the only person on whom to fix his suspicion on account of her visit to the barn and he accordingly told her that he must take her into custody on a charge of stealing a pocket book. Mr Fowler then told her that he must place her in the lock-up at Brampton. She appeared to be the worse for drink and Mr Fowler gave her into the custody of Constable Birrell, and instructed another constable to guard the barn all night, in order to carry out a search in daylight the following day. A witness – a neighbour of Mrs Brown stated that The pocket book was found hidden amongst the coals.

Council for Mrs Brown proved that at the time, Mr Holliday was intoxicated and she had seen Mr Holliday go into the barn and that his waistcoat was flying open.

Other witnesses were called to say that Mrs Tamar Brown was a person of honest character. Mrs Tamar Brown was found not guilty."

Carlisle Journal, 1862

Shortly after Mrs Tamar Brown's court appearance, The Odd Fellows was again advertised – the owner looking for a new tenant!

A Case of Stabbing near Brampton

"John Boustead was charged with maliciously wounding William Thompson with a knife at a public house called The Odd Fellows at Beckside. Thompson stood in court with a bandaged head, several wounds covered with sticking plaster and Boustead had a black eye. William Thompson stated that he went to the Odd Fellows Arms, he was standing by the fire, when Boustead struck him without provocation. They struggled; Boustead thrust his hand into his pocket from which he took two instruments and struck a blow. Thompson was stunned from the blow which caused blood to flow. William Clifford a factory hand said that he was at The Odd Fellows Arms, and found Thompson and Boustead struggling with each other. He saw Boustead draw a hammer and a knife about 7 inches long from his pocket, and strike Thompson on the forehead. Clifford tried to separate them, then a man called Richard Bell seized Boustead and dragged him out."

Carlisle Journal, 1868

Despite the newspaper reports of "Riot and Affray" and "A case of Stabbing at Brampton", The Pavier/The Odd Fellows Arms was a quiet country public house that relied on passing trade, even though some of the customers were already intoxicated when they arrived like Mr Holliday. The outhouses were used as stables with accommodation for 8 horses and plenty of yard space behind for coaches, carts and gigs.

The Odd Fellows Arms continued business as a public house well into the 1880s when Mr Alexander Riddell who already owned The Jolly Butcher, and Riddell's

63. The Oddfellows and The Pavier

Spirits Vaults in Brampton took over as owner. Mr Riddell, possibly realising that The Temperance Movement was becoming too much of a force to be reckoned with, changed the Odd Fellows public house to become The Beck Brows Hotel in 1882. However this change did not save it from the ever increasing influence of the Howard family and the Temperance Movement as shown in the following report from The Carlisle Journal of October 1883:

Beck Brow Hotel ceases as licensed premises

> BECK BROW HOTEL, BRAMPTON.—This long-established inn ceased to exist as a licensed house on the 10th inst.. By the closing of this once popular place of resort, owing to its contiguity to Talkin Tarn and Gelt Woods, some disappointment and inconvenience will doubtless be caused to the numerous tourists and pleasure-seekers who annually resorted thither. Another public-house situate at Newtown, Irthington, in the occupation of Mr. John Irving, was also closed on the same day. Both these properties belong to the Trustees of the Earl of Carlisle, and we are informed that there is not now a licensed house on their estates.

From the Directories and Licence register and newspaper articles, the following landlords are shown for the Pavier/The Odd Fellows Arms;

1820 Edward Pickering	
1824 Edward and Margaret Pickering	**The Pavier**
1826 John Pickering	
1845 Thomas Pickering	
1847 Thomas Forster	
1855 John Hetherington	
1858 Tamar and George Brown	**The Odd Fellows**
1863 James Bell	
1874 Alexander Riddell	
1882 Alexander Riddell	**Beck Brows Hotel**

The current owners of Moss House believe that the public house which formerly occupied this site was locally known as "The Clickham Inn", but no record has been seen to verify this. The landlord at The Clickham Arms at Penrith, claim that the name comes from local dialect used by horse riders clipping the harness of their horse to a metal ring, whilst popping in to the public house for a drink. The following report in the Carlisle Examiner goes some way towards an acceptable explanation:

211

"A farmer refreshed at The Click'em Inn"

"A farmer set off from home with his horse and cart with wages and ample supply of beer to go to pay his sheep shearers some distance away. Passing through a village, he heard merry making coming from the hostelry and not wanting to miss an opportunity, he handed over his horse and cart to the ostler, and joined the company. Having generously partaken he went to collect his horse but could not for the life of him, remember what kind of horse he came with. He took the first one he came across and after several attempts managed to mount his steed and proceed with his mission. Unfortunately he had another public house to pass, known locally as The Click'em Inn. In he was clicked, leaving his horse at the door. More ale was swallowed. How long he remained at the Click'em inn or how he managed to stagger home he knew not, but his wife was much distraught that he had abandoned his own horse and cart in one public house, he had stolen someone else's horse which he had left tied up outside The Click'em Inn and was now raving like a maniac for its owner."

It is not known whether this is a true story, but it does refer to the practice of tying up a horse to the front of a public house whilst the owner was inside – a practice which surely must have taken place here at the Oddfellows Arms.

We need to "un–click" our horse and gig now and prepare ourselves for our return journey to Brampton town centre – but what is this? I hear someone calling "last orders."

LAST ORDERS PLEASE! – THE TEMPERANCE MOVEMENT IS COMING

It took only two years following the implementation of The Duke of Wellington's Beer Act for the very serious negative effects of drinking to begin to emerge within the Brampton community and nationally. During our tour of Brampton's public houses, we have seen for ourselves, evidence of violence, theft, cheating, degradation and moral decline resulting from drunkenness and dependency upon drink:

"Drink has become the curse of our community."

George Simms

"The working classes having been a mostly independent, industrious and thrifty community attentive to the interests of their employers, have now become disaffected, dissolute, impatient of superiority or control."

"The Water Drinkers"

In 1832 Joseph Livesey and seven Preston working men, appalled by the increase in violence accompanying drunkenness, signed a pledge that they would never again drink alcohol. Other groups of working men followed their example and by 1835, The British Association for Promotion of Temperance was formed. We have already heard at The Shoulder of Mutton about the reception that Thomas Whittaker received when he visited Brampton on a speaking tour of Cumberland to convince people to give up drinking altogether, but made little progress. Later in 1839, the following report appeared in the Border Herald of Temperance.

"The course is going rapidly on in this place – a public meeting was held in the Primitive Methodist Chapel. The place was filled and after the meeting, 21 signed the pledge."

Life in Brampton with 63 Public Houses

In 1853 a Mr Thompson of Leeds visited Brampton to deliver a course of lectures on Temperance and made some progress:

"His first address on Wednesday 23rd he was anxiously listened to by large and intensely interested audiences. He addressed the Sunday school children and delighted the juvenile audiences. On Friday he was prevailed upon to lecture again and this drew great numbers all acknowledging his eloquence and many signed the pledge. Nearly 100 signatures were gained since his first appearance this week."

Carlisle Journal, 8th April 1853

By the 1860s "drink" had become a major moral and political issue because of the increasing levels of crime and violence emanating from public houses, and by 1869, support for better licence legislation was called for by the Liberal party with further Beer Acts being passed returning the control of all licensed houses to the Magistrates. The Conservatives tended to support the interests of the drink industry whilst the Liberals were its' dedicated enemy. The situation was further inflamed when the Conservatives began to deal out peerages to rich brewers, so a National Temperance Federation was formed and became closely associated with the Liberal party. In Cumberland, rural society was reluctant to turn away from drink. The problem with being teetotal in the early Victorian period was that it was associated with radical politics, and few really wished to risk the embarrassment of joining a revolutionary cause. The Presbyterians, Roman Catholics and Anglicans chose to remain aloof from the cause, the Non-Conformists and Wesleyans showed little enthusiasm until the 1870s.

"I regret to say that most of our local leaders did not have the commitment, and instead of receiving encouragement from quarters that should have given a helping hand, the Temperance Movement was rebuffed by the Christian Church. As late as 1870 all the ministers in the town were invited to sign the pledge and to interest themselves in the Temperance Movement but only one of them would countenance or help the movement because he was already an abstainer. The movement therefore in Brampton was only kept alive by outside help."

North Cumberland Reformer, February 1892

Alderman Charlton from Gateshead and Joseph Mullins of The Good Templars visited Brampton regularly and kindled the first sparks of interest and it was the smaller churches – The Quakers, and the Primitive Methodists in Brampton who first promoted the teetotal message with vigour. The baton of these early trail blazers was then picked up by the Liberals and Non –Conformists of Victorian England, carrying the issue to the forefront of the political agenda of the 1880s.

Last Orders Please! – The Temperance Movement is coming

Lady Rosalind, Countess of Carlisle

Rosalind was born in 1845. Her father Baron Stanley of Alderley, had been Member of Parliament for Hendon and had given untiring service to the Whig party. The life of Rosalind covers that period in England of transition away from the rule and dominance of rich land owning families, to the beginnings of democracy, political and social change and the extension of voting rights to most people. To that transition, Rosalind made a very significant contribution.

At the age of 19 years, Rosalind married George Howard, the only son of The Hon. Charles Howard, MP for East Cumberland and came to live in Naworth Castle. Rosalind became a fierce opponent of the Tory cause, and despite her privileged upbringing she became passionate about the need for political and social change, hoping to improve conditions for the common man. She developed a great sense of service to others less fortunate than herself, making accommodation available at Naworth Castle for 100 women and children from deprived inner cities to stay for a month's holiday. Five farmers from the Naworth Estate were invited each year to stay at her Kensington house to visit the Royal Show and see the sights of London. Greatly moved by the plight of a family of children left orphaned by the death of an ill mother and the admission of their father to a lunatic asylum, she arranged for them to be cared for at Naworth Castle, until accommodation could be found elsewhere.

Rosalind became engrossed in politics, but favoured the more progressive and radical beliefs of the Liberals rather than the Whigs, and, regularly dressed in blue – the colours of the Liberals, she canvassed hard locally for people to vote for her husband.

The Temperance Movement in Brampton

In terms of the demise of the public houses of Brampton, it was in 1881 that the match was put to the blue touch paper. One of the preachers of the National Temperance Federation had come to the tiny hamlet of Lanercost near Brampton, and Lady Rosalind, together with her children was in the audience:

> *"There I had the chance of hearing the great work that was being done, and forthwith, my children and I took the pledge."*

Life in Brampton with 63 Public Houses

So convinced was Lady Rosalind, that she called for further meetings to be held at Lanercost, and when the number of those having signed the pledge had reached 299, she persuaded her husband to provide the 300th signature.

> *"Then followed work in our small and ancient town of Brampton. We carried the crusade there with the enthusiasm of those who rejoice in having found a new and better way of life."*
> Lady Rosalind's diary, 1882

Monster meetings were held in the Tweed Mill at Brampton, owned by Lady Rosalind, and were addressed by leading members of The Temperance Movement.

> *"The Movement is revolutionising the social life of our town and district. Great crowds have been attending these meetings, and this has bound together so many people to a common cause."*
> North Cumberland Reformer

Rosalind and her two daughters, Mary and Cecilia, set up and taught in a "Band of Hope." This was a series of meetings for children and young people to learn about the evils of drink and to encourage them to be pledged to temperance for life, before they became adults. Meetings in the years 1882–1883 were held fortnightly and, as a consequence, 331 children of the Bands of Hope had signed the pledge. Between them, Rosalind, George, Mary and Cecilia bombarded Brampton with speeches and meetings, and their impact was remarkable. At Christmas time 1882 the Brampton police stated that:

> *"Never has such a sober Christmas at Brampton been seen, so little drink was going and the gas company say that gas consumed is much less because the public houses are so much emptier."*

Lady Rosalind and George Howard, being landowners of many local dwellings, exercised their authority and influence as landlords and in one stroke, closed 8 licensed houses on their Naworth Estates. In their place they established 15 reading rooms, meeting places where families could socialise and discuss local issues, read newspapers and where, of course, all alcohol would be prohibited.

Rosalind bought outright the premises of a public house in Hallbankgate and closed it immediately. The deal was not a good one for her financially. A letter appeared in the local press accusing her of high handed exploitation of her privileged position as a wealthy land owner and going against the wishes of local people. Being astute enough to appreciate that it would be helpful to have public opinion on her side, Rosalind arranged for petitions to be signed – for or against the idea. The result was a majority of 2 to 1 in favour of closure of the public house. Similarly, at Banks in Lanercost she closed the Plough Inn resulting in the brewers accepting defeat, and on the evening before the Plough finally closed its doors, there was a ceremonial burial of the signboard with the brewers reciting over the grave:

> *"From ashes to ashes, from dust to dust,*
> *If the Countess won't have you, the Devil must."*

Beck Brow Hotel closed

> *"Beck Brow Hotel has ceased to exist as a licensed house and this will cause disappointment and inconvenience. Another public house at Newtown Irthington was also closed on the same day. Both of these properties belong to the Trustees of The Earl of Carlisle and we are informed that there are now no licensed houses on their estates."*
> Carlisle Journal, 16th October 1883

By 1883 over 2,500 people had signed the pledge in Brampton and district:

> *"Our mission this week was very interesting. 300 more people have pledged themselves, but it is not the pledges alone that give us encouragement – it is the reverent, thoughtful*

and profound looks on the faces of the lower classes who come night after night to listen to the speeches and hymns which promise a better life ahead without the scourge of drunkenness."

Lady Rosalind's Dairy, 1883

Lady Rosalind then persuaded her husband to banish all alcoholic drink from Naworth Castle. George by this time had become passionate about the Temperance cause. As well as being Member of Parliament for East Cumberland, George Howard had been a Pre-Raphaelite painter and now strongly believed that the drink trade had brought great ugliness to England. After closing public houses on their Naworth Estates, he claimed that the beauty of the neighbourhood increased and showed itself with a better class of house and cottage gardens and prettier clothes. This, he believed, was evidence enough to show that by spending less money on drink, improvements in home comforts and a better standard of living could be achieved.

"When we compare the Brampton of the past with its large number of public houses, drunkenness and poverty, with the present with our temperance movement, educational facilities, we can arrive at no other conclusion but that poverty was a direct result of the liquor traffic. Now with the spread of education and social programmes adopted by the Liberal Party, I am hopeful that the world on the whole and Brampton in particular is much improved."

North Cumberland Reformer, 1892

In Brampton a Temperance Association Brass Band was formed, and Lady Rosalind provided the funds for instruments. Only players who had signed the pledge were accepted as members of The Brampton Total Abstinence Society Band – as shown in their rules:

List of Members.

Last Orders Please! – The Temperance Movement is coming

Sir Wilfred Lawson, a very influential political figure in Cumberland, was also dedicated to the Whig-radical cause, supporting votes for all men, land reform, and above all, strict control of the drink trade. A wealthy landowner, Sir Wilfred not only gave sums of money to help any organisation that promoted temperance, but also paid speakers to hold public meetings preaching about the effects that drink was having upon society. Lady Rosalind recruited the help of her political ally, and records in her diary:

"Sir Wilfred spoke last Friday and we had an audience of 2,700 – think of that in Brampton 2,700! Our Society is now 1300 strong.

I have taken a small public house (the Shepherd Inn on Front Street) on a 7 years lease to make a working men's free and easy coffee house. It won't pay but I can't lose much.

The new landlady of the Howard Arms says that she certainly cannot pay the rent that she agreed when she came, as she is making nothing, and we now expect in a few months time, she will give up for want of custom and that we shall get that as a farmer's Temperance Inn."

The diary goes on to record:

"The Publicans are really angry now – one of them made only 9d last market day; another only 4s and 6d for the whole week. The Spirit Vaults close early and the liquor trade is for the present ruined – – –"

Lady Rosalind was not prepared to leave it there – power and influence spurred her on to work feverishly to her goal:

"We have not won our victory yet, until all the public houses are shut up entirely will we have won."

Her plan to achieve this was through her husband George, who meanwhile had become appointed Chairman of the Brampton Licensing Authority. Many questions could be asked as to the "How and Why" George Howard – a confirmed teetotaller, whose influential wife was known to be a passionate disciple of the Temperance movement, could be appointed to such an important position.

It was through this mechanism that the fate of many of Brampton's public houses was secured. In one fell swoop, the following public houses had their licences withdrawn:

The Blue Bell	The Sportsman	The Coach and Horses
The Samson	The Black Bull	The String of Horses
The Half Moon	The Wheat Sheaf	The Moorcock West Hall

The meeting convened to discuss these licensed premises became a grim battle between the brewers and licence holders on the one hand, and the police and Magistrates on the other. The new Police Station was much too small for the large numbers who wished to attend and the court hearing was transferred to St. Martin's Hall and sat for three days. By 1903, the number of licensed public houses in Brampton had been reduced to ten, as had existed some 100 years earlier.

Lady Rosalind – a passionate reformer – or a bigoted teetotaller?
There is no doubt that Lady Rosalind's personal influence secured a major reduction in the number of public houses in Brampton, which led to a marked decline in the number of convictions of drunkenness and drink related crime.

A vast improvement in the quality of life at the turn of the century was due to a number of factors, but a more responsible attitude to drinking played the major part. But why did Rosalind have such a strong dislike for alcohol? She was certainly not an ascetic wanting to deny other people pleasure, and had no hankering for the simple frugal and self denying existence of monastic or puritan life. She had been brought up to appreciate and partake of fun, frolic, amusement and entertainment and to enjoy life to the full. The great influences upon her life were from the strong Whig and Liberal philosophies and the full enjoyment of love, beauty and nature, exemplified in her husband's painting and lifestyle of the Pre-Raphaelites.

Rosalind appreciated the good things in life and strove passionately to achieve these, not only for herself, but for others much less fortunate than her. She was convinced that the moral character and happiness of all ranks of society were being destroyed by drink, and had seen at first hand that drinking had caused misery, too many family tragedies, violence, dishonesty and the very serious decline in the quality of many people's lives. Rosalind was convinced that poverty and lack of opportunity could be tackled through politics, and that her upbringing, her ability to inspire others, and her position in the local community could all be pressed into action to bring about that change.

Rosalind achieved much in her lifetime, but never achieved her ultimate goal of getting the Government of the day to accept the idea of total abstinence and the closure of all public houses – this was a step too far for her reforming colleagues. The power and influence of wealth, vested interests, and private business were too strong an opposition, but very major changes had been achieved. Rosalind was instrumental in setting up School Boards, Co-operative Societies, Reading Rooms, improvements to housing conditions, but most important of all, her efforts led to the closure of many public houses with the consequent reduction in crime, poverty and social degradation.

From the 1890s there was a period of increasing wealth and hope in the Brampton community. Although most people had more money to spend than before, the consumption of beer dropped by 15% and of spirits by 36%. The greatest change was felt in the Magistrates Courts where crime resulting from drinking fell by 22%.

And finally:

Magistrates warn Government of alcohol fuelled crime and violence

"Judges have warned the Government that there will be an inevitable explosion in alcohol fuelled violence and crime when the licensing laws are relaxed this year. Documents issued by The Home Office say that they told ministers that it was simply wishful thinking to believe that the new laws would lead to a reduction in drinking.

The judges said those who routinely see the consequences of drink fuelled violence, grievous bodily harm and worse, on a daily basis, are in no doubt that an escalation of offences of this nature will inevitably follow the relaxing of the liquor licensing laws which the Government have now authorised.

The Council of Circuit Judges made its comments in response to the Government's consultation document "Drinking responsibly." The Judges comment that, had they been asked they would have emphasised from their experience as full-time judges sitting in the Courts, that relaxing of drinking laws will certainly result in many more cases coming before them of drink related crime, violence and anti-social behaviour. The judges say that the only way to deal with the problem is to make drink significantly more expensive.

The judges commented that excessive drinking turns some people into savages, becoming angry and brutal. If it were not for the widespread availability of alcohol, the judges believe that crimes of violence would be at a fraction of their recent level. The situation is already grave and by making drink more available is close to lunacy. It simply means that our towns and city centres will become abandoned at night to pugnacious, drunk noisy vomiting louts.

The Association of Police Officers has also warned ministers about the likely consequences of the Act. One only has to look at the overwhelming evidence of the strong link between drinking and disorder with the explosion of late night premises. The Association has seen no evidence to support the argument that by allowing licensed premises to stay open longer will see a reduction in crime and violence.

Judge John Samuels Q. C. Council of Circuit judges quotes one judge "I sit on 3 benches and in all three the lists contain a substantial quantity of violence and it is rare for any of these offences to be committed by someone who has not been drinking.

It is not just the illiterate and inarticulate underclass which does this; quite bright people in well paid jobs do it, with a surprising number of women. Their sole idea is to get drunk as possible. Fights ensue usually over minor or trivial matters – if not, they roam the streets in malign short fused hostility until some unfortunate victim suffers. In our view there is a need for a lot less provision of drinking facilities not a lot more."

Daily Telegraph, 14th August 2005!!!

BIBLIOGRAPHY AND PRIMARY SOURCES

Ashbridge, Ian. Cumbrian Crime from a Social Perspective 1834-94. Redburn Publishing 1999
Burn, Peter. Brampton as I have known it. B.J. 1880
Davidson, Steven. Carlisle breweries and Public houses. P3 Publications 2004
Tames, Richard. The Victorian public house. Shire Publications Ltd. 2003
Parsons, Iain. Brampton Old and New. Netheray Books 1999
Roberts, Charles. The Radical Countess 1962
Felc, Joanna. A History of Theatre in Carlisle
Longmate, Norman. The Water Drinkers 1968

Newspapers:
Carlisle Journal 1800-1900
Carlisle Patriot 1800-1900
North Cumberland Examiner
Pierce Egan's life in London 1827
North Cumberland Reformer 1892-1895
Cumberland News "Onlooker" 15/12/1934
Daily Telegraph 14th August 2005

Other Sources:
Cumberland Trade Directories of 19th Century: Jollie; Parson and White; Jackson; Bulmers; Pigot; Mannix and Whelan; Kelly; Slaters
Penn, Rev. Arthur. Notes: Brampton Public Houses in the nineteenth Century. 1971
Militia Lists Eskdale Ward 1808
Public house License Register 1822-1826
Ordnance Survey maps 1865, 1899
Tithe Map and Schedule Brampton 1841
Return for Public houses and Beer houses 1892
Wills: Edmondson; Modlen; Snowball; Sinclair; Halliburton
Census: 1841; 1851; 1861; 1871; 1891

Bibliography and Primary Sources

Brampton Parish Magazines 1889–1892 DX 442, DX 148
Plans Couch's Shoe Shop DXI 64/2
Poor Law Union 1837-1930 3/Pu/B
Brampton Total Abstinence Brass Band 1892-1899. Minute Book and Rules
The Independent Coach. Daybook 1837 D/CL/P/8
Issac Bird Spirit Merchant Account Book D/CL/P/8/38
Thomas Modlen Spirit Merchant Book D/CL/P/8/14
An Innkeepers Ledger D/CL/P/8/64
Laws and Rules: Brampton Independent Order of Oddfellows D/Hod/11/154–171
Archives: Howard of Naworth Durham University Library
A Builder's ledger D/CL/P/8/53
Indenture Edmondson 1818 D/Hod/17/3

INDEX

Admiral Nelson Inn, 67
Alehouses, 31
Allen, Hannah, 50
Alma, 63
Anchor Inn, 156
Ancient Order of Forresters, 95
Apprenticeship, 89
Armstrong, James, 2, 5
Armstrong, John, 51, 79, 122
Armstrong, Mary, 99
Armstrong, Joseph, 80, 105, 114
Armstrong, Robert, 17, 22, 101, 166
Armstrong, William, 65, 122, 124, 177, 185
Atkinson, Edward, 2, 112
Atkinson, Francis, 1
Atkinson, Robert, 146
Atkinson, Thomas, 112
Atkinson, Elizabeth, 114

Barker, Elizabeth, 62
Barker, James, 62, 196
Barley Stack/Barley Mow, 53
Batey, James, 52, 126
Batey, William, 186
Bay Horse The, 190
Belted Will Rifles, 74
Blue Bell Inn, 48
Bell, Elizabeth, 109
Bell, George, 122
Bell, James, 122, 211
Bell, Jane, 45
Bell, John, 14
Bell, Joseph, 97, 103

Bell, Margaret, 95
Bell, Mary, 72, 94, 97
Bell, Thomas – Howard Arms, 72
Bell, Thomas – Lion and Lamb, 45
Bell, Thomas – The Grapes, 94
Bell, Thomas – The Bush, 169
Bell, Thomas – The Shepherd, 45
Bell, William, 109, 124, 169
Bird, J., 59, 62
Black Bull, 21, 194
Blaylock, George, 13, 183
Blue Bell Inn, 48
Board Inn, 85, 102, 166
Bonnie Prince Charlie, 19, 65, 162
Boustead, S., 130
Broom Inn, 84
Brown, George, 211
Brown, James, 77, 80
Brown, John, 2, 5
Brown, Joseph, 93, 172
Brown, Tamar, 209
Buckingham Palace, 73
Bulman, W., 70
Burn, Peter, x, 16, 19, 39, 68, 72, 133, 151, 176, 178, 179, 185
Burns, J., 98
Burrows, W. J., 39, 97
Bush Inn, 169

Carrick, George L., 117, 121
Charlton, N., 171
Cheesebrough, M., 41
Clark, William, 54
Coal Waggon The, 188

224

Index

Coach and Horses, 147
Commercial Inn, 173
Conservative Party, 20, 21, 25, 33
Corbett, Mary, 163
Corbett, Thomas, 163
Crouch, M., 66
Crown Inn, 58
Crown and Anchor Inn, 68
Crown and Cushion Inn, 70
Crown and Thistle Inn, 70
Crozier, Ann, 50
Crozier, Mary, 16, 179
Cullen, Isaac, 175
Cullen, Joseph, 174

Dawson, Arabella, 66
Dickinson, Whitfield, 60
Dodd, Ann, 6, 103
Dodd, Ellen, 69
Dodd, John, 106
Dodd, Richard, 103
Dodd, Walter, 171
Dodd, William, 172
Dodgson, Ralph, 196
Dufton, Samuel, 122, 126, 172
Dunwoodie, George, 122, 126
Dunwoodie, John, 126

Earl Grey, 181
Edgar, Martha, 11
Edmondson, John, 78
Edmondson, William, 12, 15, 84, 85, 165
Elliot, Joseph John, 94
Elliot, John, 50
Elliot, George, 115
Elliot's Spirit Vaults, 115
Elsdon, Robert, 49
Errington, George, 122

Fat Ox Tavern, 81
Fisher, Elizabeth, 129
Fisher, William, 122
Forester, James, 103, 173

Forester, Dinah, 173
Foster, John, 153
Foster, Thomas, 208
Freemason's Arms, 162
Friendly Societies, 140

Gaddes, Sarah, 197
George and Dragon Inn, 8
General Wolfe, 153
Ghosts, 20
Gill, John, 8, 11, 38
Gleed, Henry, 126
Globe Inn, 99
Goodburn, Chistopher, 85, 102
Goodburn's Spirit Vaults, 102
Goodfellow, Christopher, 103
Good Samaritans, 54
Graham Arms, 109, 203
Graham, Elisabeth, 55
Graham, George, 11
Graham, Hannah, 11
Graham, Joseph, 11
Graham, James, 50, 99, 101
Graham, Joseph, 149
Graham, Margaret, 56
Graham, Thomas, 11, 126
Grapes Inn, 93
Gray, Mary, 122
Greyhound Inn/Hare and Hounds, 56
Grindley, John, 55

Half Moon Inn, 18, 25, 26
Hall John, 101
Halliburton, Ann, 128
Halliburton, John, 127, 170
Halliburton, Robert, 128
Halliburton, Thomas, 101
Harding, Charles, 150
Harding, Christopher, 23, 47, 97
Harding, Hamilton, 47
Harding, Robert, 168
Hardy, John, 17
Hardy, Mary, 17
Hare and Hounds Inn, 56, 200

Harrison, Mr, 110
Hartley, N., 193
Haston or Hastings, James, 12, 14
Head, John, 187
Hetherington, Arthur, 153
Hetherington, David, 152
Hetherington, James, 198, 204
Hetherington, Elizabeth, 187, 198
Hetherington, John, 132, 168
Hetherington, Margaret, 45, 68, 204
Hetherington, Thomas, 202
Heward, Esther, 196
Heward, Hugh, 196
Hewetson, Mr, 157
Hewitt, George, 69
Hewitt, Robert, 148
Highland Laddie, 117
Hogg, George, 39
Holliday, Isaac, 126
Hope, David, 119, 122, 163
Hope, Elizabeth, 69
Horse and Farrier Inn, 58
Horse and Groom The, 190
Horse's Head Inn, 2
Howard Arms Inn, 71
Howard Rosalind Lady, 47, 74, 215
Hudspith, John, 73, 187
Hudspith, George, 167
Humbel, George, 39
Hutchinson, Robert, 30, 155

Independent Coach, 4
Inns, 31
Iredale Brewery, 22
Irving, William, 183

Jackson, William, 50, 191
James, John, 37
James, Joseph, 62
James, Robert, 190
Jamieson, George, 122
The Jolly Butcher, 15
The Johnson Arms, 197
Joiners Arms, 95

Johnstone, Mary, 61, 114
Johnson, Thomas, 61, 114
Jolly Butcher, 21

Kings Arms, 119
Klondyke Bar, 30, 154
Knott, Elisabeth, 186
Knott, Sarah, 186
Knott, Thomas, 200

Laidlow, John, 198
Laidlow, June, 198
Lamb, Fergus, 73
Law, Jane, 95
Law, Mary, 95
Lawson, Daniel, 50
Lawson, Robert, 132
Lee, Joseph, 5
Lee, Mabel, 73
Leonard, Mrs, 57
Lightfoot, William, 11
Lion and the Lamb Inn, 44
Little, John, 120, 122
Lockups, 90
Lord Brougham, 32
Lord Nelson, 67

Mark, Joseph, 171, 173
Marrs, Mary, 160, 161
Marrs, Thomas, 112, 156, 160
Mawbray, Joseph, 114
Mc Gregor, David, 57
Maxwell, Martha, 104
Maxwell, Mary, 105
Maxwell, Margaret, 105
Mewse, Elizabeth, 203
Mewse, Ridley, 201
Militia List, 2
Miller, Isabella, 196
Mitchinson, David, 132
Mitchinson, Thomas, 41, 55
Modlen's Spirit Vaults, 41
Modlen, Arabella, 41, 43, 44
Modlen, Jane, 43, 44

Index

Modlen, Robert, 41, 43, 44, 167
Modlen, Thomas, 43, 44, 81
Moffat, George, 106
Moffat, James, 106
Moses, Thomas, 172
Mounsey, Elisabeth, 55
Mounsey, William, 54, 66
Mulcaster, Thomas, 101

Nag's Head Inn, 1
Nag's Tail, 6
Nichol, Mr, 95
Nicholson, James, 39
Nixon, George, 14, 19
Nixon, John, 2, 5
Nixon, Joseph, 125
Norman, Ann, 193
Nursery Arms, 51

Oddfellows Arms, 206
Oddfellows Friendly Society, 79, 106, 141
Oliphant, Hannah, 76
Oliver, John, 23
Ord, Elizabeth, 183

Packhorse Inn, 77
Park, Isaac, 39
Parker, Edward, 21, 23, 101
Parker, Ann, 23, 101
Parker, Joseph, 122
Parker, Mary, 126
Parker, Thomas, 50
Parker, William, 126
Patterson, James, 30
Pavier The, 206
Pearce Police Supt., 13, 16
Pearson, Thomas, 177
Pearson, William, 51
Penn, Rev. Arthur, viii, 98, 153, 160
Phillips, David, 50
Phillips, John, 23
Phillips, Mrs. A., 132
Pickering, Edward, 207

Pickering, John, 207
Plough Inn, 107
Porter, 49
Pratt, Thomas, 179
Professor Scott, 50
Punchbowl, 147

Quarter of Mutton, 37

Railton, William, 14
Ramshay, George, 30
Reay, James, 5, 80
Red Lion Inn, 64
Reed, John, 80, 176
Richards, William, 69
Richardson, John, 50
Richardson, Isaac, 62, 97, 126
Richardson, Jane, 62
Richardson, William, 39
Riddell, Alexander, 210
Riddell, T. R., 17
Ridge House Inn, 190
Robson, Joseph, 159
Routledge, Joseph, 14
Routledge, William, 131, 191
Ruleholme Bridge, 77
Rutherford, Mary, 122
Rutherford, Richard, 188

Salutation Inn, 98
Samson Inn, 28
Sandhouse Inn, 184
Scotch Arms, 127
Shaw, James, 158
Shepherd Inn, 44, 68
Ship Inn, 147
Shipley, Samuel, 5
Shoulder of Mutton, 37
Simpson, John, 183
Sinclair, William, 81
Slack, William, 55
Smith, John, 5
Smith, Samuel, 68, 76
Snaith, Ann, 23

227

Snaith, Thomas, 21, 23
Snowball, Cuthbert, 95, 97, 120
Snowball, Mary, 95, 97, 120
Sportsman Inn, 12
Steenson, Jwhonnie, x
Stephenson, Samuel, 183
Stobbart, Mrs, 178
Story, Henry, 181, 185, 187
Story, John, 23
String of Horses Inn, 166
Swallow, George Lawson, 13, 165

Tait, John, 14
Taverns, 31
Taylor, George, 50
Taylor, Henry, 47
Taylor, Margaret, 39
Taylor, Robert, 39, 167
Thirlwall, Thomas, 147
Thompson, Dinah, 20
Thompson, John, 64
Thompson, Joseph, 18
Thompson, Rebecca, 18
Thompson, Thomas, 18
Three Crowns, 176
Three Lions, 184
Tinling James, 150
Tom and Jerry, 145
Tom and Jerry Main Street, 144
Tom and Jerry Moatside, 179
Tom and Jerry Ewarts Buildings, 151
Tom and Jerry Central Place, 159
Topping, Miss, 117
Topping, William, 114
Turpin, W., 50

Wallace, Mrs, 48
Wallace, William, 50, 57
Walker, William, 63
Ward, Margaret, 149
Watkins, Richard, 187
Watson, James, 30, 50
Watson, Mary, 30
Watson, Thomas, 66

Wellington, The, 181
Wellington, Duke of, 33
Wellington's Beer Act, 33
Westmoreland, Thomas, 101
Wheatsheaf, 123
Whig Party, 33, 215
White Hart, 112
White Lion Inn, 104
White, Miss, 107
Whittaker Thomas, 38
Willie Brewed, 178
Wilson, Joseph, 172
Winthrop, Ann, 99
Winthrop, Senhouse Martin, 21, 23
Winthrop, Thomas, 99